DARING

SMON & SCHUSTER

New York London Toronto Sydney

YOUNG MEN

The Heroism and Triumph of the
Berlin Airlift, June 1948–May 1949

RICHARD REEVES

Simon & Schuster
1230 Avenue of the Americas
New York, NY 10020

First Simon & Schuster hardcover edition January 2010

SIMON & SCHUSTER and colophon are registered trademarks of Simon & Schuster, Inc.

For information about special discounts for bulk purchases, please contact Simon & Schuster Special Sales at 1-866-506-1949 or business@simonandschuster.com.

The Simon & Schuster Speakers Bureau can bring authors to your live event. For more information or to book an event contact the Simon & Schuster Speakers Bureau at 1-866-248-3049 or visit our website at www.simonspeakers.com.

Designed by Kyoko Watanabe

Manufactured in the United States of America

1   3   5   7   9   10   8   6   4   2

Library of Congress Cataloging-in-Publication Data
Reeves, Richard, 1936–
Daring young men : the heroism and triumph of the Berlin Airlift,
June 1948–May 1949 / Richard Reeves. — 1st Simon & Schuster hardcover ed.
      p.   cm.
Includes bibliographical references and index.
1. Berlin (Germany)—History—Blockade, 1948–1949.   2. Air pilots, Military—United States—History—20th century.   3. Air pilots, Military—Great Britain—History—20th century.   I. Title.
DD881.R435   2010
943'.1550874—dc22

2009015333

ISBN 978-1-4165-4119-6 (hardcover)
ISBN 978-1-4391-6051-0 (eBook)

This book is for Jeffrey Reeves,
who is just a great guy—and my son.

CONTENTS

THE
BERLIN
AIRLIFT

CITY OF BERLIN

SOVIET ZONE

SOVIET ZONE

FRENCH SECTOR

Tegel
Airport

BRITISH SECTOR

SOVIET SECTOR

RAF Gatow
Airport

Tempelhof
Airport

AMERICAN SECTOR

Potsdam

SOVIET ZONE

0 Miles   10

0 Kilometers   10

North
Sea

DENMARK

Baltic
Sea

SCHLESWIGLAND

Lübeck

FUHLSBÜTTEL

SOVIET ZONE

Hamburg

FINKENWERDER

Elbe R.

INBOUND

Bremen

Weser R.

FASSBERG

CELLE

Berlin

Oder R.

WUNSTORF   Hannover

OUTBOUND

NETHERLANDS

Ems R.

BUCKELBERG

Helmstedt

POLAND

Amsterdam

GERMANY

INBOUND

SOVIET ZONE

BRITISH ZONE

Rhine R.

Elbe R.

Brussels

Köln

Bonn

BELGIUM

SOVIET ZONE

LUX.

Moselle R.

WIESBADEN

Frankfurt am Main

Prague

Luxembourg

RHEIN-MAIN

CZECHOSLOVAKIA

FRENCH
ZONE

Meuse R.

AMERICAN ZONE

FRANCE

Rhine R.

Danube R.

Danube R.

AUSTRIA

0 Miles   100

0 Kilometers   100

SWITZERLAND

© 2009 Jeffrey L. Ward

INTRODUCTION

Let's make a joint effort, perhaps we can kick them out.
>   —*Soviet Premier Joseph Stalin to Wilhelm Pieck, Communist*
>   *Party leader of East Germany, March 19, 1948*

We stay in Berlin. Period.
>   —*President Harry S. Truman on June 29, 1948, after his*
>   *military and diplomatic advisors told him there was no way*
>   *for a few thousand Allied soldiers to stand up to hundreds of*
>   *thousands of Red Army troops blockading the city*

It was great fun, we were all together again doing an important job. . . . You'd be talking to some fellow and find out he had been a lawyer in Manhattan a couple of weeks before.
>   —*Royal Air Force Flight Lieutenant John Curtis,*
>   *later Air Marshal Sir John Curtis*

TEMPELHOF AIRPORT IS QUIET NOW, BEING TURNED INTO A giant park by the Berlin City Council. But there was a time sixty years ago when it was never silent, in 1948 and 1949, when American and British planes landed or took off every forty-five seconds to keep Berlin and Berliners alive.

It is an extraordinary place still, a grassy bowl enclosed on one side by a C-shaped building three-quarters of a mile long, once the largest structure in the world, a looming artifact of Hitler's architectural ambitions. In the silence, it is not hard to imagine the sights and sounds of history, the gigantic swastika flags that hung from the main terminal's sixty-foot-high ceilings and then the planes roaring in and out only three years after the end of World War II.

The far side of the greensward is bordered by a chain-link fence just in front of six-story apartment buildings and a cemetery. A United States Air Force C-54 is on a pedestal with a plaque that reads:

> For 467 days during 1948 and 1949, the City of Berlin was kept alive by an Airbridge of Allied Aircraft bringing food and other essentials from the West. This C-54 Skymaster actually flew during the Airlift and was last flown into the city in 1971 by Colonel Gail Halvorsen, the "Candy Bomber." The Airlift, called "Operation Vittles" by the Americans, was the result of a Soviet blockade of all land, rail, and water routes into the city.

I was eleven years old when the airlift began, as thrilled by the action as only a small boy could be. I thought I was on those planes far away, riding to the rescue of innocent people. Of course, Berliners were not that innocent, but that just made the effort more heroic to an American kid, particularly one who wanted to be a pilot.

I was different more than a half-century later and so was my country. The United States was becoming or being seen as arrogant, self-righteous, brutal, even a monster using our very substantial power to try to enforce a new order, a kind of global neo-imperialism. Of course, we meant well—innocents abroad—Americans usually do. After all, don't all people want to be like us?

It seemed some didn't. I have traveled enough and lived in enough places to feel the resentment, even hatred, of people who had been told America was the height of disinterested good—as long as things were done our way. I was taken by a line in a not-very-good 2003 movie, *Head of State*, in which a young black Washington city councilman is running for president against a self-satisfied senator who ends each speech by saying, "God bless America. And no one else!"

Was that the America I grew up in? That was my state of mind when I picked up Tony Judt's excellent book *Postwar*, which is subtitled *A History of Europe Since 1945*, published in 2005. On page 146, I read this:

As the Soviet troops tightened their control over surface connections into the city, the American and British governments decided upon an airlift to provision their own zones and on June 26 the first transport plane landed at Tempelhof airfield in West (Berlin).

The Berlin airlift lasted until May 12th 1949. Over those eleven months the Western allies shipped some 2.3 million tons of food on 277,500 flights, at the cost of the lives of 73 Allied airmen. Stalin's purpose in blockading Berlin was to force the West to choose between quitting the city . . . or else abandoning their plans for a separate West German state . . . in the end he secured neither objective.

That was about it. I was surprised. I thought there would be much more. I asked a few friends what they remembered about the airlift. Students said they never heard of it. People my age generally responded by asking when it happened. "The sixties, wasn't it?" was the usual guess. Many added, "It was Kennedy, right?" They generally thought the Soviet blockade was the same as the building of the Berlin Wall thirteen years later, in 1961. I generally responded by saying, "It was Truman. He was a real hero. His cabinet, the State Department, the Joint Chiefs all thought it was impossible to maintain a desperate city of more than two million people by air alone."

That was exactly what Stalin thought. Even if the Americans and the British could get the thing going, "General Winter" would defeat the airlift as surely as he had defeated Napoleon and Hitler when they invaded Russia.

Then I would babble on about the daring young men (and some women) from the States and Great Britain being pulled away from their new lives, their wives, their schools, their work for the second time in five or six years. This time they were supposed to feed the people they had been trying to kill, and who had been trying to kill them, only three years earlier. The airlift, Tom Brokaw might say, was the last act of what he called "The Greatest Generation."

It was interesting trying to bring to life the stories of Truman and Stalin, and of other men of history: Ernest Bevin, the language-mangling Foreign Minister of Great Britain; Ernst Reuter, the Mayor of Berlin; the great generals who opposed the airlift, George Marshall and Omar Bradley; and the younger ones who made it happen, Lucius Clay, Curtis LeMay, Joseph Smith and William Tunner. Great men. They are easy to find, in diaries and memoirs, films, military records, transcripts, letters, interviews—and some mythology. The other names in this book, the men the book is about, sound almost corny, like the lists of "American" names that were a staple of the World War II movies we grew up watching: Lafferty, Evans, Spatafora, Gere, Wagner, Goodman, Palahunich, Thompson . . . even Von Kaenel.

It was harder, but more rewarding, to collect the stories of those uncelebrated airmen, mechanics, weathermen, ground controllers, and uncommon laborers who were among the sixty thousand men and women who kept the airlift going for more than a year. Reading through records and hanging around at meetings of the Berlin Airlift Veterans Association in the United States and of the British Berlin Airlift Association produced some of those stories, but there are more out there. What was it like to be one of the seventeen thousand German women and men, wearing whatever clothes they had, sometimes slippers and bathing suits, using the rubble of their broken and cruelly hungry city to build a new airfield at Tegel in just ninety-two days? "It was an unforgettable sight," said an American colonel who had been a B-17 pilot bombing the old German capital. "Women in high heels pushing heavy wheelbarrows, men who looked like doctors or professors, and probably were, wielding shovels." What was it like to be one of the pilots who received telegrams from the President and were back in uniform within forty-eight hours? What was it like to be one of the American enlisted men—"high school kids," said Clay—supervising Luftwaffe mechanics recruited and retrained by the Allies to keep the C-54s flying loads of coal and fuel from eight bases in West Germany to Royal Air Force Station Gatow, Tempelhof and Tegel airports?

Those were the kids—real, live innocents abroad who refused orders to pour gasoline in the cans of trash outside Air Force mess halls so that emaciated Germans, mostly women and children, could not scrounge for leftover food. Soon enough, German mothers were telling their children that the Americans were "angels in uniform." That was hardly true—and not all Germans were devils—but this great and amazing effort did tend to bring out what Abraham Lincoln called "the better angels of our nature."

RICHARD REEVES
NEW YORK
JUNE 2009

CHAPTER 1

"City of Zombies"

June 20, 1948

THE *NEWSWEEK* HEADLINE WAS "DATELINE GERMANY, 1948: the Big Retreat."

The dispatch below was from James O'Donnell, the magazine's Berlin bureau chief, reporting on the exodus of American and

British officials and soldiers from the city as the Soviet Union took complete control of the old German capital.

After the Russians claimed control, O'Donnell reported, General Lucius Clay, the American military governor of Germany, had cabled Washington that he intended to order B-29 Superfortresses to begin attacking Soviet installations across Germany—and beyond. Washington responded, "Withdraw to Frankfurt."

Then, the *Newsweek* story continued, "At 1000 hours Saturday, the American cavalcade rendezvoused with the British . . . The bedraggled and demoralized caravan proceeded along the 117 miles of Autobahn to Helmstedt in the British zone . . ."

At the bottom of the two-column account, published on August 8, 1947, *Newsweek* added that the story was a fantasy, but still a plausible scenario:

> This fantasy does not sound so fantastic in Berlin as it does in the United States. For the German capital has been buzzing with rumors that the Western Allies would this winter recognize the irrevocable division of Germany and pull out of Berlin. The Germans probably envision some dramatic exodus. Actually, policy makers in Washington have seriously considered quietly leaving Berlin for the Russians to rule—and feed.

The magazine had found a way, an anonymous source, to tap into the cable traffic between Berlin and Washington that spring, as memos flew back and forth predicting Soviet pressure on the small occupation governments of the United States, Great Britain and France. Robert Murphy, the State Department's man in Berlin, Clay's political advisor, cabled back to Washington: "The next step may be Soviet . . . demand for the withdrawal from Berlin of the Western powers. In view of the prospect that such an ultimatum would be rejected, the Soviets may move obliquely, endeavoring to make it increasingly impossible or unprofitable for the Western powers to remain on; for example by interfering with the slender communications between Berlin and the Western Zone, taking further actions towards splitting up the city . . . Our Berlin position is delicate and difficult. Our withdrawal, either voluntary or non-voluntary, would have severe psychological repercussions which would, at this critical stage in the European situation, extend far beyond the boundaries of Berlin and even Germany. The Soviets realize this full well."

It was not fantasy anymore on June 24, 1948. That day, the final edition of the *Times of London* reported:

NEW RUSSIAN RESTRICTIONS IN BERLIN

BERLIN—Shortly after 1 o'clock this morning the Soviet military administration for Germany announced that all railway traffic on the line between Berlin and Helmstedt had been stopped in both directions. The Soviet authorities have also given instructions to the Berlin electricity company that deliveries of current from the eastern to the western sectors of Berlin are to be stopped immediately. These measures followed the announcement yesterday that the three Western powers intend to introduce the new West German currency into their sectors in Berlin.

The instructions for the stoppage of this important railway traffic which, air traffic apart, is the only means by which Allied and German supplies can now be brought from the Western zones into Berlin means that Allied zones of the city are essentially isolated.

So, the rumors were true—about half of them. Talk of the introduction of new currency by the Western Allies to replace worthless Nazi Reichsmarks, and of a Soviet blockade, had been both boiling and freezing life in Berlin for weeks. The people of the broken city, with its four occupation sectors—Soviets in the eastern sector and Americans, British and French in western neighborhoods—had been trading information and rumors of devalued currency, or the withdrawal of American, British and French troops, or even another war.

There were hundreds of thousands Red Army troops (at least twenty divisions in various states of combat readiness) in and near East Germany. The Soviets also had more than 2,500 combat aircraft, fighters and light bombers in East Germany and another 1,500 or so in Eastern European countries. That compared with 16,000 Allied troops, most of them military police and engineers, fewer than 300 American combat aircraft and perhaps 100 British fighters and bombers. There were another million or so Soviet troops in the rest of Eastern Europe, surrounding East Germany. Allied troop strength in all of western Germany was 290,000 men but only one or two combat-ready brigades.

The military imbalance was a regular feature of secret reports submitted by a Berlin representative of the West German Social Democratic Party,* which was headquartered in Hannover, in western Germany. He signed each message "WB." Willy Brandt was a thirty-five-year-old journalist who had fled Hitler's Germany and become a Norwegian citizen. He returned to Berlin in 1945 as the press attaché at the Norwegian mission. Then, in 1947, becoming a German citizen again, he began reporting weekly to West German SPD leaders on the situation in Berlin. In a secret dispatch labeled number 59, on June 14, 1948, he wrote:

> The English political officers are very nervous internally because of the new and possible Russian strangulation measures. An informant from SED [the Socialist Unity Party of Germany, controlled by the German communist party, which was in turn controlled by Soviet occupation authorities], might be interesting in this context: Walter Ulbricht, an important SED official, has

---

* Social Democratic Party is abbreviated SPD, from its German name, *Sozialdemokratische Partei Deutschlands*.

4

said (privately) that the western powers will be forced to leave Berlin before July 15. These circles obviously believe that preventing supply will make the population prefer a withdrawal of the western allies to anything else. Personally, I am inclined to believe that the Russians will not carry it to the extremes. Talking to the English and Americans I gained the impression that they by now have realized the disastrous consequences of a possible withdrawal and are therefore serious in declaring their unwillingness to withdraw. Two days ago a well-informed American again explained to me that their highest offices recognize the political necessity to keep Berlin . . . The aforementioned source confirmed that the Russians had tested the waters in the past two weeks and that high American and Russian representatives talked about the currency reform . . .

Now, ten days after Brandt's memo, which was wrong about American intentions, truck and automobile traffic from the western zones was indeed strangled. The Soviets announced that the Autobahn from Helmstedt in the British Zone, running through East Germany to Berlin, was being closed for "technical reasons." The stated technical reason was to make repairs on the dozens of bridges between Helmstedt and Berlin. With Soviets preventing rail travel through East Germany by blocking or ripping up track, and using patrol boats to blockade rivers and canals, the 2.1 million people of western Berlin were effectively cut off from the world. The lifeline to western Berlin, bringing in its food and fuel, more than 15,000 tons each day, was cut. Allied statisticians estimated that the western sectors of the city had enough food to last about thirty-five days, and enough fuel to last forty-eight days.

There were, however, six months of medical supplies stockpiled in western Berlin. Dr. Eugene Schwarz, Chief Public Health Officer in the American Sector, had been told in January by a friend, Ada Tschechowa, that when her husband had delivered a Soviet general's baby, the new father and his friends had drunkenly toasted both the infant and the day they would blockade the city and drive out "the swine"—the British and the Americans. Dr. Schwarz had passed the story up the line to General Clay, who dismissed it as drunken gossip. On his own, Dr. Schwarz had begun secretly filling warehouses with emergency supplies.

The first public reaction from the Allies came from one of Clay's subordinates, the commander of civil government in the American Sector of Berlin, Colonel Frank Howley, a former Philadelphia advertising executive. He was, in effect, the city manager of one-quarter of Berlin. An Irishman, and a volatile one, he was called "Howling Howley" for a reason. Hearing of the blockade, he rushed to the studio of RIAS, "Radio in the American Sector," on his own and announced: "We are not getting out of Berlin. We are going to stay. I don't know the answer to the current problem—not yet—but this much I do know: The American people will not allow the German people to starve."

General Clay, also the commander of all American troops in Europe, had been in meetings in Heidelberg, the U.S. military headquarters, and flew back to western Berlin, where he lived. He told his counterparts, the British and French commanders, that he was sure the Russians were bluffing, and he proposed sending an armored convoy of 6,000 men to race down the Autobahn from Helmstedt to Berlin, using American engineers to repair the bridges—if there was anything actually wrong with them.

Lucius DuBignon Clay, fifty years old, a 1918 graduate of the U.S. Military Academy, was both brilliant and aloof, a courtly but distant man, a descendant of Henry Clay and the son of a U.S. senator from Georgia. He wore few decorations on his uniform and was a chain-smoker, rarely photographed without a Camel in his hand. He usually skipped lunch—he lost thirty pounds in Germany—but was said to drink thirty cups of coffee a day. He sometimes worked seventy-two hours at a stretch, with his Scottie, George, at his feet, and was one of the very few Americans ever to become a four-star general without commanding men in combat. An engineer and administrator, he was always needed more urgently at home than on fields of battle. In World War II, he served as what amounted to a national czar of military production and procurement. He came to Europe only once during the war, at the personal request of the supreme Allied commander, General Dwight D. Eisenhower, to figure out how to move men and equipment inland from the beaches after the invasion of France on D-Day, June 6, 1944.

Clay's British counterpart in Germany, General Sir Brian Robertson, described him as "looking like a Roman emperor and sometimes acting like one." Among the Americans who served him there was a joke that Clay was a real nice guy when he relaxed, but he never relaxed. He had what amounted to dictatorial powers in the American Zone of Germany and Sector of Berlin. Believing the Russians would back down in the face of force, he wanted his troops in motion before any of his superiors in Washington—the chairman of the Joint Chiefs of Staff, General Omar Bradley, Secretary of the Army Kenneth Royall, Secretary of Defense James Forrestal and President Harry S. Truman—could order him to stop.

Clay had already discussed the convoy idea with General Curtis LeMay, commander of USAFE (United States Air Force Europe). LeMay was a bombing legend before he was forty for developing the block formation of B-17s and B-24s, Flying Fortresses and Liberators—bombers that destroyed much of Germany—and the use of incendiary bombing that destroyed Japan's cities. Characteristically, he had already prepared a contingency bombing plan to begin if a convoy was blocked by the Red Army: LeMay believed American planes could destroy every Soviet airfield and every airplane on the ground in Germany in a few hours, because the Russians routinely and irrationally made their own planes perfect targets by lining them up in orderly rows. "They vetoed the plan," said LeMay in disgust. In his lexicon "They" usually meant liberal politicians in

Washington. "The Berlin crisis," he said, "is a logical outgrowth of the God-bless-our-buddy-buddy-Russians-we-sure-can-trust-them-forever-and-ever philosophy that flowered way back in the Roosevelt Administration." And, as far as the Soviets were concerned, he said, "We could have done a pretty good job of cleaning out the Russian air force in one blow. They had no atomic capability. Hell, they didn't have much of any capability."

But before Washington knew any of this had happened, Clay and LeMay's plans were stopped by the British military governor, General Robertson. "If you do that, it'll be war, it's as simple as that," Robertson told Clay. "If you do that, I'm afraid my government could offer you no support—and I'm sure the French will feel the same."

The early hours of the next morning brought the daily American "teleconference"—Clay and officials in Washington held coded teletyped conferences most days, with the decoded words slowly tapping out on huge lighted screens in the Pentagon and the bunker under American military headquarters in Berlin. By the time he left the bunker, the American commander had received his orders: Clay was told to take no action that risked war with the Soviet Union. It was a frustrating setback for Clay. He was sure that the Soviets did not want war. He was equally sure that a stable, free Europe depended on an economically strong and democratic Germany, with an elected parliament, an executive and an independent judiciary. Clay was a hard man, but, above all, he was a true democrat. His views of Germany's future were often quite different from those in Washington—and in London and Paris—where many high officials preferred a Germany forcibly kept too weakened to begin another war. Usually he got his way by acting preemptively or threatening to quit in letters and during teleconferences. He was a man with many antagonists, beginning with Secretary of State George Marshall and his celebrated assistants, Robert Lovett and George Kennan, who usually believed Clay was trying to move too fast toward a self-governed Germany rebuilding its industrial power. All admired his talent, but few found it easy to work with him.* One of his adversaries was his superior, General Bradley, who had said secretly, back in April, "Shouldn't we announce the withdrawal from Berlin ourselves to minimize the loss of prestige?"

Clay's answer, via teleconference, was:

I do not believe we should plan on leaving Berlin short of a Soviet ultimatum to drive us out by force if we do not leave. At the time we must resolve the question as to our reply to such an ultimatum. The exception which could force us out would be the Soviet stoppage of all food supplies to German population in Western sectors. I doubt that Soviets will make such a move because it would alienate the Germans almost completely, unless they were prepared to supply food for more than two million people.

The official population of the western sectors was just over 2.1 million. The number for the whole city of 355 square miles, a bit more than the area of the five boroughs of New York City, was about 3.1 million, compared with 4.3 million in 1938. There were only 1,285,376 male Berliners after the war.

In that teleconference, Clay ended angrily. "Why are we in Europe? We have lost Czechoslovakia. We have lost Finland. Norway is threatened . . . If we mean we are to hold Europe against communism, we must not budge . . . If America does not know this, does not believe the issue is cast now, then it never will and communism will run rampant. Once again, I ask, do we have a German policy?"

Hearing of the latest temporizing in Washington from Clay, Robertson then suggested that perhaps the Allies could expand the daily

---

* Clay's most important biographer, Jean Edward Smith, did two hundred hours of interviews with his subject. Asked how well he knew Clay, Smith answered: "I would not presume to say I 'knew' him. He was not a first-name kind of guy."

flights that brought provisions into the city for their own troops. They had done that in March, three months earlier, when the Soviets briefly stopped trains from Helmstedt, using three twenty-mile-wide air corridors that had been agreed upon in a written air safety plan between the Soviets, Americans and British at Potsdam in November of 1945. The three air corridors coverged over Berlin from Frankfurt, Hamburg and Hannover, looking on a map like a hand-drawn arrowhead pointing into the city. Robertson's bold talk was backed up by a bold British Foreign Minister, Ernest Bevin, who had once been Britain's most important and outspoken labor leader. Those flights in C-47s, the military version of the Douglas DC-3 airliners with a cargo capacity of three tons, were being used to help supply food and other essentials to just over 25,000 healthy young soldiers and some middle-aged diplomats and their families living comfortably among the West Berliners.

The Berliners themselves were a totally defeated people in every sense of the word. They were very old and very young, mostly women, hungry, sick, most of them burrowed into the rubble of their old neighborhoods in basements and damaged apartments assigned as shelter for four or five families. In Charlottenberg, a central neighborhood, only 604 of 11,075 buildings were still standing.

William Heimlich was a thirty-three-year-old lieutenant colonel in military intelligence from Columbus, Ohio. He arrived in Berlin in the summer of 1945, after Soviet troops had ravaged the city—just as the Nazis had ravaged the Soviet cities—and saw this:

> Berlin at that point was a city of women. The men were dead or in prisoner of war camps. There were only the aged and the very young males available. They moved about the city like zombies. They were starving, that was clear. We saw such things as a horse dropping dead in the street and the women rushing out with pans and knives to butcher the horse on the spot to get some

food. There was no food. There were no lights, there was no power.

Henry Ries, a Jewish Berliner who had escaped Germany in 1938 at the age of twenty-one, returned in September 1945 as a photographer on assignment for the *New York Times*. He wrote home to the United States that he thought the Berliners, who were forced to step into the gutters and tip their hats when their conquerors passed, still retained a secret attitude of superiority toward their conquerors. But a couple of months later, he wrote: "Of course they deserve [to suffer] at least a good part of them. But that doesn't prevent me from feeling pain at seeing these hungry people, crippled people, diseased people, all smelling of filth . . . I saw a man with one eye and one leg moving along in a 3-wheel cart. Why him? Why not me? Of course they deserved it, but that doesn't mean I want to see it."

General Clay was more blunt, calling Berlin "a city of the dead." LeMay used the same words as Heimlich, "a city of zombies."

The Soviets had pillaged the city after they captured it in May 1945, removing 3,500 factories and 1,115,000 pieces of industrial equipment for transportation, bolt by bolt, back to the Soviet Union, along with thousands of German technicians and managers. There were an estimated one million rapes in the city during the sixty-two days between the Soviet capture on May 2, 1945, and the arrival of American troops on July 3, 1945.

Almost three years later, in February 1948, Collie Small wrote in *Collier's* magazine:

Chronic hunger has taken the worst toll. In many cases, otherwise normal Berliners have skidded mentally through a lack of food until their sense of discrimination is fuzzy, their objectivity largely gone, their reactions dangerously slow. Crossing streets, they are easily confused and frequently wander uncertainly into the paths of oncoming automobiles, or, worse yet, stand fatally entranced in the swirl of traffic, paralyzed with fear and indecision. Industrial accidents have skyrocketed. In 1938, with industry in Berlin going at top speed, there were 1,867 fatal accidents. In 1946, the last year for which complete figures are available, there were 5,342 industrial fatalities in Berlin, and those with less than 15 per cent of the 1938 factories even operating. An accountant confessed that he was frequently baffled by simple columns of figures and that a problem in simple addition or subtraction often seemed like an advanced exercise in calculus. An optician complained that he could no longer muster enough concentration even to be sure of making the correct change in eyeglasses for his customers.

At the same time, school officials in the city questioned 41 boys between the ages of twelve and fourteen. This is what they found: 22 had no blankets, 14 no bed linen, 7 no shirt, 21 no shoes, 37 no overcoat. Questioning 34 schoolgirls between the ages of fifteen and eighteen, the officials reported that 7 had contracted a venereal disease and 14 had slept with men to get food. A sixteen-year-old living in eastern Berlin, Lutz Rackow, whose family lost their house for a year when Red Army telephone linemen appeared and gave the family thirty minutes to pack and get out, said, "Teachers tried to teach us declensions, but all we thought about was food, cabbage soup from the Russians, cookies from the Americans."

Small added that cats and dogs disappeared regularly and graves were being robbed to use wooden caskets for fuel. And the city was dangerous; roving Red Army deserters were sometimes willing to kill to eat. Gerhard Rietdorff, a young man living on the streets of the eastern sector who was arrested (and beaten) more than a dozen times as a runner in the black market, carried a large cut of meat into the house where his group hid. "It looked abnormally red and smelled sweet," he said. "We debated back and forth until somebody said,

'Well maybe it's not the meat of a human being.' Our disgust, though, was greater than our hunger. We threw it away."*

What Geoff Smith, an RAF mechanic, would never forget was the sound of the bicycles of Berlin in 1948. They had no tires and scraped along on metal wheels. He arrived in the early-morning hours of June 20, 1948, at Gatow airport, then a rarely used stopover for British military flights to Warsaw. With a dozen airmen he was ordered to unload crates and sacks marked "Bird Dog" from two Dakotas, the British designation for C-47s. The next day he realized that the sacks contained Deutschmarks, the new currency secretly printed in the United States by the Allies for use in West Germany, but not in Berlin. In the city, negotiations continued with the Soviets on establishing a new currency under quadripartite control. That day, Monday, June 21, at 7 A.M., American planes were also secretly flying crates of the new money from Frankfurt in the American Zone of West Germany into Tempelhof Airport. The American airmen were also carrying hand grenades and ordered to blow up the cases marked "Clay" and "Bird Dog" if something went wrong and they were forced down in Soviet-occupied East Germany. It was a nervous flight, with men on the ground speculating about the secret cargo: Americans thought it was dog food—Clay loved dogs—and the British thought it was parts to assemble an atom bomb.

A radio announcement of the new Deutschmark in the Allied-occupied zones of western Germany was recorded by Sergeant Robert Lochner, the American director of Radio Frankfurt. He had grown up in Germany as the son of an Associated Press reporter, and his message, a civil revolution, was played over and over again beginning on Sunday night. West Germans were told that they should

---

* Cannibalism in postwar Berlin was part of the plot of *The Dark Arena*, a novel written by a civilian employee of OMGUS (Office of Military Government, United States). The book, written in 1953 and published in 1955, received good reviews but did not sell well until fifteen years later, when its author, Mario Puzo, wrote his third book, *The Godfather*.

turn in their old Reichsmarks at designated locations and would receive forty new Deutschmarks immediately and twenty more in two months. Lochner's message emphasized that the order did not apply to West Berlin. But four days later, after the Soviets announced they would produce a new currency for both East Germany and eastern Berlin, western Deutschmarks, stamped with a large *B*—the bills in the "Bird Dog" crates—were distributed in West Berlin. Berliners in the western sectors waited in line for up to six hours to get their new money. In announcing their own currency reform, the Soviets added a phrase that persuaded many that worse was coming: "Bank notes issued in the Western zones of Germany are not being admitted for circulation in the Soviet occupation zone in Germany and in Berlin, which is part of the Soviet occupation zone." Those last eight words, many believed, would lead to withdrawal by the Western Allies—or war.*

In fact, the Soviets were totally surprised by the timing of the Allied currency reform, so rather than attempting to print new currency, they pasted little stickers on old Reichsmarks, distributing them to party officials at a 1:1 rate with the new Western currency, then giving ordinary East German and East Berlin residents the same bills with exchange rates between 3:1 and 4:1, which quickly drifted as low as ten Eastmarks for each Westmark.

The currency reform was the immediate cause of the blockade of Berlin, or at least that is what the Soviets said. The headline on June 20 in *Tägliche Rundschau*, a Soviet-controlled newspaper:

---

* Lochner, fluent in German, became famous years later for an odd mistake. In 1961, he phonetically taught President John Kennedy to say, in German, the phrase "I am a Berliner!" for a famous speech the President gave in Berlin in 1963. Somehow, the phrase became "Ich bin ein Berliner" rather than "Ich bin Berliner"—and thus could be translated comically as "I am a jelly doughnut." "A Berliner"—the article is important—is not a citizen but a pastry.

WESTERN POWERS COMPLETE
THE DIVISION OF GERMANY
Separate Currency Reforms in Western Sectors—
A Heavy Blow to the Interests of Workers

Three days later, on June 23, an extra edition of *Tägliche Rund-schau* filled its front page with the official text of Decree 111:

> By the commander of the Soviet Military Administration in Germany . . . As of June 24, 1948, new notes will be introduced for the entire territory of the Soviet-occupied zone in Germany and the greater Berlin area: the Reichsmark and Rentenmark, as formerly, with special coupons stuck on . . . As of June 28, 1948, the circulation of marks issued by the Allied military authorities, as well as of the Reichsmarks without special coupons, is to be discontinued. Signed: V. Sokolovsky, Marshal of the Soviet Union.

Allied occupation authorities countered with a "special edition" of the *Telegraph*, a British-licensed Berlin daily:

> The Soviet orders to change the currency in the greater Berlin area are in contradiction to the four-power agreement on a four-power administration of greater Berlin. In the French, British and American sectors these orders are null and void and do not apply to the inhabitants of these sectors. Contraveners will be prosecuted. The necessary steps will be taken to introduce the new currency of the Western zones into the three Western sectors of greater Berlin.

At the end of the war, the four powers had decided to continue the use of Hitler's Reichsmark as legal tender in the four occupation zones of Germany and the four sectors of Berlin. The currency quickly went from being practically worthless—the Nazis had increased the money in circulation from 7 billion Reichsmarks to more than 50 billion during the war—to almost totally worthless. In addition to the German inflation, the Americans made a naive mistake in creating a new and separate Allied Occupation Currency and giving each of the four powers plates, made in the U.S.A., to print their own military money—and triggered a double inflation. The Russians used the plates given to them to print billions of occupation marks to give to their soldiers, who had never been paid as they fought for four years across the Soviet Union and Eastern Europe. For all practical purposes, bartering and a thriving black market, with American cigarettes as the preferred currency, became the real economy of Berlin. Shops showed empty shelves, their nonperishable goods hoarded in warehouses, waiting for a new currency. Men and women worked only long enough to earn enough Reichsmarks to cover what they could get with their ration cards. College professors asked for three pounds of flour from students before they began lecturing.

For the Allies occupying the western sectors, most particularly Clay, currency reform was seen as the only action that could even begin to make Berlin once again into some kind of normal city. And there were many among the occupiers and their leaders who did not want that to happen. The Soviets acted as if they believed economic chaos would deliver all of the city and perhaps the country itself to their control. The French, invaded twice by Germany in twenty-six years, wanted to see all of Germany remain a poor agricultural society. Important Americans agreed: Secretary of the Treasury Henry Morgenthau proposed a program called "pastoralization," designed to make Germany into a pre-industrial country with a daily diet of 1,600 calories per person, leaving the people too weak to even consider revolt or aggression.

In fact, in 1947, Clay's staff had estimated that the average Berliner in the American Sector was living on a little more than nine hundred calories a day. Anthony Mann, a correspondent for London's

Daily Telegraph, visited a dozen German homes and described their diet:

> Breakfast consisted of one slice of black bread and "tea" brewed from lemon blossoms or "coffee" made from acorns . . . At mid-day, each adult usually got two thin slices of bread and a potato . . . Supper was one bowl of watery soup made from carrots or barley. Occasionally there were minute scraps of various fats, and some-times a little extra (mainly vegetables) could be obtained from a farmer after a trudge, in exchange for treasures such as shoe leather, nails or string.

A month before the blockade began, Elisabeth Poensgen, a woman who had been rich enough never to work, wrote a letter to relatives in the western zone, saying:

> I had lost a lot of weight and my cousin Wergin gave me vitamin supplements that he had received from England. They did me good, but unfortunately, I was very hungry afterwards so that I nearly couldn't think of anything else than food . . . This is all I can write for today. I am completely exhausted. My eyes are squinting because I am so tired. Getting used to work (as a school-teacher) at an old age is extremely difficult, much more difficult than I had imagined.

She was forty-two years old.

The most famous diarist of the period, a forty-five-year-old book editor at the Ullman publishing house named Ruth Andreas-Friedrich, whose journals were published in two volumes in Germany, described life before the blockade this way:

> Slowly one gets used to walk rather than spend twenty pfennigs for the streetcar. Twenty pfennigs! How much is twenty pfennigs?

It is the price of the seventy grams of butter the average person is entitled to every ten days. On the black market it buys one and a third milligrams of butter. Ten grams, enough for a sandwich of bread and butter, costs fifteen marks. Seven legal butter sandwiches for every ten days will not help much and certainly will not fill the average person's stomach . . .

For a portion of the population small change is a thousand-mark bill, while for another it's a five-pfennig piece. The new capitalists are the dealers in scarce goods, the producers of scarce goods, the providers of scarce services, the black marketers, the factory owners, the farmers, the craftsmen—in food-supply terms they represent the upper classes of today's Germany. Those to whom the monthly rations are providing a basic existence, but are not the sole means of subsistence, form the new middle class. Their modest sources of capital are—in case of need—their connections to farmers, chance bargains, Sunday hoarding excursions, and the exchange of remaining tangibles for additional calories . . . Silverware from one's dowry for cigarettes, coffee, a winter coat or suiting. Great-grandma's Dresden china for ten pounds of sugar, five bottles of schnapps, three packs of tobacco, twelve hundred pounds of coal and a pair of galoshes . . . Eighty-five percent of all Berliners live on additional products beyond their ration card allotments, a recent American opinion poll revealed. That means more than three quarters of the population is now involved in the black market . . . the unemployed citizen goes gathering. Half a box of soap powder equals 5 marks, equals three beers, equals 30 marks. A quarter pound of tea equals 100 marks, equals a pound of butter, equals 240 marks.

Another diarist, Inge Godenschweger, wrote of the "foraging trains," with Berliners riding the roofs and clinging to the sides of trains going through the farmlands of East Germany, ready to trade heirlooms for food. There were stories of stables with Persian rugs covering bare earth. "We stole like crazy," she said. "Farmers hired guards, who hid in the furrows of their fields. One caught us, standing over us, laughing. Then he walked away. He was stealing, too."

As early as the summer of 1946, Andreas-Friedrich lived and understood the dangers of her city's geography:

> The Russians surround us. Only a narrow corridor, a single-track railway line, connects Berlin with the West. Our vegetables, our fruit, our potatoes—nearly all our food is obtained from the neighboring provinces. In a twinkling the occupying power there could sever our lifeline. All they need do is prevent a few trains from passing through—block a bridge, or let the single-track railway line deteriorate . . . If necessary, will the Western Allies supply three million Berliners with potatoes? With fruit, vegetables, coal and electricity? Or will they tell us that this problem, too, is a "German domestic matter"?

Andreas-Friedrich reported rumors of currency reform again and again in her diary during 1946 and 1947. But only in 1948 did the rumors become reality. Reporting on the buildup to the reform, Mann of London's *Telegraph* wrote, as early as June 8, 1948, that there would be a 90 percent devaluation of the 65 billion Reichsmarks circulating in the western zones. On the 13th, he wrote: "Trade is almost at a standstill, as nobody will part with goods for cash which may be valueless." Then he quoted a British economist as saying: "Our aim is to make money just as scarce as food so that it will be worth working for." An American added: "There will be a vast upheaval: it will be like a bomb under the economic structure."

Four-power Berlin was always a bomb, the most dangerous place in the world. The place had been ticking almost from the beginning, when the city was divided at American insistence. The symbolism of the city, capital of the Prussians and then Hitler, was such that the United States was willing to turn over to the Red Army two "lands," provinces south of Berlin, Saxony and Thuringia, in return for part of western Berlin. An intelligence report from Berlin to Soviet Foreign Minister Vyacheslav Molotov on October 3, 1947, stated:

> Analysis of the materials at our disposal, and of the steps which were taken by the United States and Great Britain in Germany, gives grounds for the conclusion that we are not speaking about a propaganda maneuver or political blackmail, but about a real threat of political and economic dismemberment of Germany and inclusion of West Germany with all its resources in the Western bloc knocked together by the United States.

The report was essentially correct and so was a briefing for President Truman on December 22, 1947, from the new Central Intelligence Agency, along with reports from the United States Embassy in Moscow warning that the immediate goal of Soviet policy in Germany was to "force" the Allies out of Berlin. On February 20, 1948, a memo to the President from Secretary of State George Marshall was practically a mirror image of the intelligence traffic reaching Molotov: "Western Germany may at some time in the future be drawn into Eastern orbit with all obvious consequences which such an eventuality would entail ... It has long been decided, in collaboration with the British government, that desire for an undivided Germany cannot be made an excuse for inaction in Western Germany. . . ."

Two weeks after the Marshall memo was written, communists in Czechoslovakia, backed by Red Army troops, staged a brutal coup d'état in Prague, overthrowing a coalition government there. The world was shocked and so was Clay, who on March 5 cabled Army Intelligence in Washington with a message he later insisted was meant to be secret, to be used only by the Joint Chiefs of Staff to argue for bigger defense budgets:

For many months, based on logical analysis, I have felt and held that war was unlikely for at least ten years. Within the last few weeks, I have felt a subtle change in Soviet attitude which I cannot define but which now gives me a feeling that it may come with dramatic suddenness. I cannot support this change in my own thinking with any data or outward evidence in relationships other than to describe it as a feeling of a new tenseness in every Soviet individual with whom we have official relations. I am unable to submit any official report in the absence of supporting data but my feeling is real. You may advise the Chief of Staff of this for whatever it may be worth if you feel it advisable.

Whatever Clay's intentions, the memo was released to the press, specifically the *Saturday Evening Post*, and was seized upon by his adversaries and others to whip up war fears across the country and to question whether there was any point in clinging to Berlin at the risk of war.

Clay actually knew better. It was not war the Soviets wanted. It was Berlin. Premier Joseph Stalin, like the czars before him, believed that the city in the east of modern Germany, a city that had begun as a Slavic fortress and had been taken by Russian troops in the eighteenth century, was in fact Russian by historic right. Berlin, to both sides in 1948, was more important psychologically than militarily. On March 19, two weeks after Clay sent his war memo to the Pentagon, Stalin met, secretly of course, with East German communists, a group led by the German communist leader, Wilhelm Pieck. The German, trained in Moscow, told Stalin the truth, which was a rare thing. Usually, subordinates at any level, from military intelligence officers in Berlin to Foreign Minister Molotov, restricted themselves to telling Stalin only what he wanted to hear. Pieck, however, told the premier that the SED, the communist-controlled Socialist Unity Party in Berlin, was certain to lose badly in city elections scheduled for October, setting back the efforts to force the Allies to leave the city. Stalin responded: "Let's make a joint effort, perhaps we can kick them out."*

Stalin's decision had probably been made a couple of weeks earlier, before or during a meeting with Marshal Vasily Sokolovsky, the Soviet commander in Germany, General Clay's counterpart. On March 20, the day after Stalin's meeting with German communists, Sokolovsky walked out of a meeting of the Allied Control Council, telling Clay, Robertson and the French commander, General Joseph Pierre Koenig, "I see no sense in continuing this meeting and declare it adjourned."

That was the end of four-power government in Germany. Sokolovsky left when the British, American and French commanders refused to discuss the results of the London Conference of the three countries' foreign ministers, who had convened in February to discuss the future of Germany. In fact, Russian intelligence services almost certainly knew the results as soon as the Allies did: the foreign ministers, along with their counterparts from the Netherlands and Belgium, gave up on obtaining Soviet cooperation and were ready to move toward creating a separate West German state. By April 9, Reuters in London was reporting early details of those still-secret plans:

> The United States has proposed a five point program setting up a West German government within just over a year it was learned here today. The five stages in the plan are believed to be: First the formation of a provisional government embracing the present Anglo-American Bizone and the French zone. Secondly, territorial reorganization of Länder Provisional governments ...

---

* Few Soviet documents have been found concerning the blockade and airlift, except for minutes of a Politburo meeting of June 30, 1948, when there was a short discussion of Soviet anti-aircraft readiness. One Soviet military historian, Viktor Gorbarev, spent years searching archives and concluded that, as in the case of other historical failures of Stalin's, records had been destroyed or never kept. "There was no settled Stalin policy for Europe or for Berlin," said Gorbarev. "It was all action, counter-action." Norman Naimark, author of *The Russians in Germany*, came to a similar conclusion: "Soviet documents never refer to a blockade except when describing Western propaganda."

Thirdly, election of constituent assembly. Fourthly, the drafting by this assembly of a constitution. Fifthly, the formation of a new West German government.

Two months later that proposal and decision were made public when the conference adjourned on June 6, 1948.

After the walkout in Berlin, Soviet troops began a sort of rolling blockade, unpredictably and intermittently stopping Allied trains and vehicle traffic down the Autobahn to the city. That was when Clay and Robertson responded by using the three air corridors to fly nineteen C-47s a day into Tempelhof and RAF Gatow with supplies for their troops and diplomats. Russian Yak fighters, named for the designer, Aleksandr Yakovlev, entered the corridors, buzzing and otherwise harassing Allied traffic, until April 4, when a Yak-3 collided with a British Viking airliner, killing all nineteen passengers and crew aboard as well as the Yak pilot.

The Soviets, claiming the airliner deliberately rammed the Yak, considered that first mini-blockade a significant success. Military commanders cabled Molotov on April 17, saying:

> The plan drawn up, according to your instructions, for restrictive measures to be taken regarding communications between Berlin and the Soviet Occupation Zones and the Western Occupation zones is applied from 1 April, except for restrictions of communications by air, which we intend to introduce later . . . Our control and restrictive measures have dealt a strong blow to the prestige of the Americans and British in Germany. The German population believes that this testifies to the Russians strength . . . Clay's attempt to create "an airlift" connecting Berlin to the Western zones have proved futile.

"Prices are rising. One scarce commodity after another disappears from the black market. Currency reform seems certain now," wrote

Ruth Andreas-Friedrich in her diary on June 1, 1948. Her family piled all the Reichsmarks they had on a little kitchen table and decided to spend it all before the old currency became worthless.

> The stores are crowded as they are in peaceful times. Apparently we are not the only ones, these days, who are inclined to stockpile toys, bulky kitchen utensils and ugly lamps.
>
> "What are we going to do with all this junk?" I grimly inquire as we walk along Steglitzer Hauptstrasse loaded down with our purchases. Six kitchen knives that do not cut, six tin spoons with edges that do, a useless soap dish, four wooden ladles full of cracks, two lamps without socket or switches, but with nightmarishly patterned lampshades, and in spite of all, six tubes of cement toothpaste, six crumbling tubes of lipstick, and toys—enough toys to open a toy store.
>
> "Don't worry," Heike [her daughter] tries to comfort me, "at least we skimmed the cream. Those who come after us will fare worse."

On June 11, 1948, she wrote:

> "I buy coffee," someone says. "One can always use coffee." And he goes and buys twelve pounds of coffee at twelve hundred marks a pound. His savings from three years of work.
>
> This person buys a hundred chisels, another buys two thousand test tubes, someone else spends three hundred marks on laxatives, and the next one, ninety marks on health tea. At the municipal railroad stations discreet briefcase carriers make profits like never before, selling American chocolate, candy and caramels. They disappear as soon as the police show up, only to return all the more numerous as soon as the coast is clear again. Berlin is selling out. Berlin is in a panic . . .

On June 15, 1948:

The prices go up every hour. One pound of coffee, two thousand marks. One cigarette, thirty marks. You are lucky to find one at all because the black marketers too are beginning to feather their nests. Hoarding . . . hoarding, rather than selling at all for Reichsmarks. The last useless products and decorative articles disappear from the shop windows. "Closed due to illness . . . temporarily closed due to lack of supply."

I enter my favorite bar. The chairs are empty. One solitary customer drinking a modest seltzer. Beer—sold out, spirits—sold out, matches, cigarettes, tobacco—entirely out of the question! I ask. I beg. I implore the waiter, the porter, the owner. With great effort and distress, the latter struggles with himself, finally letting me have a crushed Chesterfield. "Because it's you! My last one!" he says, and without the slightest scruple he charges me forty marks for it . . .

June 19, 1948:

Just now the Soviet Military Administration announced: "In connection with the currency reform the Soviet Military Administration has been forced to take the following measures in order to protect the interests of the population and the economy: All travel to and from the Soviet-occupied zone of Germany is suspended. Entry is refused to vehicle traffic of every sort coming from the Western zones, including all traffic on the highway between Helmstedt and Berlin." Now we're in for it! Snap, said the mouse, finding herself trapped! We poor little mice of Berlin!

June 22, 1948:

The price for a pound of coffee is three thousand marks. A loaf of bread, two hundred marks. One Chesterfield, seventy-five marks.

One wonders where the goods are still coming from. There is a buzzing in the air as in the time of bombs. On short notice, the American military government has increased air traffic to Berlin several times over.

"We're able," General Clay tells us, "to supply the ten thousand Americans in Berlin via airlift for an indefinite period of time." And he adds optimistically: "The Russian occupation authorities will not let the German population of the Western sectors starve."

We are less hopeful.

Another diarist, a young man named Christian Seaford, wrote: "Life is empty, without color . . . There is a lead-like silence over the city. Kids collecting dandelions for the rabbits on the balcony. Everybody believes the Americans will give up Berlin . . . For many people suicide seems the only way out."

The *Times of London,* June 25, 1948:

SEVERED WESTERN LINKS
WITH BERLIN

General Clay, the American Military Governor, has stated that supply by air, on which the Western sectors are now entirely dependent, is not possible "as a long-term policy."

Clay's view, expressed in teleconferences that day with Secretary of the Army Kenneth Royall and other officials in Washington:

It seems important to decide just how far we will go short of war to stay in Berlin. We here think it extremely important to stay . . . Except for our capacity to stick it out, we have few chips here to use and future actions would appear to be at governmental level. I regard the possibility of war with the Russians as rather remote, although it must not be disregarded.

As early as May 1948, officials in Washington raised the question of evacuating American dependents, the wives and children of the diplomats and soldiers in the city. Clay replied:

The evacuation of family members from Berlin would lead to a hysterical reaction and drive the Germans in droves into the supposed safety of Communism . . . Every German leader, except SED leaders, and thousands of Germans have courageously expressed their opposition to Communism. We must not destroy their confidence by any indication of departure from Berlin. I still do not believe our dependents should be evacuated. Once again we have to sweat it out, come what may. If Soviets want war, it will not be because of Berlin currency issue but because they believe this is the right time . . . Certainly we are not trying to provoke war. We are taking a lot of punches on the chin without striking back.

Looking back on that day years later, Clay would say:

Remember this, when the war ended we were sitting over there with the greatest army that had ever been seen, nobody was ever concerned about anybody blocking us on roads and railroads . . . The Japs surrendered and then the demand for bringing the troops home was great. Within a relatively short period of time our military forces had deteriorated until they were nothing but young high school boys not wanting to be there. It was pretty sad.

"Bring the boys home" was the American chant (and policy) as soon as World War II ended. The total strength of the U.S. Army in February 1948 was 552,000 men; the new Air Force, replacing the Army Air

Force in 1947, had 346,000 men. The strength of the U.S. Navy was 476,000 men, including 79,000 Marines. There were just over 90,000 American soldiers in Germany and fewer than the 103,000 British soldiers in the country. The French had 75,000 men. The Soviet strength was estimated at close to one million men in East Germany and eastern Berlin. Said Secretary of State George Marshall, chairman of the Joint Chiefs during the war: "This is the disintegration of not only armed forces, but apparently of all conception of world responsibility."

Added Clay: "It was under these conditions that I am sure the Russians made up their mind that it was time to push; that our actions didn't indicate any desire on our part to stay in Europe."

Still, there were East-West factors, having nothing to do with military strength, that the Soviets did not understand. As early as late June, a series of vivid "Top Secret" memos from the Central Intelligence Agency to the President emphasized the interdependence of the economies of the two halves of Berlin. In fact, though it had never been announced publicly, during the spring of 1948, the Allies ordered West German manufacturers to gradually reduce industrial exports to East Germany—and increased those measures, again without announcement, throughout the airlift. It was a tactic Soviet military officials did not take into account until it was too late. As the CIA reported to Truman on June 30:

> A conference was held in Karlshorst on June 28 between Russian officials, and German members of the German Industrial Committee. Sokolovsky asked the industrialists what was the influence on the Eastern Zone of Germany of the [counter] blockades from the Western Zone.
>
> A German representative stated that being cut off from the West meant a complete stoppage of production in sugar refineries for lack of 50,000 meters of steel piping on order in the West-

ern Zone; it also meant a complete closing down of canneries since all raw material was received from the West; and a certain discontinuance of the Baltic fishing fleet in a short time because of a lack of machinery parts . . . The German member then stated that heavy industries, particularly the steel mills in Hennigsdorf, could not produce without the West and that other heavy industries in the Eastern Zone would be equally affected . . ."

American officials estimated that before the blockade eastern Germans were importing 320,000 tons of processed steel, 400,000 tons of chemicals and 110,000 tires from the west during the last year.

Sokolovsky was in a rage, reported the CIA. "He replied that the Russians had been led to believe the East could be independent of the West."

Another Russian general shouted: "We had no idea of this situation; Russia is suffering from heavy droughts and is counting on German food supplies this year . . . If we had known this, we would not have gone so far."

Angrily, Sokolovsky said this meant only three possibilities were available now:

"Start a war.

"Lift travel restrictions on Berlin.

"Leave entire Berlin to the West, giving them a rail line."

After the meeting, Col. Serge Tulpanov, head of the Soviet Information Division in Germany, said that war was impossible due to bad harvest prospects and that lifting travel restrictions would make the Russians lose face. The third possibility was that the West would have to feed all of Berlin and would have more on their hands than they had bargained for.

Field comment: The above information is an indication that the Russians mean business in the present crisis. Having gone this far, it is difficult to see how they could back down.

In some ways, that Monday, June 28, 1948, defined the Berlin Blockade and then the airlift. The Soviets had gone too far on too little information. Later in the day, the President of the United States took his own leap of faith. At lunchtime in Washington, Truman called in Defense Secretary James Forrestal, Secretary of the Army Kenneth Royall and Undersecretary of State Robert Lovett, representing Marshall, who was ill. They all dismissed the idea of an airlift, with Lovett beginning to list options for leaving the city. He was cut off by the President:

"We stay in Berlin. Period."

CHAPTER 2

"Absolutely Impossible!"

June 28, 1948

"302, GIT MOVIN'. YOU GOT YOUR TAIL IN MY PROP."

Lieutenant William Lafferty, a twenty-three-year-old Air Force pilot, was stationed at Rhein-Main Air Base, seven miles south of Frankfurt, the field that German Zeppelins flew to and from in the 1930s. He had already made a midday C-47 flight to Tempelhof Airport in Berlin on June 26, 1948, carrying food, cigarettes and other supplies for the American men and women who made up the small force occupying one of the four sectors of the broken capital. The airport, in the center of the American-occupied sector of the Allied half-city, stood as an island surrounded by East Germany—and by the Red Army. When he returned to Rhein-Main, which was also functioning as the largest commercial airport in Germany, he was surprised to be stopped by an operations officer, his friend Lieutenant Herschel Simmons, who pointed to another "Gooney Bird," as the old C-47s were called. "When it's loaded with those cartons of food," Simmons said, "get a crew together and fly that one to Berlin."

"Too dark," said Lafferty. Allied pilots rarely used the three twenty-mile-wide air corridors over Soviet-occupied territory at night. The pilot said he would take off at first light and began walking away.

"You've got to go now," the ops officer called.

"No, it's not safe," Lafferty repeated.

"Lieutenant!" a scarier voice bellowed. "You get your ass out to that plane now and take it to Berlin as soon as they finish loading."

He turned around. It was the base commander, Colonel Walter Lee, coming toward him.

He quickly recruited a copilot, a guy making his first flight into Tempelhof, and they landed in almost total darkness. Lafferty wanted to stay in the airport for the rest of the night, but he was told to turn around again after the plane was unloaded. They took off in the early gray dawn of European summer. Lafferty's copilot saw for the first time the six-story apartment building a hundred yards from where they had touched down in the dark.

"Did we go over that when we landed?" the new man asked.

"Yep," said Lafferty.

"Jesus!"

"Welcome to Berlin."

The clearance above the roof was just seventeen feet and pilots swore there were skid marks on that roof. The approach pattern was just one of the problems with the airport, a grass bowl that had originally been built as a parade ground at the turn of the century, then enclosed on one side by a Hitler-approved terminal with seven underground levels that had included not only a full hospital but also a Focke-Wulf aircraft factory. The other side of the field, the southern rim, was guarded by the apartment buildings, which were separated by a cemetery.

Lafferty had been ordered back to Rhein-Main, so at least he and his crew would get to sleep in their own beds. But the first voice they heard on the radio as they exited Soviet-controlled airspace over East Germany told them to keep going twenty-five miles farther west to another American base, Wiesbaden.

"But," Lafferty began to say.

"No buts! Understand! You've been diverted to Wiesbaden, get over there."

This time they were greeted by another colonel, Bertram Harrison, commander of the 60th Troop Carrier Group, based at Wiesbaden.

"Congratulations, Lieutenant."

"What for?"

"You don't know what you did? Didn't you get a briefing? Didn't anyone tell you the Russians said they'd shoot down anything that came down that corridor?"

"Nobody told me anything."

"Well, congratulations again, Lieutenant," Harrison said. "You've just flown our first mission of the Berlin Airlift . . ."

The airlift was a British idea. On June 23, Royal Air Force Commodore Reginald Waite submitted a memorandum to Major General Otway Herbert, the military commandant of the British Sector of

Berlin, saying that food (1,700 calories per day, per person), and fuel too, for the more than two million civilians of the western sectors could be supplied by a joint British-American air operation. In fact, Waite had been thinking about the possibility of an airlift for weeks. In a chatty letter on June 9, 1948, to Lady Tedder, wife of Sir Arthur Tedder, the British Chief of Air Staff in London, the Air Commodore thanked her for some sunflower seeds and said his tomatoes were coming along splendidly. Then he wrote: "Our Russians, particularly General Alexandrov, who went to the opera with us, are being naughty and exasperating, but in the air we have their measure and there is nothing they can do, if we play our cards properly, to control the air as they have completely controlled road, canal and rail traffic. If the RAF had not come to the rescue of the transport system we might soon have to consider abandoning Berlin."

After listening to Waite's idea of keeping the city alive by air, Herbert responded: "That is impossible." Then Waite asked the general if he could get him ten minutes with the British governor the next day. Waite stayed up all night with a slide rule, working out load weights and frequencies of flights. He concluded that planes could fly 4,500 tons a day of food and fuel to provide some heat and power, enough of it and enough raw material to give Berlin manufacturing operations a chance to continue functioning. He persuaded Robertson, another very capable man, son of a Field Marshal and a former director of the Dunlop Rubber Company's South African operations, that it was possible, at least in good summer weather. Robertson called his American counterpart, Lucius Clay.

The Americans were more skeptical. Marguerite Higgins of the *New York Herald Tribune* had asked Clay if it would be possible to supply the citizens of western Berlin by air and his answer was short: "Absolutely impossible." On June 13, Clay had cabled the Joint Chiefs of Staff: "We can maintain our own people in Berlin indefinitely, but not the German people if rail transport is severed." But, in his June 24 call, Robertson emphasized that the British were ready to try it alone. Meanwhile, in a call from Washington, Secretary of the Army Kenneth Royall had already told Clay not to undertake any action—such as the armed convoy—that might provoke a shooting war.

Robertson reported Clay's reaction back to London, where it happened that Lieutenant General Albert Wedemeyer, the U.S. Army's chief of planning, was meeting with British officials. It also happened that he had played a major role in the planning of the only successful airlift in history: the flying of supplies to Nationalist Chinese troops fighting the Japanese over "The Hump," the 16,000-foot-high Himalaya Mountains between India and China. At its peak, that operation involved 350 airplanes, mostly C-47s, making 600 round-trips each day, delivering 71,000 tons of ammunition and gasoline each month for just over a year in 1944 and 1945.

Visiting with British Foreign Minister Ernest Bevin, Wedemeyer explained in great detail why a Berlin airlift would almost certainly fail. Bevin was a rough and burly man, the son of a servant girl and an unknown father. He was orphaned at the age of six, had dropped out of school at ten, working at anything he could get before driving a mineral water delivery truck for ten years. Then he turned to trade unionism—Samuel Gompers, the American labor leader, said Bevin's hands were so big his fingers looked like a bunch of bananas—and soon enough he was Britain's dominant labor leader. He was the organizer of the huge Transport and General Workers Union and a leader of the great General Strike of 1926. He was a socialist who called most everyone "me lad." During the war he had served as Minister of Labour in Prime Minister Winston Churchill's unity War Cabinet. When Labour and Clement Attlee, Deputy Prime Minister in the War Cabinet, defeated Churchill and the Conservatives in 1945, Bevin became Foreign Minister, a most unlikely diplomat, but one of England's greatest. He was famous for mangled metaphors— "Don't open that Pandora's box, you never know what Trojan horse will get out"—but he learned on the job as he had always done. "Last night I was readin' some papers of ol' Salisbury and 'e had a lot of sense," he once told an American diplomat, Dean Acheson. He thought a lot of the Americans. When one asked why he kept a life-size painting of George III behind his desk he answered: "'E's my hero. If he hadn't been so stupid, you wouldn't have been strong enough to come to our rescue in the war."

But he was not waiting for an American rescue in Berlin. He had responded to the blockade by asking the United States to send its most powerful warplanes, B-29 bombers and F-80 jet fighters, to scare the Soviets. When Wedemeyer hesitated before committing to the airlift, Bevin mocked him a bit, saying: "Well, me lad, I never thought I'd live to see the day when an American general exclaimed that his men can't do what the RAF is going to do." The Royal Air Force was going to continue to supply British troops in Berlin—and were ready to try to feed Berliners as well. The loyal opposition, the Conservatives, agreed immediately. Their leader, Harold Macmillan, stood in Parliament to say: "We must, if we are frank with ourselves, for this is a serious and solemn moment in this house, face the risk of war. Grave as that risk is, the alternative policy—to shrink from the issue—involves not merely the risk but almost the certainty of war."

At noon the next day, Robertson called Clay to say eight British transports were on the way from England to Germany. This time Clay said, "Okay, I'm with you!"*

Clay called Curtis LeMay. The conversation may not have been

---

* There are several competing American claims to initiating the idea of an airlift, including one by Clay in his memoirs. Some of them actually refer to the "Little Lift" of material for the military and diplomatic representatives and their families living in Berlin. Undersecretary of the Army William Draper said this in an oral history interview in 1972, describing a flight to London from Washington with General Wedemeyer: "After we had breakfast on the plane, we read our cables and learned the blockade was on. On the way over we planned the airlift . . ." In Draper's version it was the Americans who persuaded Bevin to approve the plan. Scholars at the Alliierten Museum in Berlin have pretty conclusively shown that Waite was way ahead of the Americans.

exactly as Air Force and Army information officers presented it to the world. This was their version:

"Curt, have you any planes that can carry coal?"

"Carry what?"

"Coal!"

"We must have a bad connection. It sounds as if you're asking whether we have planes for carrying coal."

"Yes, that's what I said."

"General," said LeMay. "The Air Force can deliver anything, any-time, anywhere."

Bill Lafferty, from a small town in Illinois, did not know what the Berlin Airlift was, but he had flown two of the thirty-two flights carrying food and other essential supplies to West Berlin that day. The thirty-two C-47 flights brought eighty tons of cargo into blockaded West Berlin. It was the first day of the Allied attempt to feed, heat and preserve not only their own twenty-five thousand personnel but the more than two million people living in the American, British and French sectors of the old German capital city—after Russian troops, tanks, and speedboats blockaded the highways, railroads and canals crossing East Germany into the western sectors more than 100 miles inside the Soviet Zone. The Berliners, defeated and emaciated, called themselves *Die Insulaner*, "The Islanders."

On that day, June 26, there were forty-eight old C-47s—the twin-engine plane designed in the early 1930s—in West Germany, and only ninety-eight in all of Western Europe. Each one could carry a maximum cargo of three tons. U.S. Air Force base commanders in West Germany were desperately calling the old birds into Rhein-Main and Wiesbaden to deliver goods to West Berlin, loading them with just about anything they could get their hands on—295 tons were delivered on day two, 384 on day three—and flying them into Tempelhof around the clock. The battered planes, many still painted with the vertical stripes that identified them when they were used to drop supplies on D-Day, had barely been used since the European war ended in the spring of 1945. Others were painted a dusky pink, the camouflage color used over the deserts of North Africa in 1942. The young pilots and crews who had flown them and the other planes into France and then Germany after the D-Day landings were long gone, demobilized within months after the Nazis surrendered. They were the men who had fought off the Luftwaffe, and destroyed it, and then along with Great Britain's Royal Air Force, had dropped 750,000 tons of bombs from B-17s, B-24s and Lancasters on Berlin, turning it and dozens of other German cities into stony and dark wastelands. The few pilots who stayed in the military switched to the uniforms of the new U.S. Air Force, created in 1947. But most went home as fast as they could. Their war was over, and now they were busily picking up civilian lives on hold for four years. They went to work for airlines or the family business, back to their hometowns, back to colleges, settling down with wives they barely knew and children they may have never seen.

Most of their planes, at least the transports, were sold to small commercial airlines around the world or abandoned on desert land the military called "boneyards," to sit, empty, in long rows in the dry heat of Arizona, Oklahoma and Nevada. The DC-3, or C-47, was the most successful airplane ever built, having flown more miles and more passengers than any other plane in history. The first of 10,500 DC-3s, sleek and silvery machines, the first "modern" airliner, rolled out of the Douglas Aircraft hangar in Santa Monica, California, in 1935. It was the first plane to have bathrooms and food service. It was the first airliner to offer coast-to-coast service, doing it in fifteen hours, including three stops for fuel. They were the first planes that allowed passengers to stand and walk through the cabin. When General Eisenhower was asked what won World War II, he cited the bulldozer, the jeep, the half-ton truck and the C-47. After the war ended in 1945, a British pilot described the ten-year-old C-47s, which the

British called "Dakotas" for *Douglas Aircraft Company Transport Aircraft*, this way: "A collection of parts flying in loose formation."

The airlift began with those leftover American C-47s, sleek no more, and whatever planes, usually old bombers, the British had standing on abandoned airfields—flown by any pilots they could find. The first calls, the easy ones, were to the men still on active duty. Lieutenant Harry Yoder, a B-24 pilot during the war, was on leave, visiting his parents in Boyertown, Pennsylvania, when the local police chief appeared at the door at 2:30 A.M. on June 26, saying, "I have a cable here from the Air Force. They want you back right away." He flew his first flight to Berlin before the end of the day on June 30. Lieutenant J. B. McLaughlin, a fighter pilot during the war, was the air attaché at the U.S. Embassy in Athens. Someone noticed that he had also logged three hundred hours piloting C-47s and so he was ordered immediately to Wiesbaden. The same kind of thing happened to Captain William A. Cobb, who was passing through Wiesbaden to test one of the Air Force's new Lockheed F-80 Shooting Stars. A personnel officer noticed that Cobb had an engineering degree. New orders were immediately cut for him and he became the maintenance control officer at Rhein-Main, scheduling repairs and overhauls, first for the old C-47s and then for newer C-54s, four-engine airliners designed in 1939 and known as DC-4s back home, which were already being stripped of seats and bathrooms to become transports. "The airplane I had was 'The City of Denver,' an American Airlines flagship," said Corporal James Spatafora, who was in charge of rebuilding hydraulic systems at Rhein-Main. "We had mixed feelings as we ripped out those fancy seats and the carpeting and put in skyhooks and belts to hold down coal and flour."

No plane was immune. A British Dakota took off for Berlin with the loading crew still on board in the back. An American diplomat high-ranking enough to have his own C-47 flew to Frankfurt for meetings, then came back to Rhein-Main and found that his plane had been stripped and loaded with three tons of flour. In London, the RAF requisitioned two C-47s from Ciro's, the fanciest nightclub in the city, which had been using the planes to ferry customers to the pleasures of the French Riviera. The U.S. Air Force too grabbed civilian planes that happened to be on the ground in Germany. Jack O. Bennett, the chief pilot of American Overseas Airlines, part of American Airlines, was persuaded to strip his polished and refurbished DC-3 of its seats and other amenities, to haul a load of coal in Army duffel bags. Other airlines, including Pan American, Alaskan and Seaboard & Western, were pressed into service transporting aircraft parts, particularly wheels and engines, from the United States to Air Force bases in West Germany.

The DC-3's big sister, the four-engine Douglas DC-4, could carry fifty-five passengers—or ten tons of cargo, more than three times the capacity of the C-47. But only two of the Air Force's four hundred C-54s were in Germany. Most were thousands of miles away, transporting men and supplies from country to country, island to island across the Pacific Ocean. Lieutenant Fred V. McAfee, a B-24 pilot during the war, got the word at Hickam Field outside Honolulu, Hawaii, that he was going to Germany—back to the country and city he had bombed on more than twenty runs in 1945. One group, twelve planes, was based in Guam, more than 3,800 miles west of Hawaii and more than 11,000 miles from Germany. The news got there during a large party at the base. Just before midnight, a sergeant came in as a band played Glenn Miller and officers and their wives danced away the tropical night. He was looking for his group commander, a colonel, who took the papers and moved to the side of the room to read them. "Gentlemen!" said the colonel, taking the microphone from the bandleader. The room became silent and he read the order: "Your group is asked to leave for Hawaii immediately, from there to California, Massachusetts and Wiesbaden, Germany, from where you will participate in the airlift to West Berlin. Take your ground personnel, your radio operators, your technical personnel. All arrangements have been made for your arrival in Wiesbaden. Confirm receipt of this message."

"We fly in two hours, gentlemen."

"What about our families?"

"The Air Force will take care of them," was the answer.

Not very well, at least not in the beginning. Pilots and other airmen kidded about "The Lost Wives Club." First Lieutenant William J. Horney of Vineland, New Jersey, flying east from Manila, looked down and saw a transport ship headed the other way. He figured his new wife was probably on it. He told his copilot, "My future just passed." The wives of men in the crews ordered to Germany, particularly the wives of enlisted men, were left for weeks without money, begging local merchants and landlords for credit until they finally saw their absent husbands' paychecks. Mary Widmar, who was nineteen years old and had a six-week-old son, was the wife of an officer, Navy Lieutenant Charles Widmar, but she could not even get his paychecks at Hickam Field, because she had no power of attorney in her husband's name when he left for Berlin. She headed for his hometown, Livingston, Illinois, to live with in-laws she had never met before. On the three-day train ride east from California, she never left her small compartment, because she was afraid she would drop the baby as the train rocked along. Mrs. Earl Von Kaenel, pregnant and with a two-year-old son, arrived at Hickam twenty-four hours after her husband had left to pilot a C-54 on the long route to Rhein-Main.

The *United States Armed Forces Medical Journal* reported later: "Seldom, even in time of war, have persons been so rapidly removed from their homes or from established society as they were in the early phases of the airlift. Believing their departures would be for a matter of a few weeks, some left their families in tourist courts, some left cars parked under trees, hiding the keys . . ."

Meanwhile, at Hickam Field, which was also being stripped of all its C-54s, Lieutenant McAfee and his two-man crew—copilot Lieutenant John McNeill and navigator Lieutenant William Skelly—were already in the air. They left Hawaii on July 1, landing first at Fairfield, California; then on to Chicago and Westover Air Force Base at Chicopee Falls, Massachusetts, before taking off over the Atlantic Ocean, arriving at Rhein-Main on 5:15 P.M. on July 6. McAfee was briefed for an hour and took off for Tempelhof at 8 P.M., carrying ten tons of flour.

Arthur Lidard was a very bored mailman in Baltimore after his wartime service as a flight engineer on the Army Air Force's biggest and fastest bomber, the Boeing B-29 Superfortress. He reenlisted as a sergeant the first chance he got, on December 26, 1946. On July 28, 1948, he was playing second base for his squadron's baseball team in Alaska when the game was broken up by a loudspeaker announcement that all personnel were to report to a hangar. The twenty C-54s stationed at Fairbanks were ordered to leave immediately for Germany. Three days later, in a plane with an orange tail—to make it visible in a crash in the Arctic snow—he was riding as a flight engineer on the way to Tempelhof, sitting on the jump seat between the pilot and copilot.

The same announcement blasted over Bergstrom Field in Texas— "All personnel report immediately to operations"—where Lieutenant Colonel Forrest Coon was returning stateside after two and a half years in the Philippines. What he wanted most after hours of flight was to hit the base swimming pool. He never got there. Within three hours Coon and forty-seven other officers and eighty-eight enlisted men were in nine C-54s headed for Westover and then Frankfurt.

At Brookley Air Force Base outside Mobile, Alabama, Lieutenant Guy Dunn was on his way to the golf course for a Sunday round with a couple of buddies when he heard the voice of the base commander, Colonel George Cassady, on loudspeakers calling all C-54 pilots and navigators to operations headquarters. The colonel mentioned the Berlin Airlift and then read a list of thirty-six pilots who were being reassigned immediately to Germany. Only one man on the list was not there, Lieutenant Peter Sowa, who was in the air, returning from a flight to Panama. His friend, Lieutenant Gail Halvorsen, a Mormon farm boy from Garland, Utah, called Sowa's wife to give her the news. "Oh, my God!" she said. "Berlin." She would be alone, off the base, with newborn twins.

Halvorsen, who was single and had graduated from piloting C-54s to the new and larger C-74s, transports too heavy for Berlin's grass airstrips, said perhaps he could do something. He went back into the meeting and volunteered to take Sowa's place. An hour of paperwork later and after hiding his car, a new red Chevrolet, in a grove of pine trees near the base, Halvorsen was in the air. Dunn was his copilot. They were part of a group of four C-54s headed for Westover and then Newfoundland. A message was waiting for them as they refueled at Harmon Field in Newfoundland before heading out on the 1,450-mile flight over the Atlantic Ocean to the Azores and then Rhein-Main: "Press on as fast as you can, ignore minor maintenance."

One hour and fifteen minutes after arriving at Rhein-Main, the first of the Brookley C-54s, piloted by Captain John Kelly, was on its way to Berlin. Halvorsen and the other pilots were taken to tar-paper shacks being vacated by "Displaced Persons," some of the eight million Eastern Europeans roaming the continent. These were the luckiest of the DPs, scooped up by the Americans and the British to load and unload the flour and coal being jammed into the planes. The shacks smelled lousy, so Halvorsen and a couple of other pilots trekked through ankle-deep mud to set up cots in a barn a few hundred yards away. Then they began scrounging around for showers and for winter clothing; northern Europe is a lot colder than Alabama or Hawaii in the spring. Halvorsen made his first flight at 11 A.M. the next day. He was shocked coming over the apartments but more shocked when he stepped out of the plane. The waiting DPs and German loaders, dressed in grimy old U.S. Army overalls dyed black, stuck out their hands for a handshake. "They looked at us like we were angels from heaven," he told Dunn. "I never expected that."

Halvorsen, who wanted to take some photographs of Berlin, was shocked again when he walked outside Tempelhof. "All I saw were starving women and children," he said. "I came from a dirt farm. We were religious people. I felt a lot better feeding people than killing them."

Private First Class L. W. "Corky" Colgrove, who had just turned nineteen, went straight from training in Biloxi, Mississippi, to Rhein-Main, arriving the same day as Halvorsen and Dunn. He was surprised by the same thing after being assigned on his first day to supervise a crew of ten German loaders. "One of my guys was a Messerschmitt pilot with twenty-six kills—of American planes!" he wrote home. "It's tough to hate these people when you work with them. It wasn't long before we totally trusted them."

That, however, did not stop Colgrove, a joker by nature, from patiently tutoring a janitor in his hangar to say, in English: "Good morning, Major, you son of a bitch . . ."

The British also used German loaders at RAF Gatow in Berlin and six RAF bases in their zone of western Germany. One nineteen-year-old RAF airman, Peter Izard, was put in charge of a crew that included a former Luftwaffe squadron commander and a U-boat captain.

With all the wild energy of the first two weeks of the airlift, there were only so many pilots still in uniform, only so many flight engineers, ground crewmen, weathermen and ground control operators still on active duty in both England and America. The British were closer to the action—and adventure—so RAF mechanics just grabbed their toolboxes and hitched a ride with any plane headed to Germany. It took British officers weeks to figure out who was where. In the United States, the telegrams were arriving all over the country, calling up Air Force reservists. "TDY," temporary duty for thirty days—that's what they said. One of the first called up was Arlie Nixon, the chief DC-4 pilot of Trans World Airlines. In a day, he was First Lieutenant Nixon again. His pay dropped from $550 a month to $180.*

Noah Thompson, a farm boy from Colchester, Vermont, who

---

* The Air Force pay scale during the airlift ranged from $75 a month for an airman (private) to $733 for a major general.

had logged more than 414,000 pilot miles as a bomber and transport pilot in the Air Force, had just passed his airline pilot's examination, which meant he could fly for any civilian airline in the country. And he had just brought his wife, Betty, and their new son, Glenn, to meet his parents on the family farm when the notice came. TDY. Ninety days. He kissed Betty and Glenn good-bye, then took off for Germany with other pilots and crewmen of a new Military Air Transport Service squadron based at Westover. For some reason, he was sent to Fairfield, California, and boarded a C-54 that was sent back across the country picking up pilots, stopping at Kearney, Nebraska, before coming to Westover again. Then came Bermuda and Lajes Field in the Azores before the final leg to Rhein-Main. The pilots took turns in the cockpit. There were so many of them on board that they spent most of their time in the back, sleeping, reading, playing bridge. Within twenty-four hours of arrival, Thompson was piloting ten tons of coal toward Berlin. He knew the landscape below from twenty-one bombing missions over Germany in the B-17s of the Eighth Air Force. More than 40 percent of his group's 450 crew members had been shot down or just crashed. Below him now were the people who beat to death his buddy, Lieutenant Don Dennis, the man in the bunk next to him in 1945, who had parachuted onto farmland from his burning B-17 one spring day. What happened next was not unusual: civilians on the ground, local farmers, enraged by incessant Allied bombing, killed Dennis with pitchforks and clubs, and probably set dogs on him as well.

"And now I'm bringing them food," Thompson thought. "What a world."

The mission already had an official name by then. That came from Brigadier General Joseph Smith, the base commander at Wiesbaden, who was put temporarily in charge of the thing by General LeMay. It was Smith who named the operation. "Hell's fire, we're hauling grub," he said. "Call it 'Operation Vittles' if you have to have a name."*

---

* *Vittles* is a slang version of *victuals*, an old English word for stocks of food.

The radio in Thompson's C-54 crackled with a controller's voice: "You are cleared for Berlin's Tempelhof Airfield. Climb out on the Darmstadt leg of the Frankfurt Range, at the beacon marker home in on Aschaffenberg, pass through that beacon at 900 feet altitude, then turn on a heading of 33 degrees, and climb to your assigned altitude of 3500 feet. Report in when over the Fulda checkpoint."

Air traffic control was stacking planes over the field. A *Time* magazine correspondent inside the control tower described the scene and recorded the dialogue:

Thirteen GIs worked around the clock surrounded by Coke bottles, cigarette smoke and the brassy chattering of radios: The chaotic chorus of American voices was tense but happy. "Give me an ETA on EC 84 . . . That's flour coming in on EC 72 . . . Roger . . . Ease her down . . . Where the hell has 85 gone? Oh, yeah overhead . . . Wind is now north. Northwest . . . The next stupid C-47 has nothing on his manifest . . . Are you in charge of putting de-icer fluid in aircraft? Well, who the hell is?"

Thompson was shocked when he broke through the clouds and saw the grass bowl of Tempelhof for the first time. Like Lafferty, he worried that his wheels would hit the roofs of the surrounding apartment houses. He was also frightened when he saw how short the runway was—6,100 feet of perforated steel planking laid out on the grass. He called for full flaps from his copilot and cut the throttle back as far as he could. Pilots coming into Tempelhof did not exactly "land," they dived for the ground. The minimum glide slope path for American military planes after the war was 40 to 1, that is, a pilot was expected to reduce altitude one foot for every forty feet of flight. At Tempelhof, because of the apartment buildings and short runways, the path was 16 to 1 on the primary runway and 10 to 1 on a secondary runway.

Below him, Thompson saw small crowds. Maintenance crews, Germans, men and women, more women than men, were filling in holes in the single runway and replacing bent Marston mats—two-yard squares of perforated steel weighing fifty-five pounds each—then scurrying away with their wheelbarrows and shovels as Thompson touched down. "Christ," someone said, "What if they drop one of those wheelbarrows and leave it there in front of us." That didn't happen but tires were regularly cut to ribbons by broken planking.

After the dive to the first few feet of the runway, pilots used full brakes to avoid the real danger of rolling off the far end into grass and mud. The wheelbarrow people Thompson saw were running back out just behind him. The men and women, some of them wearing their best clothes, maybe their only clothes, were filling holes—more than a thousand times every twenty-four hours—before the next plane popped out of the low cloud cover typically blanketing Berlin.

Across the city, eight miles away at a former Luftwaffe base called Gatow in the British Sector of the city, Royal Air Force planes of all kinds were landing. The first one, a Dakota, landed at 4 P.M. on June 26. It was followed by twenty-nine more that day. Two days before, there had not been a single British transport available anywhere in Germany. The Air Ministry ordered one hundred old transports, tankers, bombers and even seaplanes to Berlin. Dakotas, Hastings transports, old Avro York transports and Lancaster bombers, giant Sunderland seaplanes, even chartered civilian aircraft were flown over from England and from as far away as South Africa and New Zealand to German bases, taking off again as soon as they were loaded. They were off for RAF Gatow, all flying dangerously at different speeds and at different altitudes. It was an airborne version of the heroic and chaotic use of boats and ships, small and large, to evacuate Allied soldiers from the beaches of Dunkirk, the French port surrounded by German troops in 1940. The Sunderlands were based in Northern Ireland. Their crews, most of them at a base dance, were given two hours to pack up for Germany, and eventually landed on the Havel See, where they were stunned to see dozens of small boats and canoes, covered with flowers, manned by singing Germans, coming out to unload their cargoes. "My God, it looks like we've landed in Hawaii," said one airman.

For the first few days, the British aircrews, many of whom had left their lunch or dinners on mess hall tables when they were called to action, had to load and unload their own planes, smearing kitchen fat on loading ramps to help slide hundred-pound loads of coal stuffed into duffel bags in and out of their motley bunch of old planes.

"It was great fun, we were all together again doing an important job," said a British navigator, Flight Lieutenant John Curtis. "There was no proper maintenance—if you had four engines and a compass, you went. Beer was a penny a pint, and you could have a girl for a chocolate bar." One of the British commanders described the early days this way: "Pilots full of doughnuts and tea went forth to seek any aircraft which happened to be fuelled, serviced and ready to fly. Hot was the competition, and great joy when one was found. Soon the summer skies were full of a monstrous gaggle of aircraft headed in the direction of Berlin." When Soviet fighters, Yaks, came up to harass the transports, British pilots pulled back their sliding side windows and thumbed their noses.

Curtis added: "The Americans were amazing to us. We were professionals, they were amateurs, but they were just as good as we were. You'd be talking to some fellow and find out he had been a lawyer in Manhattan a couple of weeks before."

General Smith, the first American commander of Operation Vittles—the British name was a pun, "Operation Plainfare"—was ordered to create an operation that would last forty-five days, though he thought two weeks was more likely. The conventional wisdom was that the so-called airlift was a show to buy time while Allied and Soviet diplomats negotiated some kind of compromise solution regarding Berlin's future. The other possibility, Smith thought, was war. He was wrong on both counts. By the end of two weeks, aircrews could not find their planes in the confusion at American and British bases in the west. Then, in Berlin, they sometimes waited two hours for unloading gangs to appear. Pilots and crews, loaders and controllers were exhausted—and planes were breaking down, many of them with their controls choked by corrosive coal dust and powdery flour. Even in the rain, and there was always plenty in northern Europe, the crews were flying with windows and doors open to prevent build-ups of coal or flour dust, because both could be explosive in closed spaces. Some cockpits were never dry, some pilots' clothes were almost always wet, leading to chronic conditions, embarrassing ones like rashes and hemorrhoids. Lieutenant John Townsend of Lompoc, California, wrote home of airmen having terrific problems with dust in their eyes, some of them literally spending days in hospitals where doctors had to remove eyeballs from sockets to clean out coal dust.

Actually, the first name the British used for the airlift was "Operation Carter-Paterson," after a popular English moving company. That was quickly changed when East Berlin newspapers used it as "proof" that the Allies were preparing to move out of Berlin. In fact, on the American side, there was great pressure on Clay to evacuate "dependents"—women and children—from the city. In a teleconference, Omar Bradley informed Clay: "We are receiving many inquiries from Members of Congress as to why we do not evacuate dependents from Berlin. Evacuation now might be plausible because it would reduce the number supplied by air. What is your thinking on this subject in view of the new situation?"

Clay, who had already issued orders that any officer could move his wife and children out of the city, but if he did, the officer himself must leave as well, responded: "I do not believe we should evacuate now. In emergency we can evacuate quickly. However, evacuation now would play into Soviet hands and frighten rest of Europe. I propose: (A) To sit tight; (B) To let dependents who are nervous go home; (C) To gradually move unessential [civilian] employees to Frankfurt . . . Our people are calm and continuing their everyday life normally. Our women and children can take it and they appreciate import. I cannot overemphasize my fear of consequences . . ."

American and British families stayed. The British ordered their men to plant vegetable gardens around their houses as evidence that they would be there to harvest the crop in the spring and summer. The only family moved out was that of Bradley's daughter, Elizabeth, her husband, Air Force Captain Henry "Hal" Beukema, and their two children. Beukema protested bitterly, but his father-in-law said that he was afraid that having his grandchildren in harm's way would affect his decision making.*

In Washington, the Air Force, having used up much of its personnel around the world, was preparing long lists of reservists and of civilians working for airlines. Edwin A. Gere, Jr., who had just graduated from Alfred University in the upstate New York town of that name, was woken by a phone call at dawn.

"Lieutenant Gere?" said a sweet-voiced Western Union operator. Nobody had called him that since he had returned home after flying B-24s, bombing the Japanese in the Pacific. "You have a telegram from the Air Force. I'll read it and send it right on to you: 'By direction of the President, you are ordered to active duty for the Berlin Airlift, reporting to Camp Kilmer [in New Jersey]' . . ."

"How can they do this to me?" Gere complained to his wife, Doris. He had just been accepted by the law school of the University of New Mexico.

"What about me?" said Doris, an Alfred graduate who had just

---

* In his second memoir, *A General's Life*, Bradley referred to his daughter and son-in-law, writing: "Lee, Hal and the grandchildren . . . were still in Berlin. If the Russians overran the city and captured them, the personal blow to me might be incapacitating. I made the decision to remove them from danger . . . The Air Force willingly consented, assigning Hal to the Air Staff in the Pentagon."

signed on for a teaching job in Albuquerque. "Wherever you're going, I'm going. I have to give up that job."

The orders that came to him were part of a new call-up of reserve officers and airmen from all parts of the country. He was one of many. First Lieutenant Edwin A. Gere, Jr., MOS 1024, which meant Military Occupational Specialty, multiengine pilot. He was at Kilmer for a week for medical exams, shots and new uniforms and was then sent by train to Westover. His next stops, on a C-54 being delivered to Rhein-Main, were Newfoundland and the Azores. Then he was in the air to Berlin piloting a C-47—"I was wandering all over the sky in that Gooney Bird," he told Doris in a letter. He was shocked when he saw Berlin for the first time. It seemed to be one huge pile of crushed stone and brick. Where were people living? Mostly in basements and caves dug into the rubble.

On the ground, a ten-ton Army truck rolled up to the Gooney Bird's door—a tough plane to unload because without a nose wheel, each C-47 rested on a small tail wheel. Loaders and unloaders, supervised by teenage Army privates, slipped around going uphill and down inside a fuselage sitting at a twenty-five-degree angle. "The loaders, the Germans and the others, were really in charge, they knew what they were doing and I didn't," said one of those privates, N. Dean Carter, who was eighteen and whose older brother had been killed in combat by Germans at the Battle of the Bulge less than four years before. "I never think about hating them," Carter told someone. "They're good, my job was to see that they did not steal anything and they never tried." A German named Kurt Friebish became one of Clark's closest friends. They met when the private caught the former Wehrmacht sergeant digging into garbage cans outside the enlisted men's mess, scavenging for bits of food to feed his family. One of the first nonfraternization orders given the American occupiers was to pour gasoline over the garbage so the Germans could not eat any of it. Clark and others refused to do that. All they saw were shivering, skinny people trying to get something for their children.

Corporal Spatafora, who saw nuns from a local orphanage searching the garbage, was among those who filled extra trays with food and then stacked them neatly in the pails.

It was different with the British and French. British soldiers were generally correct around Germans, who had bombed their country; Frenchmen, whose country had been occupied, hated the Germans—and it showed.

"I had no feelings about Germans, we were too busy to feel anything," Staff Sergeant Robert Evans told his family. "Then a buddy of mine who had a German girlfriend brought me to dinner at her house. All they had was bread, potatoes and cabbage. After that, I'd get Band-Aids, cold medicine and stuff at the Post Exchange and give it to the children on that block. I walked out of the PX one day holding a banana. A German I knew said, 'What's that?'—guess who got the banana?"

Roger W. Moser, Jr., had piloted a C-47 during the war, ferrying men and supplies around the European Theater, then was demobilized in early 1946. Like most of the millions of men returning to civilian life, he came home ready to forget about war and start a family and a career. Like many, however, he missed the planes. He loved aviation. He tried to become an inspector with the Federal Aviation Administration, but, at twenty-three, he was too young. The FAA official who interviewed him suggested he think about becoming an air traffic controller. That age limit was only twenty-one. So, many tests, interviews and months of training later, Moser was working the 4 P.M. to midnight shift at the Washington Air Route Traffic Control Center, then located in the terminal building at Washington National Airport, across the Potomac River from the Capitol. One Saturday that summer, as he arrived at National, he was told there was a man from the Civil Aviation Authority in New York who wanted to talk with him. The CAA official told him that the Berlin Airlift, only a few weeks old, was going to last a lot longer and require a lot more people than anyone had thought in that last week in June.

It was not going to be a two-week wonder, as General Smith had thought.

"We're looking for volunteers to go over there," said the man from the CAA.

Moser volunteered on the spot. His old rank, First Lieutenant, would be reinstated for TDY of ninety days. Eighteen other controllers from New York, Boston, Pittsburgh, Cincinnati, Detroit, Chicago, Jacksonville and Miami signed on the same day. Five days later the nineteen of them were at Westover, boarding a C-54 for Rhein-Main. Moser's first shift in the control tower at Fassberg, an old Luftwaffe base being run by the RAF, was scheduled for 7 A.M. the next morning. He worked a twelve-hour shift and when he was relieved he headed for the mess hall, which was running twenty-four hours a day, seven days a week. Seeing how many pilots were falling asleep as they ate, Moser volunteered to fly as a copilot and made three trips to Tempelhof and back before climbing into the tower at Fassberg for his second shift the next day. It was obvious to him that the operation would break down, probably within weeks, maybe days. In Washington that did not matter so much—the idea was still to buy some time and then work things out with the Soviets.

The flashing headline of UNIVERSAL-INTERNATIONAL NEWSREEL for the third week in June, backed up by pounding martial music and the deep voice of Ed Herlihy:

BERLIN CRISIS
Capital Blockaded
World's Powder Keg

"A complete rupture dividing the capital into two armed camps," said Herlihy. "Rumors of communist seizure of the city. Violence everywhere . . ."

There was film of fighting outside a meeting of the anticommunist Social Democratic Party of Berlin. "High point of the meeting: Ringing defiance of Red Domination. Berlin will be held at all costs." The highlight of the newsreel was film of a Russian soldier lowering the red hammer-and-sickle flag in front of the Kommandatura, the building where representatives of the four occupying powers in Berlin, the victors over Germany, had met regularly, if not always amicably, since 1945. On June 16, the Soviet city commandant, General Alexander Kotikov, walked out of the weekly meeting of the four-power body that officially ruled occupied Berlin—just as Marshal Sokolovsky had walked out of the Allied Control Council in March.

Or, perhaps it was the American city commandant, Colonel Howley, who did the walking out. After another of many long Russian monologues, Howley had stood up at midnight and said, "That's it for me. I'm going home to bed. My deputies can handle this." With that, Kotikov stood, too, and walked toward the door. The city commandant presiding at the moment, General Jean Ganeval of France, said no date had been set for the next meeting. Without turning around, Kotikov said, "As far as I'm concerned, there won't be a next meeting."

And there was not: four-power rule of Berlin ended. Herlihy's last line, voice rising dramatically, was "Three flags remain—the American, the French and the British—and there they will stay!"

Newsreels in Great Britain were a bit more subdued, with long scenes of quiet railyards and empty highways. An announcer said: "Trucks, barges and rail traffic were stopped . . . The alternatives before the West were to leave Berlin ignominiously or stay and allow the people of the British, American and French sectors to starve. The only way in: The sky above . . ."

On the evening of June 25, Clay invited Ernst Reuter, the leader of the city's Social Democratic Party, to his house in the Darmstadt district of western Berlin and said, according to American spokesmen: "I may be the craziest man in the world, but I'm going to try the experiment of feeding this city by air . . . This is going to impose terrible hardship, even at its best, people are going to be cold and people are going to be hungry. We may not have enough planes."

Reuter's reported answer was: "You take care of the Airlift. I'll take care of the West Berliners."

It was a little less dramatic as reported by another German in the room, Willy Brandt, who served as Reuter's assistant as well as the national SPD's man in Berlin. He wrote in his weekly report to national party leaders in Hannover:

> "At the end of June, I accompanied him to a conversation with several gentlemen from the American administration. They wanted us to 'take courage'—maybe it would in fact be possible to supply Berlin more or less satisfactorily by air. Reuter smiled skeptically. He could not really believe that this would succeed. But—and he spoke without any sharpness of tone—'We will in any case follow our own path. Do what you can. We will do what we feel duty-bound to do.' Berlin would take on every sacrifice and would resist, come what may."

It was an unusual meeting. Clay rarely fraternized with Germans. The American was polite and gracious, a son of the South, even as he kept his distance from the city's most important political leader. Reuter had been chosen as mayor after citywide parliamentary elections in 1947, but the Soviets used their veto in the Kommandatura to prevent him from serving. After that, he carried a card that identified himself as the "Elected but unseated Mayor of Berlin."

Reuter was fifty-nine years old in 1948, a man of the world in every sense. He was the son of a Prussian merchant marine captain, who ended their relationship (and Reuter's education) when the son joined the Social Democratic Party as a pacifist just before World War I. One of six children, three of them killed in World War I, one a

Lutheran pastor and one who would become a devoted Nazi, Private Ernst Reuter was wounded in southern Russia in 1916. In telling that story, he said that his life was saved by peasants before he was forced to work in coal mines as a prisoner of war. Not only did he quickly learn to speak Russian, he openly agitated for socialist causes among his fellow prisoners. Legend, which he never denied, had it that his political activity brought him to the attention of V. I. Lenin, who made him the commissar of the German-speaking Independent Soviet Republic of the Volga, where he reported to the Minister of Nationalities, Joseph Stalin.* He returned to Germany from that war as a Communist and in 1921 became General Secretary of the German Party, a job he quit within three months—he was succeeded by Wilhelm Pieck, the same man who would later become the East German leader who met with Stalin about a possible blockade of Berlin—and rejoined the Social Democrats.

Reuter became the director of the transportation system of Berlin. He was elected to the Reichstag, and then, in 1931, elected mayor of the city of Magdeburg. He was arrested three times after the Nazis came to power, twice being released because of his connections with foreign pacifists, particularly Quakers and the American religious thinker Reinhold Niebuhr. The third time, Reuter was put in a concentration camp, but he managed to escape to Turkey, where he became, in effect, that country's transportation minister after learning the language, his fifth.

Reuter survived it all. "It was like being in the army all over again. In the German Army a soldier survives, if he is lucky, by looking stupid, saying nothing and obeying every order. And always standing at

---

* Reuter's estimation of Stalin, whom he met in 1918: "The man has the mentality of a drill sergeant . . . 'The Little Father' is narrow-minded and equipped with monstrous blinders. His mistrust is the surest sign of his weakness, which shows itself when he encounters real opponents. More courage and firmness are required for this." It was also commonly said that he had been praised in a letter by V. I. Lenin—"Young Reuter has a brilliant and lucid mind but he may be a little too independent"—but that story is a myth, according to one of his biographers, David E. Barclay of Kalamazoo College.

attention when anybody is watching. I decided, if I was not to go mad, I must imagine myself back in the army again. The Nazis respected anybody who looked stupid enough to make a good soldier . . . and besides, I cleaned the latrines so beautifully!"

After 1945, the Soviets, who despised Reuter as a traitor and feared him as an exceptionally capable politician, were able to prevent his return to Germany for more than a year. Their fears were justified when Reuter finally returned. On June 24, 1947, the City Assembly, under control of the four occupying powers, elected Reuter to be Oberbürgermeister (Lord Mayor) of Berlin by a vote of 89 to 17, with only SED members (the German communist party) opposing him. The Soviets immediately exercised their veto power under the occupation agreements and denied him the office. Still, Reuter was the most important political figure in western Berlin. He had a vision, which he laid out in an interview during the airlift with James P. O'Donnell, the *Newsweek* correspondent who wrote a profile of the German politician for the *Saturday Evening Post*. Said Reuter:

> Airplanes, wonderful. Something you Americans understand so well. But it is unfortunate that it has been called Die Luftbrücke (The Air Bridge) because the days when one dreamed of building a bridge between East and West are over. Here in this Western outpost of Berlin we yearn not for a bridge but a magnet— something in the West strong enough to pull Germany together in that direction . . . While you debate about the dangers of splitting Germany, the reality is that the Soviets have already done so . . . We in Berlin will fight to join you. The political currents in Europe will then be reversed from East–West to West–East. The magnetic pull of the West will someday pull Berlin and the Eastern zone back into a united Germany.

Reuter did not get along particularly well with Clay, but that was not unusual. One of Clay's three secretaries, Mrs. Ann Slater, said, "Everyone was afraid of him. Those black eyes. You just trembled."

Reuter's assistant, Willy Brandt, thought the American commander considered even the most democratic of socialists as "Reds," too much like communists.

The Clay-Reuter meeting of June 25 came the day after Reuter had addressed a rally of more than fifty thousand Berliners to protest the blockade, saying: "People of Berlin . . . With every means possible, we will utterly reject every attempt to make us slaves and harlots of a particular party. We experienced that sort of slavery in the Reich of Adolf Hitler. We have had enough of it. We do not want a return to it!"

The speech was legend already, and the conversation at Clay's house became legend, too.

Reuter, perhaps unintentionally, often irritated Clay. In this meeting he did it by saying food and fuel were not enough, that the Allies would also have to bring in industrial supplies to keep Berlin factories and shops working at some level. Clay already knew that, of course, but it was difficult to find and fly such material. By July 15, half of Berlin's workforce had been laid off because there was not enough electric power for many industrial operations. "If the people have no work," he told Clay, "they will lose heart whether they have enough to eat or not. Then they will surrender to communism."

So, both of these proud and talented—and testy—men knew that the future of Berlin depended on the people of Berlin.

By June 29, according to Andreas-Friedrich's diary, planes were going over her place every eight minutes. She was not sure what was happening because electricity had been rationed to two hours a day, midnight to 2 A.M. in her neighborhood. "Loudspeaker vans from RIAS"—Radio in the American Sector, the 20,000-watt station often drowned out by the 100,000-watt Radio Berlin on the Soviet side—"have been driving through the streets of the Western sector, substituting for the news service. It's quite annoying to be at the focus of world affairs and to be informed about them only between midnight and two in the morning. So we run outside when the RIAS van appears. It reports the latest and most important news: 'The airlift has increased to one hundred flights daily. Swimming prohibited in lakes and rivers because they are likely to be polluted with sewage due to the power cuts. More people arrested in the Eastern sector for possession of Deutsche Marks.' . . . 'We will dry out the Western sectors like a tied-off wart,' the Soviets have supposedly said. And this time they no doubt mean it."

They meant it. The Soviets were never able to completely cut off electricity to the western sectors, but not for lack of trying. Before the British and Americans arrived in July 1945, the Soviets had already dismantled the city's largest power plant (Berlin West) and shipped it to Moscow. At the beginning of the airlift, the western sectors of the city generated only 11 percent of their own electricity. As in most big cities, all the utilities and services of Berlin were interconnected in complicated ways. In the case of both the S-Bahn and U-Bahn, the elevated trains and the subways, respectively, it was impossible to cut off western service without also shutting down eastern trains. The same was true of parts of the city's electric grid. When the blockade began, the power available in the western sectors was cut to 700,000 kilowatt-hours per day, which amounted to less than a quarter of the preblockade daily usage of up to 3 million kilowatt-hours.

A younger woman, Christa Ruffer, who was nineteen, wrote in her diary that same day: "The war ghost is going around. If the Americans give up the western part of Berlin, we will be communistic and that will be awful, or we will have war . . . If we are fortunate, the Russians will give up, and then everything would be OK. But I don't think the Russians will give up."

An even younger girl, twelve-year-old Ursula Erika Yunger, ran out to hear the loudspeakers on American jeeps and met her father coming back from Tempelhof, where he had gotten a loading job. " 'The planes are bringing us food and supplies,' he said. 'We are not being attacked. The Americans and English are coming to rescue us. Do not be alarmed. We are going to be free' . . . Mama said that God had heard our prayers and sent angels to help us. Angels in uniform."

CHAPTER 3

"Cowboy Operation"

July 29, 1948

"HE'S THE NEW NOSE AND THROAT SPECIALIST FOR THE COAL FLIERS, SIR!!"

F OR THE NEW UNITED STATES Air Force, THE AIRLIFT REALLY
began on June 29. General Joseph Smith, who had been told
by General LeMay that the whole thing would be over in two
weeks, called a meeting of the officers under him that day. One of

them, Major Edward Willerford, a B-29 pilot during the war, remembered it this way:

> I was made the air cargo officer. I wasn't even sure just how much
> of a load a C-47 could fly, but I soon learned. The weather was
> foul and Captain Solomon of Ground Control worked out the
> instrument flying procedure. Everything was soup from Rhein-
> Main and Wiesbaden, all the way down the corridor to Tempel-
> hof . . . I knew the C-54's were coming in from all over the world.
> When we got to the point in the meeting where it was necessary
> to make a forecast on our potential future performance, I was
> ready. General Smith called on me. I stood up and said, "I esti-
> mate by July 20 we'll be flying in 1,500 tons every twenty-four
> hours."

It was a pretty bold goal, considering the Americans had flown around the clock that day and managed to deliver only 384 tons to Tempelhof. Some of that, the C-47 pilots learned, was wine for the French soldiers and officials in Berlin. The pilots were already complaining loudly about that and it became Willerford's problem. "It became a cause célèbre," he said. "The French were outraged. They sent in a delegation armed with their dietary history through all times. Their chief contention was that wine was to them equally as important as potatoes to a German, black bread to a Russian or ketchup to a Texan. I thought their argument was pretty impressive."

The Americans adapted. Lieutenant Leonard Sweet, another farm boy from New Hampshire, brought some of the wine into Berlin, but a French officer came on board and said three bottles were missing. A bilingual argument ended when Sweet told the Frenchman, "We're leaving. Get off my plane or I'm taking you back to Wiesbaden with us." On landing, Sweet said with a laugh, "I was absolutely amazed to find three bottles of good French wine right under my seat."

The first C-54s did begin arriving at Wiesbaden the next night, June 30—just in time.

On July 4, 1948, in good summer weather, the Americans and the British gave it everything they had with the Gooney Birds, but the tonnage they were able to deliver to Berlin was just less than 1,400 tons, about a fourth of what was needed to keep the western sector going—and less than 10 percent of the preblockade import tonnage of 15,500 tons by railroad, trucks and barges. But the strain on men and machines of around-the-clock operations was showing. On July 7, three Americans were killed in a crash on a mountainside in Soviet-occupied eastern Germany: First Lieutenant Leland Williams of Tuscaloosa, Alabama; First Lieutenant George Smith of Abilene, Kansas; and Carl Victor Hagen of New York, a German-born civilian, grandson of a founder of BMW, who had been working on currency matters. That was cover for his real work; he was a CIA agent. On the British side that same week, twenty-six Dakotas were grounded in one night because, in the wet weather, water was leaking into planes and causing multiple electrical problems. Group Captain Noel Hyde kept a diary that made for pretty discouraging reading:

> July 1—Well behind schedule chiefly owing to loading difficulties . . .

> July 3—Gatow asked if we could speed up rate of flow at night to one every ten minutes. Petro and Fuel could not cope . . . Plumbers behind with serviceable aircraft . . .

> July 4—Combined Ops room not working well as Flying control cannot cope with traffic . . . there were not enough men to man the telephones . . .

The airlift was dramatic, exciting—and failing. General Smith's best efforts and the willingness of pilots and crews to do whatever was needed was not enough. On July 17, even as the newspaper was reporting on the building of a new five-thousand-foot runway at Tempelhof, a *New York Times* front-page story by Hanson W. Baldwin began: "The Berlin Airlift—magnificent achievement in logistics though it is—is a losing proposition . . . Food and medicines are adequate, but lighting and power in the Western zones are greatly curtailed and industry is to a considerable extent shut down . . . [There are] all sorts of difficulties to which the Russians could easily add others—barrage balloons, fighter 'buzzing' or other interference, radio jamming."

The most prominent columnist in the United States, Walter Lippmann, writing in the *New York Herald Tribune*, said much the same: "To supply the Allied sectors of Berlin is obviously only a spectacular and temporary answer to the ground blockade. The operation can only be carried on for a while in the summer months. But in the long run, especially in the fog and rain of a Berlin winter, the cost in lives of the pilots and crews of planes which would have to be replaced, and of the money, would be exorbitant."

The message from London was as gloomy. The *Economist* magazine, attacking Truman, editorialized: "The Western countries have blundered into this crisis and are only beginning to realise the intensity of the dilemma with which they are faced. They have every right to be angry with the so-called leaders who put them there. But anger will not get them out. Only hard thought and high courage will do that."

That clearly was the conventional wisdom in Washington and London. The Assistant Secretary of the Air Force, Cornelius Whitney, told the National Security Council that the airlift was "doomed to failure." On Capitol Hill, Senator Arthur Vandenberg, of Michigan, the Republican chairman of the Foreign Relations Committee, said in a note to Royall: "Let's keep in mind that our 'basic position' is that we cannot be forced out of Berlin by duress. It's not that we will not get out of Berlin voluntarily under satisfactory circumstances."

The Secretary of Defense, James Forrestal, was telling Truman that the logical decision was for the Americans to get out of Berlin on their own terms—before the Soviets drove them out. He told the President the decision had to be made before mid-October, the beginning of winter in northern Europe.

"Jim wants me to hedge—he always does," Truman wrote in his diary that night. "I have to listen to a rehash of what I know already and reiterate my 'stay in Berlin' decision . . . We'll stay in Berlin—come what may."

As to the airlift operation itself, Smith had established, first, that each of the three corridors into Berlin would handle only one-way traffic. The middle corridor, the shaft of the arrow, would be used only for "Willie" flights, that is, flights returning west to American and British fields in the western zones. The northern corridor was for British "Easy" flights, flying eastward from six British fields and from England itself. The southern corridor was for all American "Easy" flights from Rhein-Main and Wiesbaden. To account for the different cruising speeds of C-47s and faster C-54s, Smith created a "block" system, with similar planes flying together at five different altitudes, separated by five hundred feet vertically, and by fifteen minutes horizontally at each altitude. It was all too much for controllers in Berlin trying to guide and protect planes stacked in circles over the city as they waited for permission to land, so the altitudes were reduced to three and then the separation at each altitude could be reduced to nine minutes. Weather permitting and crews available, under the Smith plan an airplane would appear over Berlin every six minutes in the early days.

The one man who understood such problems best and thought it could be done more efficiently was in Washington, far away from the action. Major General William Tunner was the deputy commander for operations of MATS, the Military Air Transport Service. Forty-two years old, handsome, arrogant, cantankerous, efficient to an almost inhuman point, he had directed the Hump operation over Himalayan peaks almost 20,000 feet high during the war.

MATS was less than one month old when the airlift began, the new service combining the transport units of the Army and Navy into the Air Force—a move understandably opposed by senior officers in the two older branches of the military. The Air Force was not much impressed with it, either. The former combat pilots who ran the Air Force designated MATS as a "Service" rather than a "Command," a gang of aerial truck drivers, many of whom, during the war, were women, ferrying planes from factories to military bases inside the United States. In the war, it was a Command, ATC—Air Transport Command—but its men (and women) were mocked by combat airmen. "Allergic to Combat" and "Army of Terrified Civilians" were two of the more polite names used by the men who flew small fighter planes or bombers into the wild blue yonder and over enemy cities.

Tunner, who had rejected lucrative business opportunities after the war to stay in the Air Force, was furiously lobbying to get to Germany and improve (or scrap) the LeMay-Smith operation.* One of many trial-and-error failures was a LeMay plan to drop coal like bombs into the city. A single B-29 Superfortress flew in low over the Berlin Olympic Stadium—where little more than a decade earlier a black American, Jesse Owens, had embarrassed Hitler by winning four gold medals—and dropped bags of coal before an audience of American and British dignitaries. The coal was pulverized into a cloud, turning the spectators and their uniforms black—as black as coal.

And Tunner was not at all shy in saying these people did not know what they were doing. "It's a cowboy operation that's going to col-

---

* The MATS general had considered going into business with the former Army Air Force commander, General Harold "Hap" Arnold. Part of the business plan was to buy large numbers of surplus C-54s for $75,000 each. He would have made a fortune, because as domestic airlines and the airlift increased the demand for the planes, the price of each C-54 gradually rose to $675,000. Tunner was also dealing with great personal problems. His wife, Martha, was comatose, suffering from a brain tumor, and he was raising two sons alone.

lapse," he told his boss, MATS overall commander, Major General Laurence Kuter. He wanted Kuter to demand that the airlift be turned over to MATS, meaning to Tunner himself. "That's not the way to do it, Bill," Kuter said more than once. "Let's just sit tight and see what happens."

Smith's Operation Vittles was an heroic and frantic mission, stretched to the breaking point, with pilots and crews running out to any plane that was loaded. The British operation, Plainfare, was even wilder. Crews sat in the Malcolm Club, as British military canteens were called, for hours at a time until a serviceable plane was loaded and ready. When one was available, an operations officer would come into the club and say: "You . . . you . . . and you . . . go to Berlin."

On that same July 4 in 1948, Private Tom Henshaw, a loader at the RAF base at Wunstorf, was drinking tea at 2 a.m. in the canteen with the men he worked with, when he suddenly said, "It's my birthday, I'm twenty years old." A pilot overheard him and said, "Bring your gang, Private. We'll fly to Berlin."

Henshaw and six of his mates climbed into a Dakota, sat down on top of a load of flour and off they went. After unloading at Gatow, the pilot asked whether Henshaw knew how to fly a plane.

"No, sir," he answered. "This is the first time I've ever been in one."

"Well, sit in here," said the pilot, pointing to the right seat, the copilot's seat.

"It's easy, all you have to do is worry about the horizon and the compass, just get those two right and it's easy." After about ten minutes, the pilot said, "I've got to go to the loo. Carry on."

Henshaw's friends were jeering and he bumped against the automatic pilot control. The plane started sliding off to the left. "What are you doing?" said the pilot, hobbling up front with his pants around his ankles. The Dakota was flying directly toward two Russian Yaks waiting near the edge of the corridor back to Wunstorf.

The pilot took over again and brought the Dakota back toward the center of the corridor. Then a few minutes later the right engine shut down.

"What's happening?" Henshaw said.

"Actually, I don't know," said the pilot. "It always does that about now, and only on the way back."

By late July, the Allies were hiring thousands of men and women in western Germany and in Berlin, England and the United States. Temporary duty was temporary no more for the Americans and British. The Germans were setting up labor companies to find and hire loaders and unloaders at the ten American and British airfields in western Germany and Berlin. Brigadier General Williston Palmer was in charge of ground transportation from depositories to the airfields in western Germany—transporting coal from the Ruhr Valley and food from western farms, loading it onto trains and trucks to Rhein-Main and Wiesbaden, where the German loaders took over. At those two American bases, the loading job eventually required eight hundred American enlisted men supervising 1,500 Germans and Displaced Persons. Tens of thousands of civilian and military personnel across the world were soon working on the airlift, Germans, British and Americans, driving, loading and unloading trucks and coal trains from the Ruhr twenty-four hours a day to the eight American and British airfields in the western zones. In western Berlin, at Tempelhof and Gatow, other trucks and loaders waited to distribute the coal and food to warehouses, small power stations and stores in western neighborhoods. There were also more than two thousand workers on the fields, many of them women, building new, longer and safer runways at the city airports. Back in the United States and Britain, parts, from windshield wipers to engines, were again being manufactured at a wartime pace.

One of the great problems of the airlift was the building of new runways—including a third one at Tempelhof used only for takeoffs—and strengthening the old ones. The Soviets had removed almost all of the construction equipment in the city, shipping it back to Russia before the Allies arrived. The engineers supervising the huge German work crews needed more than wheelbarrows and shovels. However, the planes of the airlift were too small to transport bulldozers, rock crushers and steamrollers. The solution was to use oxyacetylene torches to cut the heavy equipment into numbered parts and then weld them back together in Berlin, ready to roll.*

At Tempelhof, a new approach to the principal landing strip was built, allowing airlift planes to go over the Saint Thomas cemetery between, rather than over, the surrounding apartment buildings; on clear days the crews could see families inside at tables through the glassless windows of the shattered city. The planes themselves, first C-47s, the transports, tankers and converted bombers used by the British, and then more and more C-54s, were maintained, kept flying in a long line of bases and repair fields from the two Berlin airports back to Burtonwood, a World War II base overgrown by weeds in England, then to the Pratt & Whitney engine plant in Connecticut, and all the way to Oklahoma, where American planes were completely overhauled after a thousand hours in the air.

But still, on July 23, the food and fuel reaching Berlin in American and British planes was only 2,500 tons, enough food, perhaps, but nowhere near the coal required for power plants and factories—and, at a lower priority, homes. The Americans, led by General Smith, now

---

* The story is that all this—including the transport of eighty-one rock crushers—was done under the supervision of a civilian worker, a genius of the torch named H. P. Lacomb, who had learned his trade as the Army Air Force–built airfields in Brazil and other South American countries before World War II. All of the many accounts in books, magazines and newspapers of Lacomb's heroics, including the Federal Bureau of Investigation searching for him in junkyards and small airports, seem to have originated in *Der Monat*, a German-language magazine subsidized by the Central Intelligence Agency. Although Tunner was said to have remembered him from his own service in South America, Lacomb is not mentioned in Tunner's memoir, "Over the Hump." In two years of searching, including interviews with some of the pilots who flew in construction equipment, I was unable to find Lacomb, his family or anyone who actually met him. The Deputy Director of the Air Force Historical Studies Office, Roger Miller, laughed when I asked him about Lacomb, saying that hundreds of cutters and welders were involved in preparing and moving construction equipment, but some service historians loved to personalize their work. The FBI refused to comment on its role, if any.

had eighty C-47s and fifty-two C-54s, each flying two round-trips per twenty-four-hour day. But both the planes and the men in them were breaking down—or close to it. A six-month reserve of windshield wiper blades lasted just two weeks. Lieutenant Robert Miller, the flight surgeon of the 60th Troop Carrier Group, the first Air Force unit to fly the lift, reported back to Washington after the first month: "It's a seven-day-a-week schedule, with most of the pilots lucky if they get seven hours' sleep out of thirty-two hours . . . Lt. Donald Ahle flew seven and one-half hours, and in addition had duty for sixteen, then slept eight. Lt. Cole Bacon flew seven and one-half, had duty for fourteen and slept eight-and-a-half . . ." The names went on: Clinton Hillman, Elmer Murphy, Adolph Loeck. Hollow-eyed heroes. Some of the overworked communications people would come to meals talking to themselves in Morse code. There were reports later of airmen jumping out of windows—second- and third-story windows—breaking legs to get themselves sent home. Dr. Miller continued:

> Toward the close of the third week, the dangerous level had been reached. A couple of the crews came in where both the pilot and co-pilot had dozed off, awakened by the change of altitude of the plane. Fatigue was shown in their irritability, and they were jagging badly on too much coffee . . . Exhaustion and weather are causing a lot of colds and a lot of flier's ears. Not a guy quit, and a lot of them were being crucified by plugged ears.

Dr. Miller's boss, Lieutenant Colonel Harry Mosely, deputy air surgeon of the Air Force, added that the conditions at RAF Fassberg were "similar to those found in Nazi concentration camps."

Robert Murphy, the State Department's man in Germany and Clay's principal political advisor, reported daily to Washington. The summary of his report on July 21: "The physical and economic plight of the western sectors of Berlin, now completely dependent on the airlift for both food and raw materials, is worsening daily. Sufficient food is being received to sustain life but not to maintain morale over an extended period, and the curtailment of industrial activities is leading to greatly increased unemployment."

Even as Secretary of State (and former chairman of the Joint Chiefs of Staff) George C. Marshall told President Truman that it would take the United States more than eighteen months to prepare for war—and that standing orders in case of Soviet attack were to retreat quickly to the Rhine River to set up a defensive perimeter—the view from Washington was both more optimistic and more tentative. At a cabinet meeting two days later, Secretary Marshall reported to the President that what was happening in Berlin had to be seen as an inevitable reaction to Western successes beginning in June of 1947 with the Truman Doctrine—"containment" of communism and military aid to Allies battling insurgencies—and the impact of the "Marshall Plan," the European Recovery Plan channelling United States aid to western European countries. As recorded in Cabinet minutes: "Present tension in Berlin is brought about by loss of Russian face in our successes in Italy, France, Finland and added to this is the Tito defection in Yugoslavia. It is caused by Russian desperation in face of success of the European Recovery Plan."*

Two days later, July 23, Wedemeyer, the Army general who had overseen the Hump operation, persuaded Air Force Chief of Staff Hoyt Vandenberg that the Berlin Airlift might last only until winter set in but had already reached its peak as a cowboy adventure. Vandenberg agreed and called in Tunner to say: "OK, Bill, it's yours. When can you leave for Berlin?"

---

* On July 28, 1948, the same day Truman told his National Security Council that he intended to stay in Berlin, the Soviet Cominform announced the expulsion of the Yugoslavian Communist Party from the body because Marshal Tito, the country's leader, refused to follow Stalin's order to confess sins against Communism. At the same time, however, communists were winning a civil war in China.

"Right away" was the answer, of course. Tunner asked for, and received, permission to take about a dozen officers he knew, most of whom had served with him on the Hump, and one woman, his secretary, the lady he always referred to as "Miss Katie Gibson."

Robert Murphy, who had also been the political advisor to Clay's predecessor as Allied commander in Europe, General Dwight Eisenhower, set up a team to assess the economic impact of the blockade on the island city. By the second week in July, a memo from his staff concluded: "West Berlin's economy is headed toward an almost total breakdown." An analysis done at the same time by the Central Intelligence Agency estimated imminent closure of "80-percent of plants in French sector, 60-percent in the British sector and 50-percent in the American sector."

In the first three weeks of the blockade, more than 3,200 companies in Berlin shut down because they could not get the material or power. Another 4,600 cut back production, operating only part-time. An estimated 35,688 Berliners had already lost their jobs. On July 12, Konrad Adenauer, the former Mayor of Cologne and a founder, in 1946, of the new Christian Democratic Union, stated that the western Berlin sector economy would soon be reduced to the conditions of May 1945. Reporting back to the Foreign Office in London, Clay's British counterpart, General Robertson, warned that unemployment might be getting serious enough to cause civil unrest. The dark streets got darker, as the level of working streetlights dropped below what it had been a year after the war ended.

General Clay was in Washington when Tunner got the word that he would be going to Germany. The President wanted to know his man better and he wanted to see if Clay could stand up to all the advisors and "wise men" who were telling him the airlift would not work, some of them still arguing strongly that the best policy was to leave Berlin now before being humiliated and forced out by the Soviets. Most of them, cabinet members and generals, were already angry at Clay for pushing ahead with what they considered a doomed effort.

In her diary, Andreas-Friedrich, speaking of Colonel Howley's frequent RIAS broadcasts, wrote:

> The American commander of Berlin, has assured us that despite the fact that the delivery of goods from the Eastern zone has been suspended, despite the suspension of interzonal traffic, despite the suspension of the milk supply from the Eastern zone to infants in the Western sectors, we should not despair . . . "We shall not let the people of Berlin starve," he affirms loudly and clearly. We are relieved. So it is not just the occupying forces, but we too who have reason to hope . . . We hope again!

Clay, who spent a certain amount of time and effort trying to get Howley to keep his mouth shut, had attempted at a press conference on the day the blockade began to tone down the colonel's pledge, but only slightly this time, saying, "They cannot drive us out by any means short of war as far as we are concerned." And there was no doubt in his mind that driving the Western Allies out of Berlin was the real reason for the blockade. On July 3, he reported to the Pentagon on a meeting of the three Allied commandants with the Soviet commander, Marshal Sokolovsky, in Potsdam, in the Soviet Zone, saying that when Robertson brought up the possibility of compromise on currency reform, "Sokolovsky interrupted to state blandly that the technical difficulties would continue until we had abandoned our plans for West German government. This was the first admission of the real reason for the blockade."

Now, on July 21, almost a month after the blockade began, Clay arrived in Washington to explain, defend and propose. It was not an easy trip. The general was in great pain, probably from a pinched nerve in his neck. Or perhaps it was just tension. He spent the night at the home of Secretary of Defense Forrestal, who believed war with the Soviet Union—nuclear war—was inevitable and that the United States was woefully unprepared for conflict. Even Clay, who had been among the very few American officials who believed accommodation with the Soviets was possible, told Forrestal that night that he believed there was a one-in-four chance of war beginning in Berlin.

He woke up on the morning of July 22 in so much pain that he could not turn his head. At 11 A.M. he was at the White House, in the Cabinet Room. The President was there, but said little. Clay was alone, defending the airlift and the determination of the western Berliners, then pleading for more C-54s. There were still only fifty-two in Germany and the Americans and British combined had carried in 2,250 tons on their best day—exactly half the calculated minimum required to keep the city going. Almost every man around the table was against him, including Secretary of State Marshall; Undersecretary Lovett; George Kennan and Charles Bohlen, the State Department's Soviet experts; General Bradley, the chairman of the Joint Chiefs; and General Vandenberg, the Air Force chief, who was concerned that a total effort in Berlin would strip his service of its emergency transport service everywhere else in the world. A National Security Council memorandum to the President before the July 22 meeting read: "[The airlift would] involve our entire transport reserve and will require the dispatch of a great many troops. We will then have everything over there and it would be a serious question as to how many would be caught on the ground and destroyed, if hostilities broke out."

There was a real difference between the American people and their leaders over Berlin. Except for the President, those leaders did not believe that the Allies could prevail against all odds in Berlin. Lovett offered this opinion, using the same time frame as Forrestal: "It is obvious that the Soviets know that flying weather will be too bad for this operation to continue beyond October . . . We should clearly recognize that the airlift is a temporary expedient." Air Force officials added: "The airdrome situation is critical since Tempelhof's breaking up under its present load."

Marshall's concern, as expressed in a telegram to Ambassador Walter Bedell Smith in Moscow, was about the American people:

> There has been a definite crystallization of American public and Congressional opinion over the Berlin issue and any agreement we make which appears to have sold out any of our basic rights in Berlin or Western Germany in exchange for lifting the blockade will be received with violent indignation here. From all reports the country is more unified by its determination not to weaken in the face of an illegal blockade than on any other issue we can recall in time of peace.

That was the setting when Clay was asked: "How many more planes do you want?"

"Another seventy-five." He did not add that even more would be needed in the winter.

"That's more than half our fleet," said Vandenberg. He repeated that Clay's demands would strip American defenses around the world. He did not add that he and Bradley had already prepared a memo for Truman, saying: "The withdrawal possibility should at least be borne in mind. Neither air transport nor armed convoy in themselves offer a long range solution to the Berlin problem."

Clay, his head turned oddly but unmoving—he had to move his chair around to see anyone speaking—tried to counter one argument after another, finally summing up: "If we move out of Berlin we have lost everything we've been fighting for. The airlift has increased our prestige immeasurably . . . Two months ago the Russians were cocky and arrogant. Lately they have been polite and gone out of their way to avoid incidents."

The others were unmoved. They were ignoring Clay and, actually, ignoring Truman's June 28 declaration that he did not intend to withdraw under any circumstances.

"Mr. President, have you thought this through?" said Lovett.

"We will have to deal with the situation as it develops," Truman interrupted him. "But the essential position is that we are in Berlin by terms of an agreement and the Russians have no right to get us out by either direct or indirect pressure."

Truman spoke more softly than Howlin' Frank Howley, but there was some similarity in the decisiveness and instinctive nature of the two men. At the June 28 meeting, Truman had approved an order sending sixty B-29 Superfortresses to England along with 2,500 maintenance men to service both the bombers and transports in Germany. That suggestion had not come from his own men, but from the British—Foreign Minister Ernest Bevin had told Robertson to ask Clay to request the B-29 deployment—who had already secretly extended and reinforced several military runways to handle the big bombers. The point of the thing, still secret until the full British Cabinet met to give their formal approval, was obvious: the Soviets did not have "The Bomb," and the Superfortress was the plane that had dropped the two atomic bombs that Truman had already used to end World War II in the Pacific. When the decision to send the B-29s was announced on July 18, the public, the press and the United States Congress were told that the B-29s sent to England were not Silverplate, the code name for planes capable of carrying atomic bombs.

Whatever the official story, much of the public in both the United States and Europe believed the B-29s were carrying atomic bombs—and there is no doubt that such information was deliberately leaked through intelligence channels known to be linked to the Soviet Union. And the public may have been right.

"We put B-29 bombers in England and took our weapons with us. We hauled these old weapons called 'Fatman,'" said Colonel Anthony Perna, who commanded two United States Air Force bases and two B-29 squadrons in England during the airlift.*

Truman excused himself after an hour of the July 22 meeting. Clay was sure he had lost. As he reached the door, the President turned toward Clay and said, "Drop by my office before you leave, General."

"You look like you feel bad, General," said Truman when Clay came to the Oval Office the next morning.

"Mr. President, I'm very disappointed. Without those planes I just don't think we're going to make it in Berlin."

"You're going to get them," said Truman, grinning. "I overruled the Joint Chiefs."

"Mr. Truman, as I leave here there are going to be reporters out there asking me what's happened. May I tell them that?"

"You may."

Clay, his neck suddenly mobile, told the reporters more C-54s would be heading for Germany.

Then Clay went up to Capitol Hill and visited for a bit with important members of Congress, including Senator Arthur Vandenberg, who was General Vandenberg's uncle. Clay stood for a press conference to announce again that more C-54s would be on their way to Berlin.

"How are your nerves holding up in Berlin?" a reporter asked.

---

* The United States did have a plan, secret, of course, code-named "Charioteer," for using 133 atom bombs on seventy Soviet cities and industrial centers. "The information was closely guarded," said Perna in an August 1992 interview for the Foreign Affairs Oral History Collection of the Library of Congress. "The way it came about was that Truman and his Chief of Air Staff, [Hoyt] Vandenberg, and Attlee, the Prime Minister of England, and his Chief of the Royal Air Force, a guy named Lord [Tedder], the four of them got together without any staff . . . Congress did not know it, Parliament did not know it. It was an agreement between the two Heads of State with their two Air Force chiefs. They went ahead and did it. . . . Our job was to hold this deterrent over the Russians' head by having the B-29 capability to bomb out of England."

"It's a lot better on the nerves in Berlin than it is here in Washington."

Truman's decision was formalized two days later in a teleconference message from the Joint Chiefs to the bunker under Clay's headquarters in Berlin: "We have ordered our planes all over the world to fly to Europe. You have our full support. God Bless Berlin."

Back in Berlin that same week, Ruth Andreas-Friedrich wrote of a real ambivalence among sophisticated Germans: "Every three minutes there is an airplane. As of recently they supposedly are even flying in coal. 'We shall stay,' the Americans assure us daily. But what's their reason for staying? 'Because the airlift gives them a great chance to train pilots for an eventual war,' gibe those who are anti-West. 'And because by expanding the Berlin airports they are building the best air bases right under the Russians' noses. Or did you believe they were staying because of you?' "

Her friends, the cynics, were not the only ones who thought they were living through the prelude of war between the victors, between the United States and the Soviet Union. Sergeant William Palahunich of Lexington, Kentucky, whose family spoke Ukrainian at home, was one of the few Americans who could actually hold a conversation with Soviet soldiers. One day he asked a Soviet sergeant why they were not cleaning up the bomb damage in eastern Berlin. The Red Army man answered: "Why should we? You'll just be bombing us again soon." Although he was only a farm boy from Kentucky, Palahunich thought he saw tremendous differences between American soldiers and the Russians he met: "We were taught to think. They were taught to do what they were told."

A German on the ground, ironically, did not show the pessimism of Russian soldiers and most of official Washington. Willy Brandt, reporting to SPD officials in Hannover, saw reasons for optimism in a secret memo he sent that third week in July:

Despite the unsettled situation the atmosphere among the population and our [SPD] comrades' attitude continues to be good. Citizens' meetings in the various districts have great attendance. After six weeks of assembly ban the district group in Friedrichshain [in eastern Berlin] on Thursday could again hold a public meeting which was attended by at least 3,000 people . . . The English have reports that economic negotiations by Pieck and another SPD leader, Otto Grotewohl, in Eastern Europe were unsuccessful. As a consequence the eastern zone was—more than ever—dependent on exchange of goods with the western zone. An employee of the Wirtschaftskommission [Economic Commission] who recently visited me confirmed that the so-called Two-Year-Plan has been duct-taped together very quickly. Electric industry has the following shortages: dynamo sheet metal, ball bearings and material for a gilded copper roof. In addition they lack management personnel. As a consequence they now want to seriously endeavor to recruit engineers from the western zones.

Three days later, Brandt added:

People here have been talking about a report of the British chargé d'affaires in Moscow which apparently says that the important Russian offices were and are still convinced they could get Berlin without a war. The Russians are currently willing to take a far greater risk in Berlin than anywhere else. The British representative did, however, deem it possible that the Russians would budge if the opposing side clearly showed their decisiveness.

That was the day, July 20, the Soviets made their most determined attempt to undermine the airlift by formally offering food and fuel to western Berliners who registered for ration cards in the eastern sector. Front-page headlines in Soviet-controlled newspapers proclaimed:

THE SOVIET UNION TAKES OVER SUPPLY OF
POPULATION OF ALL BERLIN

and

SOVIET HELP FOR BERLIN

Under the headline "There Can Be No Talk of a Berlin Blockade," *Neues Deutschland*, the newspaper of the SED, said that thousands of tons of foodstuffs from the Soviet Union, Poland and Czechoslovakia were now available in the east. Talk of a blockade, the paper stated, was "irrelevant . . . a fabric of lies . . . rabid, inflammatory tirades."

The Soviets also set up a series of "Foreign Shops" in eastern Berlin. Operated by Polish merchants and others from communist countries, the shops offered liquor, tobacco and other luxuries—for a price, in Westmarks only, a way for the Soviets to collect Western currency worth four or five times their own Eastmarks.

It did not work. In the first few weeks of the new program, in Treptow, in the east, cards were signed for by only 20 of the 285,000 western Berliners invited to register. In Pankow, the number was 19; in Prenzlauer Berg, 16. West Berlin officials played as tough a game as the easterners, holding the numbers down by warning or implying that West Berliners who registered in the eastern sector risked losing their jobs or apartments.

It was a close thing. Five days after the Soviet offer, on July 25 in a dispatch numbered 71, Brandt emphasized that he was not at all sure that the Soviet move would fail, writing, "The new round of the Eastern currency reform and its negative effects on people's mood must not be underestimated . . . In my opinion, we should point out to the Allies that we cannot guarantee the inner front in Berlin to remain as steady as it is today, should the blockade last for a long time. For the rest, I am not afraid of difficulties, such as threats that may arise during winter—in case the Russians should decide or be forced to withdraw partially or completely. In the meantime, we could gather supplies and even a partial pullback would mean a striking defeat of the Russians . . ."

By the end of the year, 85,000 of more than 2 million western Berliners had registered. Most of those were people who worked in the east and had usually shopped there before returning home to the west.

Then Brandt passed along two serious warnings:

A Russian official told a trustworthy German that the results of the politics of his stubborn party members were unpredictable. The military, the source said, is not contained and that even though it was not looking for war, it was not afraid of it. The Ministry of Foreign Affairs pursues a more moderate course, but in terms of the "Berlin question" it was convinced of the legitimacy of Russian claims.

I also want to inform you that several Englishmen here have become more and more pessimistic over the past few days. They seem to expect a military confrontation and are appalled by the lack of preparation for it. Please don't treat this report as more than it actually is: a quickly written summary of certain viewpoints that are a result of some conversations.

Tunner arrived in Wiesbaden on July 29 with an advance team of a dozen old associates. On that day American planes carried just over 1,800 tons to Berlin. The British carried another 750 tons. If there was any doubt in Tunner's mind, and there rarely was, that Clay, LeMay and Smith were hardly overjoyed about the arrival of MATS, it was erased when he reported to LeMay. The commander of the Air Force in Europe lived in a 102-room mansion, once the home of the Heinkel champagne family, later appropriated as the home of the Nazi foreign minister, Joachim von Ribbentrop.

"I expect you to produce," Tunner was told that day by LeMay, whose tough-guy image was enhanced by the cigar that was always at the corner of his mouth. It was a trick, really: the cigar hid the drooping of his mouth on the right side of his face, which was numbed by disease, apparently Bell's palsy.

"I intend to," said Tunner.

The new airlift commander was assigned to a maid's room in the partly damaged Schwarzer Bock (Black Stag) Hotel at 11 Tannus Strasse in Wiesbaden, up three flights of stairs and behind a bathroom. His men got worse. The MATS offices were in an abandoned bombed-out apartment building. And, in Tunner's hard eyes, the airlift did not look much better than the accommodations. Starting from scratch with different kinds of aircraft, Smith, a fighter pilot by training, had devised a workable but rough system of flying blocks of C-47s and C-54s together, to avoid collisions between the smaller and slower (140–150 mph) C-47 and the speedier (170–180 mph) C-54s. What Tunner saw were planes parked at crazy angles all over the fields, while overworked aircrews were grabbing a little food and maybe a little sleep, too, inside the terminals. Very few planes were coming or going on schedule. In fact, both pilots and mechanics did not seem sure what their schedules were supposed to be, when they were supposed to work or when they were supposed to eat. They slept pretty much wherever they were—worse, there were a lot of near misses in the air and on the ground. Lieutenant Halvorsen, the pilot who left his Chevy in Mobile and made his first Berlin flight three weeks before Tunner arrived, had trouble finding his plane after that first run. The American operations officers and the German unloaders were both long gone when he wandered back out of the terminal after some hot chocolate and a quick tour of the wonders of Tempelhof.*

· Tunner also saw very little maintenance being done and was convinced planes would soon start falling out of the sky. The man from MATS thought airplanes were useful only in the air and aircrews useful only in airplanes. When Tunner arrived, the airlift fleet totaled more than 250 mismatched planes: the Americans had 54 C-54s and 105 C-47s. The British had 50 Dakotas and 40 York transports—and were also using dozens of chartered commercial planes operating with their own crews and their own rules, and often their own substantial liquor supplies.

"Willie-the-Whip," as he had been called back in Burma, had been in Germany less than seventy-two hours when he issued his first orders to American aircrews. No one would be allowed to leave their plane or the area immediately around it after landing at Tempelhof or Gatow. Three jeeps or small trucks would follow the giant trucks that carried the twelve-man unloading teams up to the side doors of the transports. While the sacks of flour and coal were swung man to man from the planes into the trucks, an operations officer would brief the pilots on conditions in the corridors and any problems back at their home bases. Then weathermen—there were 570 working the airlift—would arrive with information collected by land stations and from B-17s and B-29s collecting data on a continuing basis across Europe and over the North Sea. Finally came a small canteen truck with the coffee, sandwiches and doughnuts that fueled the men of the lift. Tunner personally had called the German Red Cross and asked them to staff the rolling snack bars with the prettiest girls they could find. Every once in a while, a payroll jeep would arrive with mail and

---

* General Smith was bitter and stayed bitter about being relieved of command of the airlift, saying in a 1976 oral history for the Library of Congress: "I was doing a good job . . . Tunner didn't create this command for anyone but himself, for his own glorification." Tunner's comment: "Joe Smith was a good man. LeMay was a good man, but they didn't know anything about air transport. The thing was about to fall apart . . . I had highly skilled men—they knew how to carry people rather than bombs."

pay envelopes. The turnaround time at the two Berlin airports was reduced to an average of thirty minutes for each plane.

The next Tunner trick was going to take a little longer. Studying maps on the way over from the United States, he had focused on the fact that the American fields, Rhein-Main and Wiesbaden, were farther from Berlin than British fields to the north. The two American bases were almost three hundred miles from Berlin, ninety minutes of flying time, and the southern flight corridor from those fields passed over the five-thousand-foot-high Harz mountain range. RAF bases to the north—Fassberg, Wunstorf, Lübeck and one being rebuilt at Celle—were as close as 160 miles from the city, less than an hour's flying time over flat farmland. So, two well-maintained planes operating from the British bases carried the same tonnage as three similar planes flying to and from the American bases. The way to deal with that—though he kept the idea to himself for a while—was a single Allied command with a single commander in charge of all operations. His candidate for that job was General William F. Tunner.

On July 27, two days before Tunner arrived, two more Americans were killed. First Lieutenant Robert Stuber of Arlington, California, and First Lieutenant Charles King of Aberdeen, South Dakota, were approaching Tempelhof in a light rain at 1 A.M. "Turning base, gear down and locked," radioed the copilot. Then silence. The plane crashed into the front of an apartment building three blocks short of the airport. No civilians were injured and German fire crews worked through the night as American trucks carted away the demolished C-47. In the morning, Berliners began to file by, leaving a mound of flowers with this sign on top:

"Two American flyers became victims of the Berlin Blockade here. You gave your lives for us! The Berliners of the west sectors will never forget you!"

Surprisingly, the American occupiers and German civilians had gotten along pretty well almost from the beginning. Despite the hat-tipping rules, the American occupation troops—the "high school kids," as Clay called them—had been taught to hate Germans but had never actually fought them or had their homes smashed or families wiped out in the war. The "Anti-Fraternization" rules, JCS 1067, printed first in 1945, stated: "Every German is a potential source of trouble; therefore there should be no fraternization with any of the German people. Fraternization means making friends."

In case any GI misunderstood that order, he was shown a short film, made by a pair of Hollywood legends, Frank Capra and Walt Disney, which showed a Frankenstein-like hand superimposed on a crowd of German faces as a voiceover said: "That is the hand that dropped the bombs on helpless Rotterdam . . . that held the whip over Norwegian slaves . . . that murdered Greeks, Czechs, Jews . . . that killed and crippled American soldiers . . . Don't clasp that hand."

American posters everywhere in Germany showed a soldier bend-ing for a handkerchief dropped by a pretty German girl—with a swastika-decorated man ready to stab him in the back. The star of the campaign was "Veronika Dankeschoen," VD for short, a fictitious seductive lady of the night. Most airmen and soldiers, and German workers, too, called the real young German women around the air-bases by that name, "Veronikas." And real venereal diseases were a significant problem, infecting as many as one-third of the Americans in some areas.

The British were a bit classier, showing a girl in a picture frame and the legend " 'Will you forget me?' Avoid VD for Her Sake. Or don't you care?"

The orders were routinely ignored from the beginning by the hundreds of thousands of young men of OMGUS, far from home, boys with far more money and power than they had ever had at home—particularly where the hungry young women of Germany were concerned. Nature took its course: prostitution, casual affairs, love and marriage. It all happened every day and night, everywhere in the city. A CBS correspondent, Howard K. Smith, reported: "There might as well be laws requiring the moon to come up square."

A popular American movie made during the airlift, starring Paul Douglas and Montgomery Clift, focused on two love stories between American men and German women. *The Big Lift* showed one affair growing from contempt to true love and marriage, while the other slid from innocence to betrayal. The title in the German-language version was changed to *Es Begann Mit Einem Kuss*—"It Started With a Kiss"—and the film was thirty minutes shorter with translated dialogue that somehow provided happy endings for both affairs. Most of the small parts were played by real airmen and soldiers. The professional actors seemed real enough and the days were gray enough that Douglas, playing a master sergeant, was stopped by a sentry who told him to tuck in his shirt and pull up his tie before an officer spotted him. "Gee, Mac," said the actor, "thanks, thanks a lot."

But more than sex was going on. Sergeant Robert Lochner, the radio announcer who also worked as Clay's interpreter, said: "We were lectured and indoctrinated about non-fraternization. For me that lasted fifteen minutes. We landed in Frankfurt and were loaded into a weapons carrier. A small boy, about five years old, ran after us smiling and waving. We did what we were told. Nothing. The smile and the hand dropped. I was so furious at myself that when we got to Frankfurt station, I went up to the first group of Germans I saw. I just began talking with them."

Then came the Luftbrücke, or "Air Bridge" in German. Lieutenant Arlie Nixon, the pilot taken from TWA, walked into a restaurant in Wiesbaden just as the airlift was beginning and, without a word being spoken, every German stood, left their tables and food and walked out. Two weeks later, he came back to the same place and every German stood again, walking to the bar and then lining up more steins of beer than he could drink in a week. A corporal, Louis Wagner, was huddled in a cold train headed for Frankfurt when a

German man walked up, uncorked a bottle of schnapps and said in English, smiling: "This could be poison, Captain, would you like to test it with me?"

The blockade and airlift turned Gerhard Rietdorff, who was twenty years old at the time, into a full-time black marketeer after he lost his job as an apprentice electrician in a small East Berlin factory. The problem, the situation that had shocked Sokolovsky in late June, was that the industrial life of the city, such as it was, depended on trade and business between the sectors. Rietdorff's employer closed down because he could no longer get copper from the west.

That was what made the Allied counterblockade so effective—and also created secret east-west trade throughout the airlift, a big-time black market. A smaller operator, young Rietdorff explained his new work this way:

> There were not enough coins available when the West German Mark was introduced to West Berlin. The old Reichsmark coins retained their old market value in West Berlin for a certain period of time. The goods that were bought in West Berlin with change could be sold for three to four times as much money in the East. Thus, I used my change to buy pickles with mustard seeds in the west, which we did not have in the east yet . . . I bought about ten pounds of plums at the east black market close to the Alexanderplatz, sold them at the Engeldamm in western Berlin for the same price in Westmarks. For the practically one-to-one exchanged money, I immediately bought cigarettes that would bring me multiple gains when sold in the east. I was stopped by police officers with my bags. Of course, they didn't believe me that the plums were all for my own needs. But I was lucky. I pointed at my birthday on my passport, July 23, 1930. "All my birthday guests love plum cake," I said. They let me go.

He was hardly alone in his work, which was highly organized with secret warehouses run by crime bosses. A reporter for RIAS, Juergen Graf, studied food distribution in Berlin and estimated that 10 percent of the milk and 5 percent of the meat in the western sector was supplied by East German farmers working through black markets. Lutz Rackow, also living in the east, remembered trading porcelain, crystal, silver and textiles after school, saying, "You can't eat silver." He continued: "The Allied soldiers wanted Iron Crosses; luckily the Nazis had produced them by the tons." Another eastern teenager who went on to become an important communist official, Norbert Podewin, said he spent mornings and evenings jumping onto coal trains from Poland, grabbing a few lumps, then bragging about it at school. More daring young men swam out to barges carrying coal to eastern Berlin, grabbed bagfuls and swam back to shore. "That's what we talked about then, like sports," said Podewin. "We all had to be thieves. It wasn't hard. We'd work on the Schilling Bridge between the eastern and western sectors, then run to the west when eastern police came and to the east when the western cops came."*

The airlift, said Lutz Rackow, changed everything in the black market, mainly to the benefit of easterners. "Westerners suddenly had nothing for themselves and they were afraid to come to the east, because Russian soldiers kidnapped people. We took backpacks of coal into the west and traded them for cigarettes and chocolate. I still remember the feel of the first Cadbury's chocolate I had in my hand."

Gail Halvorsen, the pilot at Brookley Air Force Base in Mobile who volunteered for TDY in Berlin, thought the airlift would be over in a

---

* I met Podewin in his sunny penthouse apartment, rented to him for seventy East-marks a month in what he called "the good old days," atop a building on Karl-Marx-Allee called Stalin-Allee before East Germany collapsed. He was an assistant to the East German leader Walter Ulbricht, and then became a prominent historian of the regime. His son, he told me in 2007, cared nothing for communism: "He's a big executive of Deutsche Telekom, a millionaire who owns two Mercedes-Benz cars."

couple of mid-July weeks or so and was determined to see the city before he was transferred back to Alabama. On a rare day off in mid-July, he hitched a ride with another pilot, his friend Lieutenant William Christian, carrying a little spring-loaded movie camera, a Revere windup eight-millimeter model. He wanted to bring back something for the family he still did not have. He'd proposed but the girl back home in Utah, Alta Jolley, had not made up her mind. The first thing he wanted to shoot was the apartment houses looming over the approach runway at Tempelhof.

He trotted around the perimeter of the field and saw a bunch of kids, perhaps thirty of them, standing on the other side of the fence watching planes land. "Guten Tag" said Halvorsen, using about half the German he knew. A number of boys and girls there, the oldest was fourteen and the youngest eight, immediately began to ask him questions about the airlift. "How many planes? . . . How much flour could they carry? . . . What about milk?" He stayed about an hour—Halvorsen loved kids—and when he was leaving he realized none of them had asked for anything and he had not given them anything. He had two sticks of Wrigley's Doublemint gum in his pocket, so he went back and broke them into pieces, handing them to the kids up front, who took their gum and then passed the wrappers back for others to lick. Halvorsen had never seen such happy children and he said, "Look, if you're here tomorrow, I'll drop some gum and candy from my plane, but don't tell anyone else about this."

He was back in the air from Wiesbaden the next day, taking off at 2 A.M. On the way to Berlin, he told his crewmates what had happened and what he had promised to do.

"You're going to get us into a mess of trouble," said his copilot, Captain John Pickering. But Pickering and the flight engineer, Herschel Elkins, agreed to go with Halvorsen to the Wiesbaden Post Exchange and let him use their ration cards to buy sweets. They also collected some handkerchiefs to make little parachutes so the stuff would float down and not break up—or crack some kid on the head.

Their next flight to Berlin was in daylight. At noon, Tempelhof was in sight and so were the thirty children. Elkins crouched at the plane's flare chute, holding the three parachutes tied to bags full of Hershey bars, Mounds bars, gum, whatever they had. Halvorsen wiggled the wings of the C-54 a bit, the signal he had told the children below would identify his plane, so get ready—and don't forget to share!

"Now," Halvorsen said, and Elkins pushed out the little chutes.

Ten-year-old Rainer Baronsky was one of the German kids at Tempelhof when the tiny parachutes opened. "One parachute got snagged in a tree, so we took a long stick and jarred it loose. My little brother and I opened up the package dangling from the chute and found candy. What was candy? We would later find out about its sweet chocolate—Hershey bars, Butterfingers." The boys brought their cache home. Their father divided the chocolate in five neat slices for the family and then let the boys chew gum. Taking it from them later, he put the little wads in a bowl of sugar, to be chewed the next day and the next.

Halvorsen and his crew did the same thing twice more over the next two weeks, candy-lifting on the days their new ration cards were issued. The crowds at the fence were getting bigger, of course, and the American flyers were afraid someone would check out their tail number—and then the trouble would begin. So they decided to stop after a final drop of six parachutes. After that drop and landing, Halvorsen had to go into the operations office at Tempelhof for a weather map. There, piled on a table, were dozens of letters, addressed to "Uncle Wackelflugel," "Wiggly Wings," and the "Schokoladen Flieger," the Chocolate Flyer. The next day at Rhein-Main, an ops officer met Halvorsen's plane and said, "Colonel Haun wants to see you. Now."

"What have you been doing?" said Colonel John Haun. He pushed a copy of the newspaper *Frankfurter Zeitung* across the desk.

"Look at this," Haun said, tapping the paper. "You almost hit a reporter on the head with a candy bar yesterday.

"The general called me with congratulations," Haun continued, "and I had no idea what he was talking about. He wants to see you to have a press conference.

"And Halvorsen, next time, tell me first."

And so it began. Halvorsen kept flying, but he had an office and two secretaries at Rhein-Main to answer the mail from grateful Germans. When he got back to his room, his cot was covered with candy—other airmen had used their ration cards—and cloth for parachutes. The crowds at Tempelhof had gotten so large that other pilots were recruited to make drops at schoolyards, at churches and hospitals—all unannounced now. They were dropping packets in eastern Berlin, too, until the Soviets protested to the State Department in Washington that the candy from the sky "violated existing propaganda agreements."

General Tunner called in Halvorsen to tell him that the Air Force was calling him back to the United States for two weeks of newspaper interviews and radio appearances, even some guest spots on that new thing, television. He returned to Germany with fifty pounds of handkerchiefs. By the time he was back in the cockpit, Halvorsen was getting tens of thousands of pounds of candy from both manufacturers and ordinary people responding to "Candy Bomber" drives at schools, colleges and churches across the country. Now trucks were delivering the candy and gum all over Berlin and western Germany.

CHAPTER 4

"Black Friday"

August 13, 1948

F ROM THE DAY THE AIRLIFT BEGAN, JUNE 26, 1948, UNTIL JULY 31, American and British transports made 14,036 flights into western Berlin, delivering 70,241 tons of food, fuel, medicines, newsprint, industrial equipment and whatever else could be crammed into the aircraft. The Americans made 8,117 flights, carrying 41,188 tons. The British flew 5,919 flights, carrying 29,053 tons—an amazing contribution, considering that the people of Great Britain, their capital and country smashed, too, were living under postwar rationing that provided them with little more food than the Berliners were receiving. And, for the first time since the end of the war, the British instituted bread rationing—after grain ships from the United States and Canada were diverted from English ports to Germany. British airmen, who could often get back home if they had a couple of days off, would stop by American messes to get milk to bring to their children.

In western Berlin during the airlift, food was allocated through local stores and bakeries, but the daily mix of cargo was determined by American and British engineers and nutritionists. On the best days that meant: 646 tons of flour (carrying baked bread would have added 30 percent water to the weight); 125 tons of cereal; 64 tons of fat; 109 tons of meat; 180 tons of dried potatoes, a tasteless product called "Pom," which weighed one-fifth the weight of the real thing; 11 tons of real coffee, because coal to make ersatz would have weighed more; 180 tons of sugar; 19 tons of powdered milk and five tons of the real thing for children; 3 tons of fresh yeast; 144 tons of dehydrated vegetables; 10 tons of cheese and 30 tons of salt. The distribution was strictly rationed for five categories:

1. Heavy workers, who comprised 3.7 percent of the population, received ration cards totalling 2,609 calories per day
2. Manual workers, comprising 30 percent of the population, 2,202 calories
3. White-collar employees and nonworkers, the largest group, just under 50 percent of the population, 1,882 calories
4. Children, roughly 1,600 calories, depending on their age
5. Others, 1,530 calories.

So, the average Berliner would receive about 1,800 calories each day. That meant 12 ounces of bread, 14 ounces of potatoes, 1.7 ounces of cereals, 1.4 ounces of meat, 1.5 ounces of fat, 8 teaspoons of sugar, 1.7 ounces of cheese, 5.2 ounces of coffee and 14 ounces of salt. All of that could be supplemented by black-market goods and vegetables that were planted and guarded on every lot and crack of dirt in the city's broken streets.

In England at the same time, rations for a family of four for a week were as low as 1 ounce of bacon, 3 ounces of margarine, 3 pounds of potatoes, 1 ounce of cooking fat, 2 ounces of cheese, 2 ounces of meat, a half pound of bread—and a pound of jam each month. And, in Germany, the RAF tried to limit its men to the same restrictions as the folks at home, sometimes only 1,882 calories per day. "The butter and margarine we took to Berlin was all produced back home in England . . . We had candy rationing in the U.K.," said RAF Flight Engineer David Lawrence. "We couldn't join the USAF guys in dropping it to the kids. We didn't have any to drop."

When General Tunner arrived, the daily airlift delivery averaged 1,985 tons, less than half the 4,500 minimum target considered necessary to keep western Berlin going. Still, it seemed that the operation would continue for only a few weeks more, perhaps even a few days. Soviet Premier Stalin invited three Western officials to a relatively friendly meeting in the Kremlin on the night of August 2. U.S. Ambassador Walter Bedell Smith, French Ambassador Yves Chataigneau and the Deputy Foreign Minister of Great Britain, Frank Roberts, came away optimistic in the early-morning hours, which was when Stalin's meetings usually ended. The Soviet leader said the blockade could be lifted immediately if the Allies would agree to a single currency in Berlin. That seemed reasonable to them, until Clay angrily informed the Joint Chiefs of Staff that a jointly administered currency (with each of the occupying powers holding veto power) would give the Soviets effective control of the city. The British had come to Clay's rescue; Robertson had been told the details of what was happening in Moscow but Clay had not been until the British governor passed along what he knew to the American. The angry American commander's next cable to the Air Force: "Berlin political leaders frightfully upset at rumor of Soviet currency becoming single currency. If we are voided of all control, they will be at the mercy of Soviet Government."

The Moscow talks went on—and went nowhere. That might have happened anyway. In the end, the Allied negotiators concluded that the Soviets were just biding their time, waiting for General Winter to win their war. The fog, snow and freezing cold of Eastern European and Russian winter had defeated Napoleon and Hitler—and the Russians thought the weather would defeat the Americans and British trying to keep a city alive with nothing but airplanes. As the talks went on, much of the American press—particularly conservative midwestern papers, including the *Detroit News* and *Omaha World-Herald*—criticized the Truman administration for negotiating at all. In a cabinet meeting, Secretary of State Marshall noted the editorial comment and said to the President, according to the minutes: "If, as suggested by the American press, negotiations were dropped by the U.S., we would really be in the fire. We either negotiate or shoot."

As early as July 3, Soviet intelligence agencies had been reporting to Moscow that the airlift could not work, and that, in fact, it was a cover for a quick Allied withdrawal from Berlin. The KI, the Committee of Information, a Soviet diplomatic intelligence service, reported that day: "The American mood has changed from warlike to dejected. The many American aircraft arriving in Berlin are taking out documents and other property of the American administration." Another KI report during the same period concluded: "Among prominent members of the American administration in Berlin, it is believed that the Western powers must give in to the Soviet Union . . . The Americans are ready to give the Soviet administration full control over the financial and economic life of greater Berlin . . . retaining only a liaison office and a small garrison."

Both were wrong. But the Soviets had several agencies that were amazingly effective, particularly in collecting information on the British. Papers that reached Bevin's desk were often copied and in Moscow within twenty-four hours. The critical question, though, was whether those intelligence gems reached Stalin's desk. A sure way to derail a Soviet intelligence career was to tell the Premier something he did not want to hear. A great deal of Soviet intelligence was revised or deliberately lost to protect underlings from the wrath of the irritated leader in the Kremlin. In fact, most Soviet intelligence operatives—one example was the chief of MGB (State Security) operations in part of Germany, Georgy Korotia—would testify later that he was never told of the plan for the blockade until it began. He said he would have told Moscow that it would accomplish nothing but turn Germans against communist rule.*

Bill Tunner, like Clay, was a driven man, another chain-smoker, who drove other men to their limits, demanding that they work fifteen hours a day, saying he was putting in eighteen himself. And he wanted the planes to work more hours as well. Smith had specified eight hours a day in the air; Tunner was demanding ten to eleven hours. Those were tough numbers that would impose tremendous strains on maintenance and safety measures—to say nothing of pilots. But soon enough, at least in good weather, Tunner exceeded his own goal; C-54s were averaging 11.5 hours per day in the air.

In recounting his experience in the Hump operation, Tunner laid out this overall philosophy: "The actual operation of a successful airlift is about as glamorous as drops of water on stone. There's no frenzy, no flap, just the inexorable process of getting the job done. In

---

* The success of Soviet intelligence in penetrating British offices is generally attributed to a single British diplomat, Donald Maclean, a Soviet agent who later famously defected to Moscow. He served in the British Embassy in Washington until the end of the summer of 1948.

a successful airlift you don't see planes parked all over the place; they're either in the air, on loading or unloading ramps, or being worked on. The real excitement from running a successful airlift comes from seeing a dozen lines climbing steadily on a dozen charts—tonnage delivered, utilization of aircraft, and so on—and the lines representing accidents and injuries going sharply down. That's where the glamour lies in air transport."

By the end of the first week of August, the lines on General Tunner's dozen graphs were already beginning to climb. More airplanes were in the air and 126 of them were C-54s, as two more squadrons made their way as much as fifteen thousand miles across the world from Hawaii and Japan in an operation called "Charlie."

The French had no planes worth using in Germany. The aircraft they had were being used in an attempt to militarily put down communist-led rebellions in French Indochina—but they did have an old Luftwaffe anti-aircraft training field at Tegel on Berlin's northern border, which they turned over to American engineers on August 5 to build a third western Berlin airfield from scratch. American trucks were collecting the rubble of the city as the base of an asphalt airstrip. Fifteen American officers, led by Major Frank McGuire, an Army engineer, and fifty enlisted men supervised the project and seventeen thousand Germans, men and women with little but shovels and wheelbarrows, provided an around-the-clock workforce. The target date for completing the work was January 1949. On the same day, his seventh on the job, Tunner began negotiating with British officers for U.S. planes to fly from British bases, particularly the RAF fields at Fassberg and RAF Station Celle, which was still being upgraded for Berlin C-54s and other transports. One of Tunner's many charts showed that twenty-seven C-54s operating from the British bases closer to Berlin could deliver 988 tons a day, compared with 588 tons using the same planes from the American fields at Rhein-Main and Wiesbaden. Within forty-eight hours the British agreed to joint operations. The RAF would operate and maintain the bases but American planes and men would do most of the flying. The RAF supervised the air control system, but USAF men manned the microphones because so many American pilots had trouble understanding British accents. The next step, quickly agreed upon, was that planes from both air forces would land at either Tempelhof in the American Sector or Gatow in the British Sector, depending on weather and how many planes were in the air.

The British had already solved the problem of bringing in the most corrosive of cargoes, salt. They used seaplanes landing on Berlin's lakes. The big Sunderlands and other flying boats were built with wiring and control lines strung along the top of fuselages rather than in or under the floor, as they were in C-47s and C-54s, where the salt could turn wiring and cables to rust and dust in a few weeks.*

The British also used thirty-five different small commercial transport companies, with very brave pilots and crews, to fly sloshing loads of the most dangerous of cargoes—gasoline and diesel oil—in old surplus bombers converted into tankers. While that was going on, a British engineer remembered PLUTO (Pipe Lines Under the Ocean), eleven pipelines totaling sixty-five miles of pipes under the English Channel. PLUTO, installed after D-Day to deliver 3,100 tons a day of fuel to supply trucks and tanks moving across France and Germany, was quickly patched up and reactivated, delivering up to seven thousand tons a day of gasoline and diesel oil to western Germany during the airlift.

Next came planning to deal with what Tunner thought was the most important of airlift problems, regular maintenance. The Americans converted Oberpfaffenhofen, an abandoned Luftwaffe base near Munich, from the main Air Force depot in western Germany to a maintenance center. Until that time not a single workstand had been built for regular maintenance anywhere in western Germany or

---

* The Sunderlands and other seaplanes flew until December 15, when the lakes began to freeze. The British continued to bring in salt, packed in panniers slung under transport fuselages.

elsewhere. Mechanics—and there were nowhere near enough of them—made do by piling old metal Luftwaffe bunks one on top of another and welding them together to make rickety ladders to work on engines and wings. The new commander began building a new inspection/maintenance chain, which would begin with inspections at each base after every twenty-five hours of flying time. After two hundred hours in the air, planes were sent for overhauls to Oberpfaffenhofen—the Americans called the place "Oberhuffin' puffin' "—and later to Burtonwood, the World War II base overgrown by weeds in England. After one thousand flight miles, American planes, nine each week, were returned to a series of maintenance and reconditioning centers across the United States, from Connecticut, the home of the Pratt & Whitney's principal engine factory, to bases from Massachusetts to Alabama and Ohio to Oklahoma, Texas and California. More than 60,000 people—40,000 of them German—would be directly working on the airlift in Germany. A half-million more around the world, in factories, offices, airbases and airports, were indirectly involved.

On August 7, the Americans and the British made a total of 666 flights, delivering 3,800 tons. Five days later, on August 12, the target tonnage of 4,500 was reached for the first time. The Americans and British flew 707 flights, 4,752 tons, to Tempelhof and Gatow in twenty-four hours.

Then came August 13, 1948: "Black Friday." It was the fiftieth day of the airlift, a dark day of scudding clouds and intermittent driving rain, not unusual in northern Europe where storms from the North Sea power east through Europe's most famous river valleys. Tunner was flying from Wiesbaden to Tempelhof in his own C-54, number 5549, the same plane he had used in Burma, piloted by his usual pilot, Captain Sterling Bettinger, on what was essentially a publicity mission. Germans came regularly to the airport with gifts for pilots—china, silverware, teddy bears, anything they had. On August 8, an old man had appeared with a heavy gold pocket watch in a velvet case, a jewelled heirloom—worth a lot of money and surely with a lot of history—and wanted to present it to the airlift commander. Tunner would not accept it, but agreed to present it to the American who had flown the most missions to that date, Paul Lykins, a twenty-five-year-old lieutenant from Brownsville, Texas, who had flown forty-six round-trips in forty-two days. A presentation stand was set up, a band brought in, and thousands of Berliners invited for the ceremony under the magnificent cantilevered roof where airliners had let off passengers before the war, a feature unique to Tempelhof.

Friday the 13th could not have been worse. Only a few planes landed cleanly that day, one of them a C-47 piloted by Bill Lafferty, who broke through the driving rain to see a C-54 in flames at the end of the main runway, and another one that had ground-looped after mistakenly coming down on the rubble of the new strip under construction. Noah Thompson also made it in, landing a C-54, but only after his plane was hit by lightning and "bounced up and down like a yo-yo"—those were his words on finally landing. The fog was so thick on the ground that the "Follow Me" jeeps that led planes to unloading areas did not move for an hour or more, for fear of driving into propellers they could not see. After Lafferty landed, another C-54 blew both tires, braking hard after landing too far down the approach runway, and was mired in mud blocking the strip. When 5549 arrived, planes were circling at twelve different altitudes in a holding pattern above Tempelhof. Tunner's plane was slipped into the eighth level at 4,500 feet. That was particularly dangerous because the air corridor restrictions allowed only circles of twenty miles diameter or less without crossing into Soviet-controlled airspace. Radar had trouble piercing the heavy rain. Visibility was sporadically and unpredictably down to "zero-zero"—zero ceiling, zero visibility. The rain, clouds and fog made it impossible to see the ground or other planes. Radio chatter was edged with panic; Tunner, whose plane was twenty-eighth in line to land, was not the only one up there thinking that one small mistake in the air or on the ground could mean a mid-air collision.

He grabbed the microphone from Captain Bettinger and said, "This is 5549. Tunner talking, and you listen. Get these goddamned airplanes out of here. Send every plane in the stack back to its home base."

There was a moment of shocked silence. Then: "Please repeat."

"Send everybody in the stack below and above me home. Then tell me when it's OK to come down."

"Roger, sir."

Then he turned to Bettinger and the copilot, Robert "Red" Forman, and said: "As for you two, I want you to stay in Berlin until you've figured out a way to eliminate any way for this mess from ever happening again—ever! I don't care if it takes two hours or two weeks, that's your job."

By the time he was on the ground, Tunner had made two decisions that defined the operations of the airlift. First, there would be no stacking; the planes would fly three minutes apart and if a pilot missed his approach or landing, there would be no second attempt. Pilots would fly their loaded planes straight back west in the center corridor. Second, all landings, no matter how clear the day or night, would be instrument landings—and if the ceiling was less than four hundred feet and the visibility less than a mile, the landing would be aborted and the plane directed west into the one-way center corridor.

That last part was more theory than practice; more pilots than not landed when conditions were a lot closer to zero-zero—as an RAF squadron commander learned one lousy night. David Bevan-John, sitting in the control tower at Gatow, heard his pilots, one after another, say they had broken through the clouds at "200 feet ceiling, 400 yards visibility." He could not even see the runway lights from his tower and called his men together. "You were lying, weren't you?" After some looking-down silence, a lieutenant from New

Zealand, Les Gow, admitted, "We couldn't even see the bleeding runway."

Landing in Berlin evolved into a three-stage operation. First, the pilots would regularly report their positions—hearing the positions of the planes in front of and behind them—and follow radio beacons into Berlin. Then, forty-five miles from the Berlin airports, the planes would be picked up by the search radars located on top of Tempelhof's control building—one floor below were controllers watching six twelve-inch radar scopes set for the two (later three) airports. At eleven miles out, planes and control would be switched to a precision radar system, a four-scope operation in a mobile station parked at the end of the approach runway, where the four operators would talk the pilots down to touchdown or abortion and the flight back west. The mobile stations, which weighed thirty tons, were actually giant, creeping trucks, with a top speed of two miles per hour and six gears to position and reposition themselves depending on wind direction or weather conditions. On landing, ground controllers directed the planes to unloading trucks and sent out a little circus caravan of operations, canteen and weather trucks and jeeps.*

The system was essentially the plan worked out by Forman and Bettinger after Tunner "locked" them in a hotel room for three days. The two pilots built an eight-foot-square sandbox and cut out a few dozen cardboard planes, to which they attached a horizontal rope and pulley system with coat hangers. The whole thing looked something like a merry-go-round over the sandbox. They called it "the bicycle chain," an airborne conveyer belt. Tunner's goal was to land one plane at Tempelhof every minute, every twenty-four hours. Ignoring standard aviation approach patterns, Tunner's men

---

* The radar used in the airlift was constantly upgraded. In fact, the use of separate search and ground-control radar stations began at Tempelhof in 1948. Another innovation perfected during the airlift was MTI (Moving Target Indicator), which, for the first time, "saw" only moving objects, which allowed ground-control operators to see planes on their scopes as far away as seventy-five miles and watch them strung out like pearls on a necklace.

recommended training pilots to make straight-in landings, rather than circling the field as part of any landing pattern. The new system made it possible to increase the number of landings from nine every ninety minutes to thirty in the same period. A landing a minute was almost impossible—though there were times planes did land every minute, especially when bad weather was coming over the horizon—and Tunner was forced to accept the one-plane-every-three-minutes schedule envisioned by Smith and LeMay. When two other Berlin airports, Gatow and Tegel, were in full operation, one plane was landing every minute in the city and one was was taking off to return west every minute. The loading time with a twelve-man crew averaged six minutes; unloading averaged thirty minutes but sometimes could be done in less than ten minutes, depending on the cargo.

On August 14, the morning after Black Friday, Sergeant Bill Palahunich, the burly Ukrainian-speaking American who could also understand Russian, went back out on the field to help clean up what was left of the three C-54s that had crashed and was stunned to see a Russian soldier standing by a wreck with his German girlfriend. The Russian asked for asylum and Palahunich turned them over to military police in the terminal. The last he saw of the couple, they were filling out papers of some sort.

"Black Friday" apparently impressed the Soviets as much as it did Tunner. Assuming that the Americans and British would be seeking a way to end the airlift, Molotov, on August 15 in Moscow, prepared a draft communiqué for Stalin that declared victory in Berlin. The draft, an audacious document the Soviets thought might be signed by all four powers, stated that the Western B-mark would be withdrawn from circulation, the Western powers would declare the end of any planning for a separate state in West Germany and a new meeting of the Council of Foreign Ministers would establish new systems for the occupation of all Germany—presumably including a provision that Berlin would become a single city within the Soviet Zone.

Tunner was a man who lived by his own time-motion graph. He was hated by more than a few young officers for his habit of dressing them down in front of enlisted men—a no-no in the service. His personal pilot, Captain Bettinger, who flew him into Tempelhof on the publicity mission on Black Friday and was the codesigner of the "bicycle chain," later waited fifteen minutes on a taxiway in 5549 so that he would not disrupt a "block" of slower C-47s. Tunner said nothing, but Bettinger never flew 5549 again.

The graphs were looking better day by day. Tunner knew what he wanted from his men, from the planes, from his superiors—and in logistics and from publicity and public relations, too. He wanted better quarters and food for the pilots, more C-54s to get rid of the C-47s, he wanted to gain control of the British fields closest to Berlin and he wanted the tools to boost the pride and morale of everyone involved in the big lift. By his third week on the job, he had made some real progress. On August 21, the British allowed the Americans, who had more planes, more men and more money, to begin moving C-54s to Fassberg and other British stations.

On August 22, Tunner's public relations officers, led by Major Hal Sims and Lieutenant Bill Thompson, began the mimeograph publication of a small airlift newspaper, a newsletter really, called *Task Force Times*, which projected an overall sense of mission and, perhaps more important, promoted competition between air bases and flight units. In the beginning, the headlines were handwritten on mimeo stencils—LIFT TONNAGE EXPECTED TO RISE was the first one—and the stories were number-heavy. A "Howgozit? Board" was a front-page feature, listing the trips and tonnage of each USAF squadron and by British units, too, to foster the competition that Tunner believed would increase efficiency and productivity.

"We rarely saw a Russian," Tunner said. "We had no enemy to keep us on our toes, and although the men knew that the cargo we were flying into Berlin kept the city alive, it was hard to keep this fact uppermost in everyone's mind, particularly if he never got within a hundred miles of Berlin. The solution was to set up competition between the units flying the lift."

It worked. Richard Malkin, the editor of *Air Transportation*, one of hundreds of the American journalists routinely flown into Berlin to see the airlift, went home to write:

> "What's the yelling about?" I asked the sergeant at my elbow.
>
> "Figures," he replied wearily. "Everybody's tonnage-whacky. He's claiming the tonnage high for the day. Somebody in Wiesbaden gave it to the 313th or some other group. You'd think this was the Kentucky Derby."

Publicity, like competition, was an important part of the airlift—and the Air Force proved to be one of the great public relations machines in the world. In August, Tunner's immediate superior, General Kuter, wrote to him in Wiesbaden, saying, "We should make every effort to have the VITTLES story told by qualified aviation writers who can appreciate the implications of such strategic air transport and who can explain both the techniques of the effort and its essential place in any plan for national defense."

Tunner replied: "No one is more aware than I of the terrific public relations potential in this operation—that this is the greatest opportunity we have ever had, or probably will have, to tell the air transport story and make certain that people will pay attention to us."

Meanwhile, a team of officers in Hollywood was already in negotiations with 20th Century Fox about producing a feature film on the airlift. "[It's] more than just an airlift," said Tunner. "[It's] a propaganda weapon held up before the whole world." He meant propaganda for the United States, the Air Force, air transport and MATS—not necessarily in that order.

Two played that game. East German newspapers daily reported that the blockade was a myth and emphasized that food and fuel rations were being offered to western Berliners if they registered with eastern authorities. And day after day, they repeated a mantra: "The Americans will leave Berlin first. Mrs. Howley has already packed her silver." That was backed up by late-night telephone calls to Germans working for OMGUS telling them they would be arrested or shot after the Americans left.

The Soviets, pushing the offer of cheap rations for western Berliners, also ran newspaper advertisements with a photograph of a noose and the headline WHY HANG YOURSELF? Said the ad: "You only have to register in the Eastern Sector and you can get potatoes and fuel for the winter." Newsreels shown throughout Eastern Europe, with soothing music on the soundtrack, featured healthy and hefty farm girls milking cows, children enjoying hot school lunches and East Berlin families sitting down for evening feasts of meat, potatoes and good German beer.

In the United States, network television documentaries, produced with money from Washington and sponsored by corporations such as Prudential Life Insurance, included one titled *The Cold Decade*, narrated by Walter Cronkite of CBS News: "People were eating out of garbage cans. Scrounging the streets. We had fought for freedom and won famine. No man's mind is free when his body receives less than 800 calories. There is no morality on less than a thousand calories a day. There is no government on less than 1200 calories per day."

The Soviets tried everything they could think of as well, beginning with stories that airlift flights were carrying caviar and champagne into Berlin and flying loot, particularly artwork, out of the city. Their greatest emphasis, though, was on unnecessary dangers of the airlift, particularly on a day like August 24, when four Americans were killed in a midair collision of two C-47s in the fog a few miles from Rhein-Main. When a British Dakota crashed in the eastern zone, the communist magazine *Berliner Illustrierte*, published two pages of photographs under the headline EINE DAKOTA WENIGER—EINE LEHRE MEHR, or "One Dakota Less—One Lesson Learned." A story on German workers in *Neues Deutschland* was headlined:

SLAVES SERVING ANGLO-AMERICANS
Dreadful Treatment of German Workers at Gatow

The weekly magazine of the *Berliner Zeitung*, the eastern sector's largest newspaper, did a series on "Grave Desecration" when the Americans began the installation of ten towers to hold high-intensity Westinghouse fog-piercing lights in Saint Thomas Cemetery— pointing the way to the new Tempelhof runway. The project required permission from German and church officials to cut down the cemetery's trees and move several graves. The *Berliner Zeitung's* take on that, under the headline COLD WAR DOES NOT LEAVE DEAD ALONE: "Recently heavy damage was done to the cemetery caused by hundreds of children chasing after candies dropped into the cemetery by American pilots prior to landing. Now in a reckless manner holes and long cable ducts have been dug and masts with position lights erected. The Americans behave in Berlin like troops engaged in a war in the enemy country."

Cartoons in the same paper regularly mocked the airlift. One showed a man shouting at his wife: "Stop! Stop! You're powdering the baby's bottom with our West Sector potato ration for August!"

Public relations, however, like instrument flying, was not a Soviet strength. *Task Force Times* countered Soviet attacks with letters, which tended to increase greatly after accidents. This one was from an East Berliner:

Dear Sirs:

Yesterday afternoon I have been standing for a while on the railroad station Tempelhof, watching the coming and going of the two and four motor airplanes. Every time, when one of the big planes appeared on the western horizon and started to land there was a light in the faces of the people. Probably you can't imagine what every plane means to us.

Gerhard Noack was a teenage private in the Wehrmacht, captured by the U.S. Army and herded into a 200,000-man prisoner-of-war holding area along the Oder-Rhine River. They were lightly guarded, and allowed to forage for food, which they cooked in the tin cans the Americans threw away. One day he was released, or just walked away, and headed for home, which was in Sachsen in the eastern zone, the Russian Zone. At the beginning of 1948 he was notified that he was being assigned to work in the uranium mines run by a joint Soviet-German company called Wismuth. The word was already out that coffins were coming back from Wismuth operations with the bodies of young miners. Noack decided to simply disappear into western Germany.

"Something is going on in Celle, there's work, the British are hiring people," he heard one day. Still only nineteen, he headed for Celle, for the German Civil Labor Organization (GCLO) offices that had been set up with the help of British and American labor union organizers. The program was supposed to aid in the process of de-Nazification; it was an organization that could investigate potential workers' backgrounds. GCLO workers were required to wear uniforms, actually old clothes dyed green if they were Germans, dyed black if they were Displaced Persons from Poland, Yugoslavia, Lithuania, Latvia and other countries controlled by communists.

He saw a lineup of men in Celle and joined it, but someone there told him the better place to go was Fassberg, just twenty-five miles away, to something called Camp Trauen. So he did. There he saw thirty men in line and he joined them. A British major walked up and down the line, saying only two words, "Left" and "Right." Eight men were on the right. The major, whose name was Hill, stood in front of them and said, "You are employed."

They were members of GLCO Company 44, each given a blue pass and a green uniform, told they would be fed, housed and paid one Deutschmark per hour. They were marched to a yellowish-brown tent city near the old Luftwaffe base at Fassberg, then told they would be loading coal into the planes flying to Berlin. Noack thought he was in heaven. There were three shifts a day. Twenty trucks carrying twelve loaders would go to the railroad spur serving the base, then take the duffel bags of coal up ramps into the trucks and then ride back and muscle them into the planes. Usually a crew would load five or six planes a shift, at least at the beginning. The British would serve them tea in the afternoon. The Americans gave them hot chocolate, as much as they wanted, at night. Cooks, good ones, were hired from all over Germany. Noack's weight went from 118 pounds to 158 in six months, all of it muscle from tossing the hundred-pound bags to the next man. Arm-wrestling and football (soccer) became the sports of choice at Camp Trauen—even Major Hill joined in the arm-wrestling. Then it was back to work together and the British were as correct as ever, talking little and insisting that they strap down the coal bags in each plane themselves because shifting weight was always a danger to air crews—and they would not trust the Germans to do jobs like that.

Fassberg had a short but amazing history. It had been built as a secret German air base—in violation of the Versailles treaty that ended World War I—by Hermann Göring in a forest. From the air the brick, red-tiled buildings and a huge greensward made it look like it had been there forever, but in fact many of the "houses" were maintenance buildings or barracks and the grass was a camouflaged training field for Luftwaffe pilots in the 1930s. The Allies did not know what it was until British soldiers arrived there in 1945. Three years later, when Noack arrived in the first week of August, it was becoming an airlift boomtown, with five thousand GLCO workers like himself and seven thousand other Germans and foreigners living there in the sprawling, muddy tent city, which gradually evolved into a neater settlement of Nissen huts, temporary round-roofed buildings of curved corrugated iron. Then there were the "Veronikas." "They were everywhere, living in basements, renting rooms or beds in Fassberg and Celle. The prostitutes worked in the cemetery. They were for the Americans," said Noack. "They wouldn't look at us and the British couldn't afford them."

By German standards, though, the loaders and unloaders were an elite, being paid totally in Westmarks and getting free hot meals every workday. The major problem with the workers was the most obvious one: pilferage. However hard they worked or however well paid they were, these were desperate men, many of them supporting cold and hungry families. The Germans were generally self-policing on systematic theft, *kameraden* preferring to deal with each other rather than informing. Many of the loaders and unloaders had been Nazis, some of them fairly prominent, but their German comrades did not betray them to occupiers.

Young Allied soldiers serving as military policemen were ambivalent about the civilian workers and often looked the other way when laborers went home from Tempelhof and the other Berlin landing fields, particularly after an eighteen-year-old British private, John Collyer, arrested a man exactly his own age for trying to steal a half pound of butter. Locked in a toolshed, the young German hanged himself in shame. But he was hardly the only one trying to sneak out some of whatever he handled that day. The preferred technique was small bags hung inside trousers—if a worker saw guards checking, he could pull the string and his contraband would drop to the ground. At Gatow one August day, a German police officer, Heinz Michael, held up one shift, determined to search every worker. His men found in pockets or trouser bags or in small piles on the ground: 79 pounds of sugar, 1 pound of tea, 4 pounds of flour, 31 pounds of butter, 10 pounds of milk powder, 3 slabs of chocolate, 129 tins of meat, 20 packs of cigarettes and 11 pounds of loose coal. Shoes were a prize too. Many Berliners or their wives and children wore homemade wooden clogs, but the Americans stopped shoe theft by shipping left and right shoes separately. There were also a few incidents of sabotage. Lieutenant Fred Hall, a pilot from Baltimore, discovered that someone had replaced the thin copper wire used to pack parachutes with stronger stainless-steel wire that would probably have prevented the chute from opening. Several other chutes were checked and the same thing had been done. The German worker charged with doing that was arrested within hours.

On August 5, 1948, Elisabeth Poensgen wrote to relatives in western Germany:

> The Airlift is admirable, but in the long run, it is a drop in the ocean . . . We don't have electricity, no means of transportation after 6 P.M. and hundreds of factories have stopped working. My passed interpreter exam doesn't help me at all at the moment. The only job available is that of a loading worker at the airport, which I don't think I have enough strength for. I use my free time to snatch some vegetables and to preserve them. Most of the time I search in vain . . . As a result of his National Socialism, Julius, my brother, has become a rotter and since his political heaven has collapsed, he has become unbearable. Is it right to let other people pay for their mistakes? Is it my fault that his Adolf failed and did not end up on the English throne?

Germans called the planes *rosinen bombers*—"raisin bombers"— because there always seemed to be small packages of raisins coming off the planes. There was a reason for that: a bumper crop of raisin grapes in California in 1948. Farmers and companies there donated a million pounds of the dried fruit to CARE, the Cooperative for

American Remittances to Europe, a charity created after the war to send food packages to Europe. When there was room on the planes, pilots and crews would fill empty spaces with twenty-two-pound CARE packages—at least 200,000 were delivered, the first one arriving on July 23, 1948. In addition to the raisins, the boxes, filled with C-rations and other food originally prepared for the expected United States invasion of Japan in 1945, typically contained: 1 pound of beef in broth, 1 pound of steak and kidneys, 8 ounces of liver loaf, 8 ounces of corned beef, 12 ounces of luncheon loaf (Spam), 8 ounces of bacon, 2 pounds of margarine, 1 pound of lard, 1 pound of fruit preserves, 1 pound of honey, 1 pound of raisins, 1 pound of chocolate, 2 pounds of sugar, 8 ounces of egg powder, 2 pounds of whole-milk powder, 2 pounds of coffee. Other CARE packages contained clothing, blankets and candles. The organization, collecting money in American schools, offices and churches, chartered planes to fly into western Germany, accounting for 60 percent of private American aid to Allied zones and sectors before and during the airlift. Among the children who received CARE packages—and never forgot it—was Helmut Kohl, who would become the first chancellor of a reunited Germany.

It was all part of a tremendous wave of sympathy and charity generated by press coverage of the airlift. President Truman personally paid ten dollars for a CARE package sent to Berlin, schoolchildren across America were making parachutes for Halvorsen, churches began special collections of toys for Berlin's children—and most every American growing up then could remember mothers saying, "Clean your plate, now. Think of those poor starving children in Europe."

In the same week of Poensgen's lament, just five weeks into the airlift, there were two articles in the *New York Times* that both reflected and drove the new attitude. NEW COURAGE RISES FROM BERLIN'S RUINS was the headline of a piece by Drew Middleton:

Trapped in the pressure between East and West, ruined by the war they started, the people of this city have no material contribution they can make. So they have turned to that courage for which Germans from the times of the Caesars have been renowned ... The stout opposition which these people have offered to Soviet pressure is a commentary on how much ground Russian Communism, or Stalinism, has lost in Germany. Does their stand augur well for the future of Germany? Some think so ... In 1945, one met many who said, "Just give us a few years on our own and we will rebuild our city." One does not hear that so often anymore. But one does hear something which was lacking in 1945: a firm resolve to build a better Germany, not to give in again to totalitarianism.

Kathleen McLaughlin's story was headlined, WOMEN OF BERLIN CALM IN BLOCKADE. She wrote:

Frau Bergerebuss is the scrawny, undersized but undismayed pivot of life in a dreary basement flat ... Up at 6 A.M., but not to use electrical current, which is available for 6 to 8 A.M. Her income admits neither electricity or gas ... Laundry must often be foregone for the lack of soap and other cleansers. She deplores her inability to keep neither the house nor her two children properly clean on the two tiny bars of soap allowed a person over a period of 13 weeks ... Conditioned to fear the police—her husband is half-Jewish and several relatives were gassed in concentration camps—Frau Bergerebuss still ventured recently into the Soviet zone and bought two pounds of plums. The portions were stored in the pockets of her six-year old and seventeen-year old sons and in a satchel carried by her eleven-year old daughter.

Germans were no longer the enemy. Germans were people.

CHAPTER 5

"We Are Close to War"

September 13, 1948

**"THIS WAY, WE HAVE 'EM UNLOADED BEFORE THEY
FINISH THEIR LANDING ROLL"**

S ATURDAY, AUGUST 18, 1948, WAS THE FIRST ANNIVERSARY OF
the founding of the United States Air Force as a service separate from the Army. In Germany, LeMay and Tunner planned
a celebration. ATF SET FOR MAXIMUM EFFORT was the headline of the

Task Force Times. For twenty-four hours, the Americans and British would carry only coal, already stockpiled and ready to go at their bases in the west. Colonel "Howling" Howley, the commandant in western Berlin, announced that families with two or more children would each get one hundred pounds of the extra coal. There were 895 American and British flights from noon to noon in cold, foggy weather. The total unloaded: 7,272 tons—far and away a new record. Germans were allowed on the fields in large numbers for the first time to watch the work. In Fassberg, a sixteen-man German team filled two C-54s with nineteen tons of coal in just over seven minutes. There was an unloading contest at Tempelhof, won by a German crew that tossed 176 sacks into trucks in five minutes and forty-five seconds.

The next night, just after 10 P.M., a British Avro York carrying coal from RAF Wunstorf to Gatow crashed on takeoff when an engine failed. The pilot, Flight Lieutenant Hugh W. Thompson, and his four crewmen were killed. The fire burned all night and the next day.

By the end of August, the Air Force had recalled to active duty more than ten thousand pilots, flight engineers and control tower personnel, all World War II veterans, for airlift Temporary Duty.

TERRIBLE TUNNER'S TIRED TONNAGE TOTERS TO TEMPELHOF was the sign put up in one of the pilots' barracks in Wiesbaden. More and more pilots were being called in from around the world. One of them was Lieutenant Richard A. Campbell, the pilot of one of thirty-six Air Force C-54s moved from Japan. His trip to Wiesbaden began in Tachikawa, then went through Guam, Johnson Island, Hawaii, Travis Air Base in California, Oklahoma City, Westover, Newfoundland and the Azores. The new men unloaded their gear, leaving it in front of the Nissen huts where they would live. But first, there was the briefing.

A major explained the routine, and then asked the pilots, most of them captains and majors, how many of them had ground-control landing experience. One hand went up: Lieutenant Campbell. He had made a number of GCA landings at Kimpo, Korea. "OK, Lieutenant," said the briefer. "You lead the first flight."

"When?"

"Now."

Campbell made five round-trips to Tempelhof before he got back to his luggage. By then the hut was filled with loaders, Displaced Persons. He and his men were put in the loft of another DP barracks—for four months. Some of the other fliers from Japan started later, but then flew three round-trips a day to Berlin for twenty-seven straight days, before getting three days off.

Captain Charles "Pat" Patterson and three other pilots went to Hamburg on their days off. He took notes:

> People begged for food and cigarettes, and young girls were willing to have sex with Americans in exchange for a candy bar. A situation many Americans took advantage of. A thriving trade in the black market existed. We were given a briefing on it. We were told what the Germans in Berlin were paying for cigarettes, chocolate and bars of soap. We were paying a dollar per carton for cigarettes at the PX and selling them to Germans for the equivalent of $35. When we reported for duty, we all carried our musette bags with whatever items we had bought at the PX . . . In Hamburg, we discovered a small pub that had a rather large string orchestra. After visiting this pub on several of our trips, we made a deal with the owner that for the time we were there we would lease the pub for our exclusive use. Although we arrived in Hamburg with a big roll of Marks, by the time our three days were over, we always were broke. We lived hard and played hard.

The lousy (literally) housing was one of Terrible Tunner's biggest gripes. The men of the occupation, ordinary soldiers and military policemen, were living like kings with their PX rations, commandeered houses and German girls. Tunner's men, airlift men, were working around the clock, and living like POWs or DPs. He had to fight LeMay to get curtains on their barracks' windows so they could sleep during the daytime. The housing was bad and the food was often worse, particularly at RAF bases, where the British seemed to get by on kippers, overcooked brussels sprouts and tea—the same rations their families were getting back home.

Tunner cared for the comfort of his men, but only up to a point. His real passion was for the health and safety of his planes. He thought most about maintenance and mechanics. There were not enough mechanics in the Air Force. That manpower shortage and the weather were screwing up his precious graphs.

Tunner was kept on a short leash at first, forbidden to talk to anyone outside the command line of the Air Force; everything had to go through LeMay or his deputies. But, like them, he was a cunning practitioner of the canny politics of the military. The transport commander took to hanging around Rhein-Main or Tempelhof when he heard that General Clay might be coming or going. Finally, one day early in September, Clay saw him, walked up and said, "Any problems, Tunner?"

"We do not have enough mechanics," said Tunner. "But I think I can whip it—if you will allow me to hire some German mechanics. They're good."

"Go ahead and do it," Clay said. "Tell Curt I said it's OK."

When Tunner told his men that he wanted to hire Germans, they were stunned. One said, "You're going to regret this. There'll be sabotage. They'll put bombs in the coal."

After his not-so-chance encounter with Clay, Tunner hurried back to his office and Wiesbaden. He told Katie Gibson: "Find von Rohden."

Major General Hans Detlef von Rohden had been the Luftwaffe's chief transport officer, the German Tunner. He had kept in touch with his men, those who survived the war, and he spoke English.

Within days, he was translating C-54 maintenance manuals into German, and trained mechanics, some of them still ardent Nazis, began appearing at the gates of Allied airfields, many of them carrying their own toolboxes. The Americans gave them sixteen pages of mimeographed sheets, most of them drawings of C-54 sections and translations: *fuselage* became *Rumpf*; *cowling oil cooler fairing* became *Ölkühlerverkleidung*.

By the beginning of September, work had begun on several of the new airlift facilities. More than five thousand Americans were at Burtonwood, the huge and abandoned Lancashire, World War II bomber base between Liverpool and Manchester that was being reconstructed to replace Oberpfaffenhofen as the main parts depot and two-hundred-hour inspection and repair center. A new 1,800-yard runway was almost ready at Celle. The most amazing of the new projects was Tegel, the airport being built in the French Sector. The number of Berliners building the airport had reached nineteen thousand. Almost half of those workers were women, many of them wearing nothing but old bathing suits in the summer heat or toddling along on high heels, their only shoes, as they pushed around their shovels and wheelbarrows. As luck, bad luck, would have it, this was the coldest September in Germany in more than thirty years. There was already snow on the Harz Mountains between Frankfurt and Berlin. With all the upbeat publicity in the Allied press, the airlift was still providing no more than 40 percent of what had been brought into Berlin by rail, truck and barge—and secret projections indicated that the total might drop by another third when winter really began. One of the options being considered by the British, who handled most passenger traffic in and out of Berlin, was to fly all western Berlin's students and teachers to West Germany for the winter. That meant 284,420 schoolchildren and 6,625 teachers. They estimated the operation would take twenty days—but it was never tried.

The work went on, even though there were rumors across Berlin that the whole thing might be over in ten days. The military governors of the four sectors of Berlin met for the first time in months, supposedly to continue the conversations between Stalin and Western envoys in Moscow, which had focused mainly on currency issues. On September 1, Ruth Friedrich-Andreas wrote in her diary:

> The blockade will be lifted. One hardly dares to believe it, but they say it is true. Yesterday afternoon, for the first time in five months, all four military governors met in the building of the Control Council to discuss the lifting of the blockade and the introduction of a uniform currency for all Berlin . . . At Helmstedt trains carrying coal and food are already waiting to roll eastward the moment the border is opened. Berliners are jubilant. No more dehydrated potatoes and canned meat. No more power cuts . . . At night Heike [her daughter] and I illuminate our apartment with four candles instead of one. Who knows, perhaps already by tomorrow we shall have light again by just switching it on.

The next day she wrote: "The rumors that the blockade would be lifted have not been confirmed. We sit around one candle waiting for the power to be turned on."

At the same time, Brandt was trying to persuade his suspicious superiors in Hannover that they might have to suspend their distrust of General Clay, who they knew distrusted them. He was another American who did not see much difference between socialists and communists. Wrote Brandt: "I have been told that Clay would by all means stay here until the American elections are over and probably until January 1. One may think of Clay whatever one wants, but it cannot be denied that he really wants to create an effective economic and political organization in the West . . ."

The politics of Germany and of Berlin had reached a breaking point. In Bonn, a West German Parliamentary Assembly was discussing a basic law, a constitution for "West Germany," a new country. In divided Berlin, parliamentary politics turned violent. The Assembly met in the old Berlin City Hall, located in the eastern sector, which meant East German police and Soviet soldiers controlled the turf. There had been demonstrations and disruptions by communist-led mobs of several hundred tough guys in August, but before the September 6 meeting, a mob of more than three thousand organized by the SED and guided by eastern police gathered outside the Assembly chambers waving red flags and banners. Exactly at noon, they broke down the doors and charged onto the Assembly floor.

A *Time* correspondent watching the mob reported back to New York that eastern zone policemen made no attempt to stop the demonstrators until a group of young men charged the doors and were stopped by an officer, who shouted: "No, no, not now. First you finish singing the Internationale, then you break down the gate."

Clay described what happened over the next forty-eight hours or so in a cable to Draper, the Undersecretary of the Army:

> They manhandled three American reporters at the scene. Today, a well-organized mob was on hand again. The deputy mayor, Louise Schroeder, foolishly and without our knowledge, took forty-odd plainclothesmen from Western sectors over to keep order. Uniformed police from the Soviet sector under direct orders of a Soviet officer started to arrest them. They rushed into the offices of the three Western liaison representatives, where some are still under siege. However, Soviet sector police broke into our office and led about twenty of the poor devils off to death or worse . . . We are being pushed around like we are a fourth-class nation. My impulse was to send our military police to restore order. . . . However, I realize the implications and am just taking it for the moment.

Forty of the western Berlin police were finally taken away in Soviet trucks. Some were never seen again. The Assembly was divided; from then on the westerners met in the British Sector. The Chairman of the Joint Chiefs of Staff in Washington, General Omar Bradley, queried Clay as to whether he actually intended to send MPs into the Soviet Sector. Clay answered: "Sometimes I let off steam to Draper which I cannot let off here. I tell him what I would like to do but am not doing."

That day the airlift set another record, with American planes carrying in 3,319 tons and the British more than a thousand.

And Berliners continued to take matters into their own hands—against American wishes. The Social Democrats, led by Franz Neumann, the chairman of the SDP; Otto Suhr, the speaker of the City Assembly; and Ernst Reuter, "the unseated mayor," called for a rally that same day, September 9, to protest the raid on the Assembly. More than 250,000 people (some of the crowd estimates reached 500,000) came to the Platz der Republik, between the burned-out Reichstag building and the Brandenburg Gate, the border between the British and Soviet sectors. Neumann opened the rally by asking for a minute's silence for victims of the Nazis. A long list of speakers led up to Reuter, who was never noted as a dynamic speaker, not that the words of anyone carried that far with the huge crowd and a tiny sound system. But that day Reuter managed to electrify the crowd as his words were passed back from the stage row upon row by word of mouth:

> Today is the day the people of Berlin raise their voice and call the whole world, for we know what is at stake in the negotiations in the Control Council building and in the stone palaces of the Kremlin ... in all this wheeling and dealing we Berliners don't want to be an object of barter. Nobody can barter us. Nobody can negotiate us. Nobody can sell us. It is impossible to make a rotten compromise on the backs of such brave, decent people. You, nations of the earth. You, people in America, in England, France and

Italy. Look upon this city and realize that you dare not give away this people, cannot give us away . . . You must not forsake us.

The crowd was getting more and more excited, shouting back *"Freiheit! Freiheit!"* Freedom! Freedom! Then as the rally was breaking up, a young man ran for the Brandenburg Gate, climbed an inside stairway to the top and tore down the Soviet flag. Three others joined him, trying to burn the flag with cigarette lighters. A Soviet jeep, carrying a half-dozen soldiers reporting for routine duty as an honor guard for the huge Soviet War Memorial on the British side of the gate, tried to drive into the crowd to protect their flag. Stones were thrown at them, and they fired back wildly, mostly in the air. The shots killed a boy of fifteen, Wolfgang Scheunemann, and nine others were wounded. The crowd surged around the soldiers, and might have killed them if five hundred men of the Royal Norfolk Regiment, hidden inside the Reichstag ruins, had not charged out to rescue the Russians and get them out of there. Their commander, Major Frank Stokes, reached the Russians and began tapping his swagger stick on their gun barrels. "Time to go," he said—and they did.

Andreas-Friedrich was there and wrote:

On Thursday thousands of Berliners demonstrated on the Platz der Republik for democratic liberties and against the scandalous events that have taken place at City Hall. Housewives ran away from their stoves, the hairdresser abandoned his customer under the drying hood, the news vendor closed his newsstand. Everybody came running, thinking: I must demonstrate. We belong to the West. We are Berliners . . . They tore the Soviet flag off the gate, and started shouting and making threats. The Russian police interfered. They fired shots. One person was left dead and several were injured. Five demonstrators were arrested. Yesterday the Soviet military court sentenced each of them to twenty-five years in a labor camp. That means death. Sooner or later, in a concentration camp or a uranium mine.

Berliners, east and west, were in a state of brave, or foolish, euphoria. Clay and the Americans were nervous and angry. The American commander had urged the British not to give out permits for the mass meeting, saying, "This is a dangerous game . . . Mass meetings against the Soviet military government can easily turn into mass meetings against other powers and can develop into the type of mob government which Hitler played so well to get into power." Then the American passed the same message along to Reuter, who agreed. A week later, a counterdemonstration on the eastern side of the gate drew eighty thousand people.

On September 14, Captain Kenneth Slaker, of Lincoln, Nebraska, and Lieutenant Clarence Steber, of Mobile, Alabama, were on a routine C-47 flight over eastern Germany, their second of the night. Slaker, making only his sixth flight to Berlin—not counting fifty bombing runs in 1944—had just received the standard briefing for new pilots at Wiesbaden, including this, read to them by an intelligence officer: "The Russians say they will shoot down any aircraft that strays out of the Berlin air corridor, and that captured airlift pilots will be treated as spies . . . If you should find yourself down in the Soviet Zone, we cannot say that you should turn yourself in, or that you should try to escape. There is no published or firm policy on this, and it would be up to you or your crew as to what action you would want to take."

Slaker and Steber had to crawl into the cockpit over fifty-five-gallon barrels of gasoline for their first flight of the night, Slaker's fifth overall. Steber piloted the run to Tempelhof and then took the left seat for the flight west. Their second flight had less dangerous cargo, flour, but both engines cut out at the same time, with Steber again in the pilot's seat flying east over the Soviet Zone. They were at six thousand feet, less than two thousand feet over the Harz Mountains. The American fliers were barely able to get out and open their parachutes before the plane crashed. But their ride down was only a few hundred feet and both were knocked out when they hit the ground. Steber was badly injured and was almost immediately captured by Russian soldiers and taken to a hospital. The Soviets informed American officials. Two American members of the Potsdam Liaison Committee, Army officers assigned as diplomats and wearing civilian clothes, drove to the hospital. There was a guard at Steber's door, and the other two Americans immediately helped the flier out a back window. They ran for their car, carrying the pilot along, and were on their way west before any of the guards knew what happened. Before they reached an East German guardhouse at the Berlin border, they put Steber into the trunk and were waved through to western Berlin.

Slaker, who was one of the second wave of World War II bomber pilots called up, landed in a muddy potato field. He was unconscious for four or five hours. Waking up, he could not feels his legs at all but he could feel tremendous pain in his back. He guessed he was about forty-five miles from the patrolled border between East and West Germany and he guessed that Steber, who followed him out the door into the night, was probably dead. As feeling came back into his legs, Slaker, in great pain, turned his Air Force jacket inside out and began limping down a country road, vomiting again and again as he walked west toward the border. He knew the direction because of something he had learned as a Boy Scout: moss grows on the north side of trees. It was near dawn and he could see shadowy figures around, farmers beginning their work. He turned into the forest beside the fields. He didn't get far before he literally bumped into an East German foraging for food in the night. "I'm an American pilot on the airlift," he said. The German, whose name was Rudolph Schnabel, reached into a coat pocket and showed the pilot his discharge papers after two years as a prisoner of war in an American camp outside Kearney, Nebraska.

"Americans were good to me," he said in workable English. "Americans capture me, save my leg." He pulled up his pants leg to show scars on his leg, which had been put back together in an American field hospital after he was run over by a tank. Then he said he would help Slaker to the border, but the American insisted on walking behind him, carrying a big stick he had been using as a cane.

"Kannath no trust Rudolph?" said the German.

"Ja und nein," said Slaker, who spoke some German—with a decidedly American accent.

Soon they were on a small road being passed every few minutes by Soviet trucks. Schnabel stopped at a friend's house, where he picked up potatoes for his family and civilian clothes for Slaker. Then he persuaded the American to take a train with him thirty miles to his home in Eisenach, five miles from the border between the Soviet and American zones. They passed through a crowded station checkpoint with Slaker pretending to be a deaf mute.

"You have to eat now," said Schnabel's wife, Magdalena, when they reached his house. Slaker said no, there was not much food.

"What feeds two will also feed three," she said.

Slaker was in great pain, so he stayed hidden in the house while Schnabel left to contact friends willing to help the American across the border. When the German returned, he said it was time to go. "Say a quick 'Our Father' and it'll be all right," Magdalena said at the door.

"You say one too," said Slaker. "Then it will be all right."

They took off at dusk with Schnabel's friends, a former German soldier and his eighteen-year-old girlfriend, who said they knew a bridge over the Werra River near the border with a guard who could be bribed. Slaker gave them the five hundred Westmarks, the amount each pilot was issued for emergencies like this one. It was a long walk. A painful walk. "My heart was in my mouth when we started crossing the bridge," Slaker recalled. "That German policeman was coming straight towards us. And about two yards from us he stopped, then he turned around and ignored us."

They could see the border a few hundred yards away on a hilltop. They would have to cross open fields and get through coils of barbed wire before taking on the hill. There were guard stations with search-lights on either side of their pathway. Halfway up the hill, Slaker got caught in the barbed wire and sentries opened up with rifle fire. His companions pulled him free and they all ran for the horizon. Slaker could not make it. He fell and began rolling down the hill.

"The Captain has fallen," said the girl. The two Germans slid back down and the three of them dragged each other up to an American guardhouse on the other side. He learned there that the Soviets had already announced he was killed in the crash. So the press was on the story. In fact, an Associated Press correspondent called the American guardhouse while Slaker was still there.

Then the story turned dark. Schnabel had lost his papers in the scramble up the hill, so the Russians would have his name. He decided to stay in West Germany and was turned over to American military police who interrogated him for three weeks because he had no papers and his brother was a communist official. They used a rubber hose as a tool, before finally releasing him to the Air Force and a reunion with Slaker at Wiesbaden.

"Kannath, they beat me," said Schnabel. "They wanted me to confess that I was a communist and I am not."

Colonel Sig Young, the Wiesbaden commander, confirmed the beating story and said that he had to call Washington, the office of the Secretary of the Air Force, before the Army would release the German. He told Schnabel the Air Force would find a way to get his family out of East Germany.*

---

* The Air Force kept its promise, and Schnabel was reunited with Magdalena and their child. City officials in Wiesbaden gave the Schnabels an apartment and provided Schnabel with a job at the post office. To protect the Army, the Slaker-Schnabel story of torture was classified for forty years.

. . .

If things seemed to be going well in Berlin, there was deepening pessimism in Washington, London and Paris. The best-connected journalist in the American capital, James Reston, the Washington bureau chief of the *New York Times*, interviewed American, British and French officials, then wrote a front-page article headlined:

WESTERN OFFICIALS
WORRIED OVER LIFT

The blockade started 100 days ago today. The function of the Anglo-American airlift was to sustain the lives of 2,250,000 Berliners and to give time for Western powers to negotiate for the restoration of their legal rights. Both of these objectives have been achieved . . .

But in the second hundred days, will it be enough to "sustain life"? . . . Can the Airlift keep the people working as well as living . . . All the avalanche of statistics on the airlift are somewhat misleading. All targets have been met, but they were emergency ration targets. When the Airlift began, there was very little unemployment in the Western Sectors . . . Now 90,000 persons [are] unemployed in the United States, British and French sectors and this figure is rising all the time.

That sense of dread had reached the White House. In fact, either Truman or Acheson was almost certainly Reston's American source. After a cabinet meeting on September 13, at which there was a discussion—pushed by Forrestal, who was irrationally certain the Soviets planned to attack—of whether the United States should use the atomic bomb rather than give up Berlin, President Truman wrote in his diary: "I have a terrible feeling we are very close to war."

Ironically, the next evening, John Foster Dulles, who was expected to become Secretary of State if Republican Thomas E. Dewey defeated Truman in the November election, was a guest at a dinner party at the home of Philip Graham, president of the *Washington Post*. Marshall, Forrestal, Lovett and Bohlen were all there, and all agreed, as Marshall had realized in August, that the American people were ahead of their leaders on how tough to be in Berlin. Forrestal, as always, brought up the question of using the bomb. Said Dulles: "The American people would crucify you if you did not use the bomb."

No one argued with him.

CHAPTER 6

"Rubble Women"

October 29, 1948

"YEAH, ALL THE WAY FROM GREAT FALLS IN THESE DAMN BUCKET SEATS."

ITS NEW 1,800-YARD RUNWAY COMPLETED, RAF STATION CELLE was turned over to American command at the beginning of October.

Almost immediately, the beautiful half-timbered city in the British Zone was overwhelmed as thousands of American airmen arrived at the same time. Good housing was so scarce that two units of mechanics were ordered to play a softball game to decide which one would be assigned to brick barracks and which to Nissen huts. (The 41st Squadron defeated the 40th, 16 to 2.) Then came 5,000 German loaders. And they were followed by two thousand Veronikas. The Veronikas were followed by reporters, who made the place notorious as "Veronika-town." Both *Time* magazine and the German magazine *Der Stern* ran photographs of some of the girls they said came to the new bars and brothels from all parts of Germany, sharing the company and money of American GIs. "Jazz everywhere," said the German journal. The mayor of Celle was quoted, saying: "The American soldiers who have come to Celle because of the airlift have brought along German women and girls whose behavior is immoral. The spread and treatment of sexually transmitted diseases causes high costs and many difficulties."

There were a couple of significant headlines in the October 4, 1948, edition of *Task Force Times*, the first one indicating that there had been a change in the way West Berliners saw the airlift:

BERLIN FOLK CONFIDENT LIFT WILL CONTINUE

"Eight out of ten Berliners," the story began, "believe that the Anglo-American Airlift can sustain them through the winter, according to an official Military Government survey." The Americans were poll-happy, constantly surveying attitudes toward the occupiers. In this case, "eight out of ten" underestimated the sentiment of Berliners. The actual number was 86 percent. The striking thing about that number was that only 45 percent had answered the same question in the affirmative in July. Support of the airlift, or at least optimism about it, had doubled. The Americans also polled constantly on German attitudes on other subjects. A survey taken by the military government during the airlift reported that 42 percent of respondents listed their principal hardship as a lack of gasoline and fuel; 35 percent cited power shortages and 23 percent said lack of food.

PILOTS IN U.S. TO BE TRAINED FOR LIFT DUTY

The dateline of this one was Great Falls, Montana, October 1. That story began: "Pilots will be given instruction in flying C-54 planes on a course set up as a replica of the air corridors into Berlin. Traffic and communications system will be similar to those used in Germany. Flight crews will learn identical communication technique and traffic control systems used on the Airlift."

"About the most bleak and dismal place this writer has seen," wrote Hanson W. Baldwin, the *New York Times* chief military correspondent, when he saw the tar-paper shacks that dotted a cold and windy high plateau 120 miles south of the Canadian border and six miles east of Great Falls itself, a "city" of twenty thousand people. The Army Air Force had put a base there for an ironic reason: to transport planes and equipment to the Soviet Union during World War II. The shipments were part of the United States' Lend-Lease program to provide material to Allies in the war against Germany. Some heavy bomber training was done at Great Falls, but the most important unit there was the 7th Ferrying Group, which was responsible for establishing an air route to Ladd Field in Alaska, where the planes—a variety of older fighters and bombers—were turned over to Russian pilots who flew them on to Siberia. A total of eight thousand aircraft, many of them flown by America's women ferry pilots, and almost a thousand tons of military and medical equipment passed through Great Falls in twenty-one months in 1944 and 1945.

Almost abandoned, Great Falls became critical again as the airlift began to run out of trained pilots in the fall. By the end of September, the Air Force began calling up thousands more reservists and contracted with several American airlines to "borrow" their pilots and air crews for the coming winter, a convenient arrangement because the commercial lines flew fewer flights in winter weather in those days. And, if it had little else, Great Falls had the same magnetic fields as Berlin and, like Labrador, was at the same latitude as Berlin—with even harsher weather. Ice, cold and fog. Perfect.*

The Air Force put up beacons for radio and light signals—duplicates of the frequencies and range of the same equipment at Rhein-Main, Wiesbaden and Tempelhof—and laid out a virtual map in the sky of the three air corridors into Berlin. Great Falls had nineteen C-54s, each loaded with ten tons of sandbags, and an exact duplicate of the main landing strip at Tempelhof and the same air-control equipment that was being used in Germany. That included simulated apartment buildings to set up conditions for the diving approaches that were often necessary in Berlin because of tall buildings and short runways. The basic course for pilots with 1,200 hours of four-engine flying was three weeks long. One feature of the training was ten hours in a Link Simulator cockpit, where smoke was pumped in, blinding the pilots to prepare them for instrument landings with engines on fire. The idea was to train fifty replacement crews the first month and then increase that to thirty crews a week. The Great Falls crews were then piled into C-54s for the five-thousand-mile trip to Frankfurt. The long journey was commemorated by Jake Schuffert, the popular cartoonist of *Task Force Times*, who drew officers climbing down from their planes in Germany with square rear ends—the backsides of the men, not the planes. The caption was: "Yeah, all the way from Great Falls in these damn bucket seats."

John "Jake" Schuffert of New Carlisle, Pennsylvania, was the best-known enlisted man in the Air Force. He had flown fifty mis-

---

* Among the U.S. airlines that provided both planes and pilots were American Overseas Airlines, Transcontinental & Western Air, Pan American Airways, Seaboard & Western Airlines, Alaska Airlines, Transocean Airlines, the Flying Tiger Line, and Slick Airways.

sions in World War II and bailed out over Yugoslavia, surviving because Chetnik partisans found him before the Germans did. He came to Berlin as Tunner's radioman, but gained fame with his cartoons. The first Schuffert cartoon, in the first issue of *Task Force Times*, showed a C-54 blowing up like a balloon and a pilot on the ground looking up and shouting, "Who the hell loaded that dehydrated food on that leaky airplane." And there were a lot of very leaky old airplanes in the airlift.

On October 8, *Tägliche Rundschau*, the East Berlin newspaper, reported that in one week, September 27 to October 3, some 420,000 *Hamsterers* (hoarders) from western Berlin had ridden S-Bahn trains east and smuggled back 7,000 tons of food and other goods. *Neues Deutschland*, also in the east, reported that 30,000 tons of potatoes were smuggled into western Berlin in September. East German police reported, officially, that from July 1 to September 29, they had confiscated more than 500,000 pounds of potatoes, 100,000 pounds of grain, 65,000 pounds of vegetables—and that did not include how much the cops kept for themselves.

Whether those numbers were accurate or not, they certainly reflected the reality that S-Bahn trains were carrying hundreds of thousands of hungry westerners to the farms of the eastern sector and zone—and then returning with briefcases full of potatoes, sacks of other vegetables and even live chickens and pigs hidden under large skirts and coats. When East German police sporadically tried to stop the trading, particularly on weekends, S-Bahn passengers would throw the food off the train to friends or accomplices waiting along the rails. Those folks would then carry the stuff on unguarded streets across the sector border into western Berlin and bring the produce home—or sell it. Another trick was to pull the emergency cord to stop trains and jump off before they reached stations and checkpoints where police might be waiting to search the passengers—and the people hanging from the sides or lying on the roofs of the cars. More-affluent smugglers or true black marketeers preferred to travel by boat into the east along the lakes and canals of the city.

None of this was secret. Ferry and tour-boat companies posted advertisements around western Berlin promoting trips to the farm-lands of the east. Streetcar conductors called "Black Market" as the cars approached the Tiergarten near the Brandenburg Gate. Each neighborhood had a "Brotybaum"—a "bread tree"—with notes attached everywhere: "Want bread. Will trade German cigarettes."

So, in the west they joked about eastern police receiving extra ration cards (which they did) because they worked so hard carrying home confiscated supplies. On the other side, communist officials tried to motivate their police, border guards and ordinary citizens with messages like this:

> If the officers of the People's Police of the Soviet Zone of occupation or if policemen of the Soviet Sector stop the smugglers' vehicles or take away someone's backpack, don't let yourself be made to feel sorry by the cry, "Oh, the poor old woman! Why? The police are so mean." Think about the fact that the transport of these goods does not only occur with trucks or by train. Rather, there are whole columns of smugglers of 120 or more persons, who are sent out with backpacks from a central point. One brings 50 pairs of stockings, another 80 pair of stockings, and they are all turned in at a central point. There, everyone of these—what should we call them—commuter black marketeers gets his wage, and the whole story goes on . . . It is necessary to tackle things firmly and to be clear what effects things have.

Gail Halvorsen, back from his publicity tour in the United States, was showing a friend around Rhein-Main when he pointed to the engine of the C-54 he had flown that day. "See that guy up there?" he said, "He's a German! He used to work on a Luftwaffe airplane. And now he's working on my airplane. Here is this man, who supported the fighters against us, or the transports or whatever else, is now working on our plane. Wow, it's a crazy world, you know . . ."

"These guys are good," Major J. G. Grier, the American chief of maintenance at Tempelhof, told a reporter after only a couple of weeks working with the Germans and their little manuals translating part names from English to German. "I have sixty-two civilians," he said. "We put the former chief engineer of Deutsche Lufthansa over them. Very skilled bunch of men. I thought I knew a little about Pratt and Whitney engines, since I've been around them in the Air Force from the beginning. But a lot of these toolmakers know them inside and out. They got to know them in commercial aircraft, both American and European."

Good, indeed. Tunner originally planned to put nine Germans in the maintenance crews of each squadron. But he kept increasing the number, ending up with eighty-five per squadron, working three shifts. Eventually there were more German than American and British mechanics keeping the C-54s in the air.

Each of the Germans had a story—or a secret—and some Americans were interested enough to find out what it was.

Günter Metzger was only eighteen when he began as a laborer at Celle before making it as a mechanic specializing in cylinder inspection and repair. He was a fifteen-year-old apprentice at Heinkel, which built German bombers. He told this story of what it was like as the Russians were advancing toward Berlin:

SS officers came around and they gave us each two anti-tank grenades, pointed east and said the Russians will come from there. Maybe they did, but I wasn't there to know. I ran away as soon as the officers were out of sight . . . They gave others pistols, saying shoot in the air when you see the Russians coming. I wasn't there, but I doubt there were any pistol shots, either . . . The Americans taught many of us what to do. We were brought to a hangar and there was a C-54 there; it began with "This is a screwdriver." We were astonished at how much the Americans trusted us. Americans accepted us as equals . . . They would take us to the canteen . . .

A mechanic at Fassberg, Walter Riggers, who had just been released from a French prisoner-of-war camp, added: "I still don't understand it. How, so soon after the war, they could just say to us, come on, work for us. I don't understand where they got the idea that it might work. I just don't know . . . I was surprised by how much responsibility Americans put in our hands . . ."

"There was a common cause," said Fred Hulke, a young Wehrmacht veteran who was twenty when he was hired at Wiesbaden. "The help for Berlin impressed me, impressed us. We were young, enthusiastic and stupid. The hostility disappeared. We had suffered a lot. The air strikes, I experienced this at first hand. In the night, it was the Englishmen, during the day, it was the Americans that came. I saw it with my own eyes, I have seen bombs dropping, and I ran when they were dropped close to where we lived. And I also experienced bigger strikes during the night. All of that was terrible. But life went on and so things changed. And the airlift was the beginning of a better relationship, and finally, we developed a friendship with the Americans."

"The British didn't trust us," Riggers said. "The Americans would give us a work dock and go have a drink. The Americans went to the latrine, which was the only place heated in the hangars, and slept or played cards . . . The British never left us alone."

He was generally right about that. RAF Sergeant John Overington, from Hersham, Surrey, saw a different war than did young Americans and did not forget it when he supervised German mechanics. "They were very knowledgeable and could speak good English," said Overington. Then he added: "None of them were ever Nazis, to hear them tell it, and although I could not forgive them for the hurt they had caused the world, individually they could be nice people. But collectively, Nazis or not, they had been a bunch of bastards!"

At Gatow one thing brought the old enemies together. With Dakotas taking off at intervals of two hundred yards, raising dust everywhere, the British and Germans would indulge their love of football (soccer) by playing against each other—and, in a way, continuing the war. "They were the roughest games you ever saw," said a British air controller, Warrant Officer David Williams. "We just kicked the hell out of each other."

After a while, Riggers was one of the Germans who was named a security officer at Fassberg, with a little extra pay. There was one at every workstation, responsible for six men working there watching for sabotage or stealing. He took the job in a Germanic way—very, very seriously, sometimes hiding in the rafters of the hangar or inside the airplane. If there were signs of any kind of trouble, the Germans almost always handled it themselves. Some of the mechanics grabbed blankets; there were four on each plane for freezing pilots and aircrews. If one was missing, Riggers would call the crew together and say he would have to tell the Americans—and the blanket or whatever else was missing would reappear.

Whatever they thought or knew about each other, the Germans would not tell the Americans. "I could have gotten killed that way," Riggers said. "The Americans did not ask about such things if a man was doing his job."

Ulrich Stampa was one of the men doing his job—quite well. In coveralls, he looked like any other German working on C-54 engines. He had been an important young man when the Nazis were in power, working with Kurt Waldemar Tank, the chief designer of Focke-Wulf fighters for the Luftwaffe. He was one of the first mechanics hired at Fassberg, where he worked on hydraulic systems. He was mechanically gifted, the son of a prominent family in Bromberg, Pomerania. "We had been there for hundreds of years, we lost everything, the land, the houses, to the communists," he said. He had ended up in two French prisoner-of-war camps, escaping from both, first in Brittany and then in Normandy. What he hated most was that the guards were Moroccans, particularly two of them who played violins together. "Creatures like them," he said, "are not worthy of such instruments." He hated Americans, too, finding it difficult to be near them. "My American supervisor was practically illiterate, a check-list was about all he could handle . . . They cheated us. I gave one of them a book, Alfred Rosenberg's *Myth of the 20th Century*. He never paid for it. And I'm sure he couldn't read it."

Kurt Dettmer, a former Luftwaffe corporal, was also in the first group of German mechanics. He was assigned to Celle. Asked what he thought of Americans, he said, "We did whatever they told us to do. They won the war, they could do anything they wanted to do . . . We were loyal to each other. One guy was late every morning, but we never did anything about it because he had won the Iron Cross. We respected that, too."

"The Americans were amazingly generous," said Dettmer. "We were given cocoa at night, even invited to hangar parties, where there was Coke and beer. They put milk powder on the floor and danced the Jitterbug. They threw us out at 9 P.M. But we were all drunk by then. Many of us, the young ones like me, had never tasted alcohol. I couldn't handle it and just collapsed."

Fog, fatigue and frost combined to make the airlift more dangerous when early winter came to northern Europe. On October 2, in the fog, a fire truck at Rhein-Main collided with a taxiing C-54, killing the truck driver, Private First Class Johnnie Orms. That cold night, one of the last C-47s flying the lift barely made it to Tempelhof. Ice on the plane's wings and a partly frozen carburetor were slowing the plane down, with others closing in from behind. Finally, the pilot, Lieutenant Howard S. Myers of Riverside, California, had his copilot go into the back of the plane and throw out the cargo one bag at a time. Somewhere in East Germany there was a trail of two tons of macaroni before Myers got the Gooney Bird down safely. The British military governor, General Sir Brian Robertson, was the victim in a similar incident. South African Air Force Lieutenant Tom Condon missed a landing in a thunderstorm and, to gain altitude for another approach or a return flight west, ordered his crew to begin throwing out hundred-pound sacks of coal. One bag crashed through the roof of Robertson's residence. Another South African, Lieutenant Duncan Ralston, reported: "This is believed to be the only direct delivery of coal to a private home during the airlift."

A pilot named John Hopkins had a rougher time. His plane had lost an engine and was losing altitude when he decided to jettison his load: fifty-five-gallon drums of creosote for airstrip construction. The drums were too heavy for one man to move, but Hopkins's copilot, on some kind of adrenaline (or fear) high, did it, pushing them out one by one. The East Germans complained this time, demanding compensation for orchards ruined when the drums burst open like bombs.

And at the British base at Celle, an American flight engineer, Master Sergeant Russell W. Koolhof, after thirty-two hours of flight duty, was put to bed by a sentry who found him standing at a gate, sound asleep. It happened all the time.

The first C-54 crashed on October 18, just three miles from Rhein-Main. Three men—First Lieutenant Eugene Erickson of Collinsville, Illinois; Captain James Vaughn of Nashville, Tennessee, who had survived a year in a German prisoner-of-war camp; and Sergeant Richard Winter, a flight engineer from Seattle—were killed when the Skymaster ran into the Taunus Mountains.

In western Berlin, the city administration finally considered an order by Colonel Howley to cut down trees in the woods and parks of the western sectors to provide 350,000 cubic meters of wood to heat homes. In the end, though, Berlin officials only approved a third of that. They wanted to preserve most of the trees left after the war. On October 10, Elisabeth Poensgen wrote to her relatives in western Germany, saying:

> I don't think private packages will be transported anymore in the winter, which will be very cold, because all planes will be needed to supply the city . . . Paulus, the good man, a friend, has sent me 200 Marks. I bought coal and firewood for that, so I have a warm house at least. Because I lack money and because of the terrible darkness in the streets, I live in complete isolation. I don't see any people. I do one-quarter of my shopping, and run back to my house. I weigh 106 pounds. I just wish I didn't have this old head. I don't have any money for cosmetics; this would have been the only aid.

On October 13, General Clay received a private communication from his friend Bill Draper, talking about the American presidential election, an election that polls, politicians and pundits had already concluded President Truman would lose to New York's Governor Thomas E. Dewey.

"It may well be," Draper wrote, "that the new Administration will have its own ideas as to commanders as well as Cabinet members." He wondered whether Clay should not submit his resignation before the election on November 2 rather than be embarrassed and dismissed publicly by Dewey or by John Foster Dulles, who was expected to be Secretary of State in a Republican administration, and was known to believe the airlift was failing and could never succeed.

Clay, who was anxious to resign, told Draper he could not do it in the middle of the crisis he was living through.

Then, Dulles himself landed in Berlin on a pre-election tour of Europe, a sort of victory lap before the victory. Clay and Dulles despised each other, but protocol was protocol, and Clay invited Dulles to his home for Sunday lunch on October 17. The general also invited Robert Murphy, the State Department's man in Berlin, and Colonel Howley, mainly because he preferred not spending much time alone with Dulles. It happened that Howley had just written in his diary: "It is generally assumed that the first act of Dewey, if Dewey wins the election and if Dulles becomes Secretary of State, would be the removal of General Clay from his present assignment."

It was an uncomfortable affair that ended only when Ernst Reuter arrived to meet Dulles. "This is your problem," Clay whispered to the German. Dulles, whose mind certainly seemed to be made up, asked Reuter, "Will the Germans stand fast during the winter? Or will they give up, accept Russian aid and get us out of Berlin rather than take any more suffering?"

"The people of Berlin are used to suffering. We are willing to suffer a great deal more to escape Russian domination."

The rest of their conversation is lost to history. But when Dulles met the press outside Clay's house he seemed a changed man, saying that all the world marveled at the airlift and said, "The morale in western Berlin and western Germany has risen to a new high."

A reporter asked Clay about his plans. "I am not requesting retirement," he said. "As long as Berlin is under blockade, I wouldn't think of voluntarily asking to leave. I'd be a damn poor soldier if I requested to leave."

That night, Clay's usual teleconference with Draper ended with the Undersecretary saying: "I suppose you realize you have become a national figure and even more, a national symbol. Keep up the good work . . . Best regards and good luck."

Clay answered: "Pride goeth before a fall and publicity leads them both."

October 15 was General Curtis LeMay's last day as commander of the Air Force in Europe. He had been promoted to lead the new

Strategic Air Command in Washington, directing the operations of all of the nation's new jet bombers and nuclear weapons. His successor was Lieutenant General John K. Cannon, who had made his name as a commander of fighter squadrons. He arrived in Germany an angry man.

LeMay and Tunner's relationship had improved over time; they had come to admire each other's talents. Their last important piece of work was to negotiate an agreement with their British counterparts to create the Combined Airlift Task Force. The paperwork naming Tunner as the commander of the task force and British Air Commodore W. F. Merer the deputy commander was signed on October 14. It was not the easiest match, even though the British and Americans had often worked under joint commands during the war. The Americans chafed under strict British rules—and they hated the overcooked food and bare housing arrangements of their Atlantic cousins. For their part, the British were astounded by the informality of the Americans. The latest indignity was the way American pilots kidded around on the radio. Lieutenant Leonard Sweet, the man who found French wine under his seat, was listening in when a ground controller at Tempelhof told a pilot he was a minute ahead of schedule and to make a 360-degree turn before landing. "A three-sixty will take me two minutes," the pilot said. There was a slight pause and the controller answered: "OK, do a one-eighty and back in."

In fact, the American chatter, all very unprofessional, was a way to fight the tiring boredom of flying the same routes day after day and night after night. One long night, on a flight from Rhein-Main to Tempelhof, in the middle of flying American jokes and laughter, James Spatafora heard a British voice identifying the speaker as a Wing Commander and saying: "You Yanks are to maintain radio silence." And there was silence for a few long seconds until an American voice was heard: "I wonder if that son-of-a-bitch is really a Wing Commander?"

Another American, Captain Anthony Cecchini, was flying in a

group of newspaper reporters, one of them a woman he gave his microphone to during a Tempelhof landing. "This is Baker Easy . . ." she said. There was silence from below, until Cecchini heard laughing and a voice asked him what was going on. "It's just a little stewardess service we've got," said Cecchini. "From Rhein-Main we go first class."

Then there was an American pilot, ready for takeoff, who used a heavy Brooklyn accent to tell a British ground controller: "Just give me the woid and I'll make like a boid."

The British had their moments, though. Master Pilot Walter Dougan, called "Dickie," was leading a block of Dakotas from Gatow west, carrying passengers, one of whom was under medical supervision and listed on the manifest as an "imbecile." As the planes approached the British base at Lübeck, a medical officer radioed from the ground, "KN566, what is the name of your imbecile." Before Dougan could answer, a pilot flying behind KN566 answered: "Master Pilot Dougan."

More important—at least to Tunner, a forty-two-year-old hotshot, and Cannon, the epitome of a fifty-six-year-old grizzled veteran—was that the new USAFE commander, unlike LeMay, would not have direct command of the airlift.

Cannon and Tunner had their first formal meeting on October 17. Cannon's greeting was "What the hell is this, Tunner? What are you trying to do to me?"

Tunner presented it as an effort to solve a problem before Cannon would be bothered by the details. To those close to him, and there weren't many of those, he said, "I wanted to be left alone—I know best how the job should be done."

They never did get along. Cannon could not do anything about joint operations, but he could, and did, prevent Tunner from communicating with his own command home, MATS. One of Tunner's new gripes after the changeover from LeMay to Cannon: "Instead of getting special personnel on the job in Germany four days after I requisitioned them, I was lucky to get the requisition through USAFE headquarters itself in four days."

Clay returned to the United States for the second time during the airlift on October 20, three days after his lunch with Dulles. The official reason was to speak at the fourth-annual Alfred E. Smith Memorial Dinner at the Waldorf-Astoria Hotel in New York. He accepted the invitation in July from the dinner's sponsor, Francis Cardinal Spellman, the Roman Catholic Bishop of New York. It was going to be awkward because, less than two weeks before the election, he would be sharing the dais with Governor Dewey.

A promise was a promise to Clay. But he had other reasons, too. He wanted to see Truman again because the Pentagon was still quietly beating the drums to get out of Berlin before it was too late— before General Winter crippled or shut down the airlift. "It is the considered opinion of the Joint Chiefs of Staff," read an October 13 memo to the National Security Council, "that our present military power cannot effectively support the supply of Berlin by airlift on an indefinite basis without such a diversion of military effort as had affected and will continue progressively to affect seriously and adversely the ability of the National Military Establishment to meet its primary national security obligations." The chairman, Omar Bradley, a five-star general, went further, saying that the time had come to decide whether to prepare for all-out war in Germany or begin planning "withdrawal from Berlin."

The Central Intelligence Agency told the President essentially the same thing: "The U.S. is now committed, in Berlin, to maintaining a strategic outpost on political grounds, when, in the final analysis, that outpost can be maintained only by force or Soviet tolerance . . . A choice will have to be made between a planned withdrawal or the eventual maintenance of the Berlin position by force."

Despite the psychological and propaganda triumphs of the airlift, official Washington and the "Military Establishment" essentially agreed with Soviet leaders: the Allies could not win and had forced themselves into a strategic corner that was getting smaller day by day. Two Americans seemed to be standing in the way of common sense, of some kind of strategic face-saving retreat: a President who was expected to be a lame duck within days and a general who had gone native, believing the Berliners could hold out through the winter. One more time, Clay went into the Oval Office—with Forrestal; Clay's State Department advisor, Robert Murphy; Secretary of the Army Kenneth Royall; and Undersecretary of the Army William Draper—and one more time Truman sided with Clay. So did the two thousand political and civil leaders who had paid a hundred dollars each to attend the Al Smith Dinner at the Waldorf-Astoria; they stood and cheered for a good long time, Governor Dewey among them, when Clay said:

> The Soviet planners failed to recognize our strength in the air. They did not understand the determination of the Western Allies to fulfill their obligation to the peoples under their charge. They did not reckon with the will of several million Germans in Berlin to resist being placed under a police state . . . The Airlift can—it must—be continued until there is stability in Europe that assures peace. If the Western Allies could be forced from Berlin, then the impression would be created that they could be forced out elsewhere.

The President took that as his cue and a week later spoke out at length for the first time in the campaign about Berlin: "In Germany, we have taken the frank and firm position that communism must not spread its tentacles into the western zone. We shall not retreat from that position. We shall feed the people of Berlin . . ."

And then he said: "You can fight communism on November 2nd with a Democratic vote."

• • •

To get more planes this time—Clay, using Tunner's figures and charts, asked for 116 C-54s—the Air Force would be stripped and the Pentagon had to turn to the Navy for help. Truman approved that request on October 22. Some U.S. Navy tankers had been used to carry gasoline to Bremerhaven in West Germany, but none had flown to Berlin. Five days later, Chief of Naval Operations Admiral Louis Denfield ordered two squadrons of Navy C-54s, twenty-four planes in Hawaii, Guam and points farther east, to head for Germany.

"It broke my heart," said one of the Navy pilots, Lieutenant Earl Moore. "I had an apartment in Shanghai with servants. Frankfurt was 'pretty bleak' compared with that. I met my wife in Guam, on her way to Shanghai. She had packed in San Francisco and I had to tell her we were going to Germany . . . I worked eight hours on and eight off. You'd bump into people in the fog and never know who it was . . . I hit a Soviet barrage balloon in the corridor, we complained, they took them down. I thought they were total chickens. Bluffers." Within three weeks, the Navy squadrons, each equipped with three aircrews and three maintenance groups, were flying at an extraordinary rate of better than thirteen hours a day. The overall goal, by the end of the year, was to have 225 Skymasters on German flight lines or on the way to or back from Berlin—with 75 more from the Air Force and the Navy out of service for a time at maintenance stations in Germany, England and across the world.

Lieutenant Moore was one of eleven pilots who reported barrage balloons in the air corridors during the airlift. Some of the Soviet tactics were rougher than others. Lieutenant Bill L. Cooley, of Miami, chief of maintenance crews at Tegel, watched from the ground as two of the Soviet's new MiG-15 jets tried to force a Skymaster down in East Germany. "They caught him on the fly and tried to make him land, but the pilot refused," Cooley recalls. "The C-54 flew over Tempelhof so everyone could see it. The MiGs were just feet from the aircraft, but he landed it anyway. The MiGs made a very low pass—maybe 10 feet above the transport as it rolled down the runway." But the worst that happened to Lieutenant Charles Minihan of Ingram, Texas, was polka music. "The Russians played the music as loud as they could," he said. "Anything to make it hard to navigate."

In the end, though, the most surprising thing about Soviet harassment of the airlift was how little of it there was. Many pilots who flew more than one hundred flights in and out of Berlin never saw a Soviet plane in the air and never experienced any of the usual harassment techniques: buzzing, random anti-aircraft bursts and other ground fire, and searchlight beams designed to blind pilots. The searchlights were the major complaints and many pilots dealt with them by simply taping newspapers inside their windshields; they were flying by instruments or in clouds or fog so they were not looking out the windows anyway. And the Soviets rarely used what could have been their most effective counter-airlift tactic, that is, jamming Western radio signals essential to instrument flying. It was obvious that the Soviets intended to take no action that might lead to all-out war—and believed that attacking American planes might have led to war.

In fact, besides the terrible weather, the major problem for aircrews was still fatigue. RAF medical officers questioned 391 British flight crews at the end of September—after almost thirty thousand sorties—and 354 complained of fatigue. More than half of those men said their major problem was "lack of sleep" or "broken sleep." Flight Lieutenant Brian Standbridge—later Sir Brian Standbridge—told a common story: "There were no navigation aids in the Soviet Zone, so for 120 minutes you could be flying without sight or sound—four days on, a day off, then four days on again. On a 1 A.M. flight, my co-pilot slipped and broke his leg coming aboard, so I ended up alone in the cockpit, flying at 1,500 feet. The next thing I knew, the navigator is slapping me awake. I looked at the altimeter. We were at 600 feet and dropping."

• • •

Willy Brandt's first son was born in Berlin on October 4. The doctors worked in a hospital without electricity. Said his father: "Peter came into the world by candlelight—a real child of the Blockade."

The new father realized that the coming of winter and the politics of the U.S. presidential election made the end of October a hinge point in Allied determination and policy. Reporting secretly to party leaders in Hannover, Wiesbaden and Bonn in a series of eight dispatches during the month, Brandt said:

> In conversations with British and American officers, one gets the impression that a resuming of talks is not out of question. This is why the issue is not (yet) submitted to the United Nations . . . The main tendency indicates that Berlin shall by no means be given up and that concessions must not be made as a result of the pressure created by the blockade. But on the other side, further tightening of the circumstances shall be avoided. This has three reasons: first, the insecurity stemming from the American elections, second, the wish of military consolidation through an extended Western union and third, the hope for a modernization of Russian policy in Europe and an acknowledgement of the changed power relations, respectively.
>
> The American side reassures us over and over again that the new administration will not bring any changes to the foreign policies. The position towards the Soviet Union could only be consolidated. In Republican circles, there is a tendency not to subordinate the German factor to the French factor any more. On the other hand, Americans have told me that surprising changes were not out of the question. In the next 6 to 8 weeks, we should remember that the situation on the American side is by no means clear.

More than one sees in official announcements and in the press, the Allies are seriously considering the possibility of negotiating about the German problem and of withdrawing. I believe that for propagandist reasons, it is necessary to formulate and point out the conditions that are necessary for a partial and eventually complete withdrawal.

By the early fall of 1948, Tempelhof and Gatow airports had reached the limits of expansion. Three runways covered with PSP, Pierced Steel Planking—also called Marston mats—had been constructed at Tempelhof and two more built at Gatow.* The good news was that work on the new airfield, Tegel in the French Sector, was ahead of schedule because the American engineers supervising the project had found a new source of foundation material: the stone ballast under railroad tracks, unused since the beginning of the blockade. Forty thousand cubic feet of rubble were trucked to the site and used as the foundation of the strips. Asphalt streets around the city were ripped up and melted to cover the crushed rubble and stone. The project also had a surprising source of other materials: construction workers in the eastern sector were secretly rolling barrels of tar and asphalt into the western sector late at night.

Tegel was dedicated on October 29, 1948, more than two months ahead of schedule, and the first load of coal was landed there six days later, exactly three months after the first "rubble women" walked onto the field. The opening ceremonies of Tegel almost turned into a riot. A changing-of-the-guard ceremony was planned by the French around the leaving of the American 503rd Engineer Company.

---

* The PSP, or Marston mats, were ten feet long by fifteen inches wide and weighed sixty-six pounds each. They were first tested, and named, near the town of Marston, North Carolina. A total of sixty thousand plates or mats were interconnected to make a five-thousand-foot landing strip.

Somehow, as the flags were lowered, an American flag dropped to the ground and was accidentally stepped on by a French officer. The Americans demanded the flag—to be burned according to protocol—but the French refused to hand it over. The men of the 503rd then tried to bring down the French flag. Words and fists began to fly and a company of U.S. military police was called in to escort the Americans (and their flag) off the base.

On September 30, eleven more C-54s from Asia arrived at Wiesbaden. C-47 number 2403, piloted by Lieutenant Luther Lyles of Savoy, Texas, made the round-trip from Fassberg to Tempelhof, one of the last American C-47 flights of the airlift. The plane had flown every day with a total flying time for the last month alone of 327 hours and 30 minutes, more than 10 hours a day. *Task Force Times*, as it always did, listed the names of 2403's ground crew: "T/Sgt. Joseph Simpson of Dearborn, Mich., S/Sgt. Thomas E. Rafferty of Haverhill, Mass., and Sgt. John P. Strange of Fort Worth, Tex."

"The gooney birds are no longer with us," reported *Task Force Times* that day. But that was not quite true. The British continued to use their old Dakotas in blocks between their Yorks and Lancasters. And the Americans were keeping a few in service, too. The day's *Times*, under the headline AIR FORCE TO RECALL SPECIAL MEN TO ACTIVE DUTY, listed the job descriptions of reservists being called back to duty, demonstrating Tunner's points about glamour or the lack of it:

Air Reserve and Air National Guard officers with military or civilian experience in the following fields, Communications—electronics and radar; Supply—procurement, production and renegotiation; Management—Financing, Accounting, Budgeting and Statistics; Inspection—technical and administrative; Air Installation—civil engineering, intelligence (especially photo-interpreters), radar navigation, aeronautical engineering; chemistry; public information; weather; law; photography and personnel.

There was, however, one touch of glamour—at Fassberg, the grittiest of the western fields. The new American commander of the old RAF base was Colonel Theron "Jack" Coulter. His wife, who often greeted pilots as they landed or ate with mechanics in the mess hall, was a movie star, Constance Bennett.

CHAPTER 7

"It Looks Like Curtains"

November 28, 1948

"CHECK THAT COMPASS, I THINK WE'RE A LITTLE WEST OF COURSE!!"

NOVEMBER BEGAN WELL FOR BOTH THE PRESIDENT WHO backed the airlift and the General running it.

On November 2, Harry S. Truman pulled off one of the great upsets in American political history, winning 24,179,347 votes and carrying twenty-eight states to defeat Republican Governor Thomas E. Dewey, who won 21,991,292 votes and sixteen states. Polling indicated that one of the incumbent's strengths was public support for his stand on Berlin. Two other candidates, both former Democrats, split, about evenly, 2.3 million votes. Former Vice President Henry A. Wallace ran as the Progressive Party's candidate, calling for the Allies to quit Berlin rather than provoking war with the Soviet Union. Governor Strom Thurmond of South Carolina headed the "Dixiecrat" ticket protesting civil rights legislation, including Truman's integration of the military. He carried four states in the Deep South: Alabama, Louisiana, Mississippi and South Carolina.

In Berlin itself, flights were coming and going as if guided by "Willie-the-Whip" Tunner's walls of graphs. In the last week of October "going" became important: rather than flying back empty to the western zones, American and British planes had managed to carry out of Berlin more than 6.4 million Deutschmarks' worth of light machinery and other local manufactures stamped "Made in Blockaded Berlin"—lamps to Switzerland, automobile brakes to Norway and phonograph records to the United States were on those returning planes. Ironically, or tactically, about 20 percent of that material was actually keeping factories open in East Germany and East Berlin—Cold War politics were always more tangled and interdependent than all-out direct confrontation.

On the first day of the month, General Clay announced that the Allies were increasing the daily calorie allotment by an average of almost 20 percent, a very bold move as General Winter approached, so that the average western Berlin resident would be given ration cards for about 2,000 calories a day, with growing children getting an extra 300 calories. On November 2, the first C-54 was sent to Burtonwood in England for a two-hundred-hour check and overhaul, and the first eleven crews arrived from Great Falls. By now, the airlift was carrying eight hundred bags of mail out of Berlin each day, and in the first week of the month, more than 129,000 pairs of shoes were being flown into Berlin, all donated by residents of western Germany. High-intensity krypton lights were ready to work at Tempelhof and, at the same time, full-time airlift service began at Tegel, even though some flights came dangerously close to two radio towers—393 and 262 feet high—near the end of the approach runway. In the complicated world of occupied Berlin, the towers were in the French Sector, but controlled by the Soviets, who had taken over the facilities of what had been Berliner Radiofunk, or Radio Berlin, the city's principal radio station under the Nazis before the Allies arrived in 1945. The French asked for permission to remove or relocate the towers, but Soviet officials refused to even acknowledge the request.

The first three of twenty-four U.S. Navy RD5s arrived at Rhein-Main and were greeted by General Tunner, standing in a foot of water from the first of the area's winter rainstorms. "We wanted the Navy to feel at home," said Tunner in a rare joke as the crisply uniformed Navy officers stepped out of their planes. Jake Schuffert greeted them with a cartoon called "Brakes On!" showing sailors tossing an anchor out the back doors of their planes. Each Navy pilot was ceremoniously handed a putty knife, which he soon learned was to be used to reach out the cockpit's side window and scrape ice off the windshield before landing in Berlin. That same day the Free University of Berlin opened in the American Sector, organized by students and teachers revolting against the Soviet and Marxist curricula of prewar Germany's greatest center of learning, the University of Humboldt on Unter den Linden in the Soviet Sector. The classrooms of the Free University, as makeshift as the early days of the airlift, were in buildings all over the western sectors; the books and laboratory equipment were stolen from Humboldt. "I was thief, a good one, stealing books for the Free University," said Frau Dr. Hanna Laurin, then one of 2,200 students who arrived and were accepted at the new school. "I am still proud of that. It wasn't lack of food and fuel that drove us, it was lack of freedom. You were never without fear."

And then there was American football, different from the kind the

British and Germans were playing so roughly. The first champion-
ship game of American teams representing several bases was called
the "Vittles Bowl." The game between the Rhein-Main Rockets and
the Heidelberg Constabulary Ramblers, both teams with more than a
few players whose college careers had been interrupted by the airlift,
drew a crowd of fifty thousand people. American spectators paid fifty
cents; Germans, one Deutschmark.

On November 4, American planes alone carried 3,976 tons, ac-
cording to the "Howgozit?" board published in each issue of *Task
Force Times*. But General Winter was already on the horizon. The
Task Force Times weather report on Sunday, November 5, began:
"Low pressure area passing over Southern England and into the
North Sea . . ." Fog was coming. The cold, wet air was coming across
the English Channel into the valleys of Germany, where it would be
trapped, as fog, by higher-pressure warm air coming north from the
Mediterranean Sea—"stagnant low" was the meteorological term—
creating a three-thousand-foot-deep fog bank moving slowly east for
weeks on end.

Airmen working on the field and crewmen leaving their planes
would sometimes crawl—for fear of walking into propellers—to the
edge of the steel runway planking and then, with one foot on the perforated metal and the other in the mud, try to get out of the landing
area and out of the way of jeeps and trucks moving around blindly.
Corky Colgrove, the teenage mechanic at Rhein-Main, was taxiing a
C-54 from one side of the base to the other in fog and snow to get to
a repair hangar—many repairs were being done in the open—when
he was ordered by radio not to cross the main runway. A long block of
Skymasters began taking off one after another. "I just sat there in the
roar for more than an hour," he said. "One C-54 would firewall the
throttle and when he got halfway down the runway, the next one
would open his throttles, so you had three planes on the runway at
one time. I was less than 100 feet from their wingtips, but I don't
think any of them could see me."

Bill Lafferty was one of the pilots who landed by mistake on the takeoff runway, the only one he could see through a small gap in the fog at an altitude of about one hundred feet. "This is Big Easy," he began when a ground controller broke in to say, "Are you the airplane on the takeoff strip?" He was, and he was lucky that no other plane was taking off. Another voice came on saying, "Some people will do anything to show off." Another said, "Forget it. On a night like this, any way you can get down is good."

Whatever Tunner thought, air transport was more than graphs. Lafferty was one of many pilots, crewmen and mechanics who had to make it up as they went along. There was very little maintenance capability at Tempelhof and overworked engines often would not start easily, especially in wet, cold weather. One way to get going, which tended to slow down the parade, was for a pilot to start the takeoff roll with only two or three engines firing until the airstream spun the propellers of the dead engine or engines and they coughed into life—the same trick as rolling a car downhill, then popping the clutch to kick-start it—then aborting the takeoff and taxiing back to start again with four engines running. That was replaced by wrapping an elastic rope (bungee cords from parachutes) around the hub of the propeller, attaching one end to a jeep and then pulling away the vehicle and releasing the cord to start the prop spinning, the way old-fashioned auto cranks did. Another mechanic figured out a way to vent the explosive coal and flour dust in each plane by throwing a hose out an open porthole, creating a suction pump—of course, the aircrews were freezing the whole time, wearing layers of leather jackets, sitting on waterlogged cockpit seats. Enlisted men supervising loaders figured out a system of laying canvas under coal bags—and then sweeping the canvas clean and collecting, in the end, five hundred tons of coal dust. If worn-out sparkplugs were the problem, mechanics would replace only the plugs in the lowest four cylinders, the easiest ones to get at without taking off the engine cowl, and that would usually do the trick. When British operations were slowed at Gatow by flocks of migrating birds, the base commander, RAF Group Captain Brian Yard, sent a plane to Malta, 1,200 miles away, to bring back several falcons—and suddenly other birds were dead or detouring.

The most dangerous tricks, as November began, involved deicing planes before takeoff. The safest way was to use J-33 jet fighter engines with their exhaust turned toward the wings of the C-54s. The alternative, used at Wiesbaden, was spraying alcohol on planes. "We just sit there and pray there are no backfires on take-off," said Lafferty. "Because if there were, there was going to be a fire." Another pilot, Lieutenant Earl Hammack, could not move his control yoke coming into Tempelhof until using both his feet and all his might he pushed it forward enough to land. Mechanics found coal dust, rags and two crescent wrenches jammed around the plane's control cables.

A famous RAF pilot, Donald Bennett, who set the world's seaplane distance record in 1938, flying from England to South Africa, and then led the Pathfinder unit that dropped flares over targets during night bombing runs, also found his controls jammed as he tried to lift off from Wunstorf. This time the problem was his own carelessness. In walking around his Avro Tudor he forgot to take out the bolt used to keep the tail elevator from flapping in wind on the ground, and the flap would not move as he reached the end of the runway. He managed to muscle the plane into the air, barely—as German construction crews working on the runway ran for their lives—using the little trim tabs on the elevator. Then he made three wide turns around the airport at an altitude of three hundred feet until he was able to use the trim tabs and changing engine speeds to line the plane up above the runway and force it down. To get the plane down again, he ordered the other three men aboard to run back and forth between the cockpit and the tail to make the plane nose-heavy and then tail-heavy as he landed.

One of the first pilots to "graduate" from Great Falls, Lieutenant

William Martin, who used a spotlight held to the cockpit windshield to melt some of the ice blinding him, said, "A general principle evolved. As long as you had one instrument that indicated something about what you needed to know, go ahead and take the plane, and if we ever get any parts for this we'll fix it." Lieutenant George H. Nelson, signing in the Fassberg logbook after a coal flight, read the entry above his: "No 4 (right outboard) engine fire warning light burns in flight. Corrected—bulb removed."

"Risks were taken by everyone to make the airlift work," said Lieutenant Harold Hendler, the pilot who had flown crates of new currency. "We just didn't talk about it." He also was ordered not to talk about a mystery cargo he flew into Tegel and turned over to French officers early in November.

Prayer was practically on the preflight checklist of airlift pilots. The RAF equivalent of the cartoonist Jake Schuffert was a York pilot, Flight Lieutenant "Frosty" Winterbottom, who did his work on the walls of Malcolm Clubs, the British officers' canteens. One of his cartoons showed his plane headed for Gatow. The caption was: "Hello, York 274. Understand you are lost in the clouds on three engines, icing up, hydraulics jammed and short of fuel. Visibility here is 800 yards. Cloud base, 200 feet. Repeat after me: 'Our Father which art in heaven . . .' "

Flying home to Louisiana as a passenger on a C-54 that November because his mother was seriously ill, Navy mechanic Hewitt LeBlanc got frustrated because the plane was sitting on a taxiway in Lyneham, England, while a mechanic tried to get the starter to work on one engine. LeBlanc got off and said, "Do you know what you're doing?"

"No. I'm a metalsmith," was the answer.

"Give me those pliers and a screwdriver," LeBlanc said. He cut the safety wire protecting the starter, took off the back plate and stuck in the screwdriver to manually push the starter plunger, a process he repeated at each stop as the C-54 crossed the Atlantic, stopping at the Azores and Newfoundland before getting to Westover in Massachusetts.

One of Tunner's first moves when he took over the airlift was to commandeer meteorologists and other weather support personnel from Air Force bases around the world and from commercial airlines, increasing the number working on the lift from 308 to 570. The weather in northern Europe is among the fastest-changing anywhere on the planet, particularly in the winter, which begins in late October and can continue into May. In addition to the fogs of winter, Germany averages 13 to 15 inches of rain every month of the year and 6 to 9 inches of snow every month of the winter. The airlift utilized more than two hundred ground weather observation posts from North Africa and the Middle East to Finland, in addition to seven permanent weather ships stationed in the English Channel and the North Sea. A dozen American B-29s and B-17s and as many British planes flew twenty-four-hour routes collecting weather data and broadcasting their numbers to Rhein-Main every fifteen minutes. The British also had developed a device called a ceilometer, which triangulated ultraviolet rays to calculate how low clouds were over the three Berlin airports. Balloons were used to calculate wind and visibility at altitudes up to ten thousand feet along the routes from western bases to the city airports. Tunner himself used a fifteen-year database of weather conditions over Berlin. He also, without asking anyone for permission, hired veteran German weathermen, some with doctorates in meteorology, who had an amazing ability to forecast where clouds would form over Tempelhof about fifteen minutes before they did. *Times Task Force* reported a conversation about that under the headline FOGGY NOTION:

"The ceiling is unlimited and the visibility is over ten miles, but the field may be socked-in in ten minutes," a controller said.

"What do you base that on?" asked the pilot.

"Experience," said a weary voice.

Finally, a corporal, Louis Wagner, a New Jersey boy, had the job of driving a jeep along Tempelhof's runway as fast as he could—fifty-five miles per hour—and then hitting the brakes as hard as he could, counting runway lights as he slowed. The number of lights he saw after hitting the brakes determined whether planes could land on the wet, icy metal—or whether sand would be spread and Berlin's five pieces of snow removal equipment would be called onto the field. At Gatow, Captain W. R. Bateman did the job himself, racing along the strip and hitting the brakes hard to see if his jeep would skid into a spin. If it did, sanding trucks would begin at either end of the runway and two more would work from the middle out, sanding a mile in less than fifteen minutes.

In addition to German weather, the airlift was slowed, quite badly on occasion, by the storms between the generals, Tunner and Cannon. The new USAFE commander was sometimes heard to refer to the airlift as "delivering groceries." He was sure that Tunner had timed the announcement of the American-British Joint Task Force to divert attention from the old fighter pilot taking over from the great LeMay, who had come out of service in both Europe and the Pacific with a reputation as the boy wonder of bombing. The new chief also resented sharing command with British officers. The younger general was both more arrogant and more direct: "I don't need advice from an aging combat general."

The two generals could not even agree on humor. Cannon wanted to fire Jake Schuffert, the *Task Force Times* cartoonist, because he thought he was lowering morale by making fun of airlifters. Tunner saved Schuffert, but then he wanted an anonymous lieutenant found and fired because he was the author of a nineteen-page mock "Fassberg Diary—Letter from an Unknown Moron." It was cast as a newspaper story written about the airlift in the year 2200, when pilots of "The Airwick Task Force" and "Operation Spittles," commanded by "General Tumbler," worked twenty-nine hours a day, nine days a week supplying the city of "Bungstarter" in "Germ-on-Knee." It went on like that:

> How does one get in a mess like this? You were out swimming . . . or perhaps sunning your cadaver on the beach at Waikiki . . . You were driving through a Connecticut summer . . . You were happy. Life was real. And then it came. The finger pointed . . .
>
> The finger pointed and you were snatched from your dreams and thrown into this. Your wife, if you still had a wife, was Lord knows where, your car was a lost cause . . .
>
> To date, our composite morale has been hovering in the vicinity of Kelvin Zero. On this memorable day, however, we have read in *Stars and Gripes* that Uncle Tumbler says our morale is very high. We did not know this . . . and here all the time we thought we were miserable.

Uncle Tunner was not amused. Cannon loved it and wanted to find the writer and hire him for his public relations staff.

Tunner may not have needed advice, but he needed cooperation—and Cannon's cooperation was grudging at best. He forced Tunner to make all equipment and personnel requests through USAFE, slowing down the process to the point that two planes a day were getting two-hundred-mile checks at Burtonwood, rather than the seven a day originally planned. Nothing if not resourceful, Tunner then switched two-hundred-mile checks to squadron level—the system used by the Navy—overworking his men even more but keeping more planes in the air.

On November 13, Lieutenant Colonel Nick Chevasse, commander of the 2105th Weather Group, reported to the two generals that the fog settled over almost four million square miles of Europe— the worst fog in recorded history—was going to continue for at least another month. Cannon and Tunner issued a joint order: "From now on, we fly zero-zero." That meant taking off and landing with no visibility. The order was something of an exaggeration—and was meant to be—but both pilots and controllers began operating with significantly lower safety margins.

Two days later, on November 15, a Navy R5D, number 5645, flying in what amounted to zero-zero, crashed and burned as it hit the runway at Tempelhof. Three German security officers, in a jeep circling the perimeter of the airport, raced to the wreck and pulled out four burning crewmen, carrying them to a fire water tank and throwing them in. Herbert Monien, one of the German rescuers, then realized he was on fire himself, all his hair and most of his clothes gone. He was in shock for days, but when he came around there was a letter and three cartons of Lucky Strikes from General Clay. "It was a fortune for me," said Monien.

On November 17—the day advanced CSP-5 radar equipment left Westover for Berlin—a British Dakota crashed into woods in the Russian Zone, killing all four men aboard, including Sergeant Frank Dowling, who was hitching a ride to meet his pregnant wife. Five days later a Lancaster fuel transport owned by Flight Refueling, Inc., crashed into a hillside in Thruxton, England. Seven men aboard were killed, and though the plane was burning furiously, it took searchers an hour to find the wreck in the fog. On one of his afternoon shifts at Tempelhof, Roger Moser counted forty-four missed approaches. At the same time, in an eight-hour shift, Joseph Haluska, a twenty-year-old controller at Wiesbaden, had to talk down three blocks of eighteen C-54s at one a minute in zero-zero conditions. "We used tractors," he said, "to pull the planes to the loaders because the pilots could not see the lights at the edge of the runway."

In Berlin, both western and eastern, life went on in a new kind of normal. Kurt Werner, a forty-one-year-old presser at a clothing factory, who looked twenty years older, was one of ninety thousand Berliners who lost their jobs because companies could not run without electricity. For five months, he, his wife and three children lived on twenty-eight Westmarks a week from city of Berlin Social Security. Then in November, through a friend, he got a job as a loader at Tempelhof, earning fifty-five marks a week and a free hot meal, part of which he was allowed to bring home in a tin can. (One of the pilfering tricks was to put bits of lard or margarine under the food in the can.) "I won't give up any hope," he said. "That is all I have. Perhaps when my son Jürgen becomes a pilot to fly to America like he says he wants to, he'll bring the rest of us with him."

That actually happened for another little Berliner named Wolfgang Samuel, who told the story years later in a letter:

In 1948, I was a young refugee living in a rotting former Wehrmacht barracks located off the end of the runway at Fassberg . . . Cold, hunger and fear of tomorrow our steady companions, there were times when we thought we wouldn't survive until spring . . . The presence of the Americans on the streets of Fassberg brought a sense of security to us that transcended all other aspects of our miraculous survival . . . They were so different from the soldiers I had known—those had been men with guns and whose faces were hard. The Airlift soldiers were not like that. They carried no guns and they looked more like people to whom life had been good and who didn't mind sharing their good fortune. When playing chess one evening, my friend the GSO worker told me: ". . . It's like an assembly line in an American automobile factory. A plane takes off right after one has landed and that cycle repeats itself hour after hour, day and night. The Russians will not get Berlin, going against these Americans . . ."

One day [when I was thirteen] my mother returned home accompanied by an American sergeant. "My name is Leo Ferguson," he said. "Call me Leo, please . . ."

Leo Ferguson became Wolfgang Samuel's stepfather. The boy and his mother moved to the United States in 1951. In 1985, Samuel retired as a colonel in the United States Air Force, a pilot.

Most of the American occupying forces, many of them with wives and children in residence, lived better than they ever had, with servants and, if they chose, local women readily available for bits of the food and liquor and tobacco flown in along with the coal and flour. Antiques, silver, paintings, even pianos were flown out to Rhein-Main for shipment back to the States. Bill Lafferty even flew several gravestones, already engraved and headed for the United States. Many of the women there set up little Americas amid the ruins, with scout troops, bake sales to raise money for The March of Dimes, recipe books and charity work of various kinds, even tryouts for the Rhein-Main Rockettes. One of their projects was a charity cookbook to raise money for German orphans; among the recipes in that one was "Block-Ade: 2 cans fruit cocktail, 1 cup sugar, 2 bottles of Cognac, 6 bottles of red wine, 6 white wine, 6 champagne. Serves 75." One of Clay's secretaries, Joan Clark, said that nearly the only contact she had with Germans came in dealing with servants and workmen. Mrs. Marjorie Clay herself made a point of having German children in her house in Darmstadt during holiday seasons, saving thank-you letters like this one: "Dear Mrs. General Clay. I'm the little girl which was there a week ago Thursday. I will thank you for the wonderful cocoa or the bread with butter and meet. The little cakes with choko-laet was very wonderful. This was my second sweeties what I have got after the war. I will never forget."

The cultural life of the city was still rich, especially the music. Free concerts among the ruins were a coveted break in the misery of daily Berlin life. American newsmen, some of them living in solid old houses on Lake Wannsee—"Westchester-on-Wannsee," they called it—hired string quartets or pianists to entertain at dinner, and, if the electricity shut down, life was more romantic with candelabras and symphonic musicians. American officers and officials usually had regular heat and electricity transmitted separately from the German grid. Ann Slater, one of Clay's secretaries, stored the cellos and violins, including a Stradivarius, of German musicians under her bed so that the wooden instruments would not be ruined by the wet cold of the winter. James Sutterlin, an American vice consul, made a point of helping distant relatives left in Berlin by giving each a pound of coffee each month, a commodity valuable enough on the black market to support a family of four for thirty days.

The Americans, of course, had the money to give them access to the black market, which operated more or less openly during the airlift. Both sides made sporadic but not very successful attempts to deal with illegal trading. Hundreds of young policemen from eastern Germany were stationed at ninety-three checkpoints at sector divisions, but they were easy to bribe or were suckers for hard-luck stories from other Germans. In the west, in a series of "chocolate raids" on cafés along the Kurfürsterndamm, western Berlin's main street, German police arrested forty-three black marketeers, one carrying more than fifty bars. But it was impossible to actually stop illegal trade. West German police watched five hundred tons of coal move through a truck garage, with one entrance in the Soviet Sector and a back entrance on the American side.

Gerhard Rietdorff, the young East Berlin electrical apprentice who became a small-time black marketeer, said it was pretty much business as usual during the airlift: "Lorries from the Balkans filled with thousands of cases of cigarettes and liquor and other luxuries would come to the big dealers. . . . Like the stock market, they could manipulate prices by holding back supplies and giving volume discounts. The big guys—everyone knew who they were, they were the best dressed people around—were rarely arrested. They were paying off the cops. People were starving, freezing, burning doors and furniture, window frames, banisters, stairs, baseboards for heat. But that didn't affect the big crooks."

Official OMGUS estimates of black market activity, reported

in March 1949, were that it supplied between 50 and 200 calories per person on average in the western sectors. "There are holes all over the place," said an American official. "We are existing on them. Anything in Berlin over the absolute minimum comes through the holes."*

In the eastern sector, for the Russian occupiers, it was quite different. "Twenty Russians would live in an apartment, destroy everything," said Rietdorff, who lived in a moldy cellar with four other people, but still embraced communism at first. "I dreamed of living in a socialist democracy," he said. "But that never happened." He was afraid of Russians, partly because Red Army soldiers would swing unpredictably from great fun and laughing to random violence. "The Russians were poor, poor, poor, they lived for the future, always the future." Bill Palahunich, the Ukrainian-speaking American sergeant who made Russian friends, also saw them as completely different from his American friends. "Those young Russians would ask me how we could live so easily with the Germans," he said. "They would tell me of the brutality to their families and how it was impossible to forget it when you lose your father and you never see a sister again."

But Americans saw it all differently. That same month, Sergeant George Gibbons of Bremerton, Washington, got the idea that he could open an orphanage in Berlin. And he did, calling it Boettgen

---

* There is still a historical (or revisionist) debate about the role of the black market in helping Berlin survive during the airlift. Volker Koop, a West Berlin journalist turned historian, author of *Die Perfekte Blockade? Über Mythos und Legendenbildung*, argues that there never was a complete blockade of the city: "I think that only five to ten percent of black market activity was ever stopped. I don't think West Berlin could have survived without it." An American military historian, William Stivers, working in archives fifty years later, wrote: "An expert assessment prepared for American intelligence in early November [1948] put the daily flow of Soviet area foodstuffs into the Western sectors at six hundred to seven hundred tons through mid-October. Taking the lower parameter of six hundred tons as a basis for reckoning, the Soviet area accounted for roughly one-third of West Berlin's food supply during the first three and a half months of the blockade . . . Answering the concerns of a committee of West Berlin industrialists, who had complained over the lack of coal, an American official had a ready solution to the problem of meager supplies: 'There was always the possibility of the firms getting coal from the East Sector and zone. Each firm was at liberty to find a way to help itself.'"

Orphanage and writing friends back home to send clothes, food and medicines, especially cod liver oil. And they did, making a new home, staffed by German women, for 120 orphans, three years old and younger. Lieutenant Gere wrote back to his alma mater, Alfred University, asking students to collect toys for a Berlin Christmas. Hundreds of packages arrived on the same day—and that story made news back home. It was the birth of "Operation Christmas," and more than ten thousand packages arrived within a week.

On November 27, Bill Lafferty and his crew were on a night flight from Wiesbaden to Tempelhof. Routine. Only one of the two radio compasses on board was working, but it could pick up just about any radio signal on the air. Lafferty had plans for that one as soon as his C-54 passed the Fulda radio range station and headed over Soviet-controlled eastern Germany. He turned the compass to the signal of the Armed Forces Network, joining the 102,500 people six thousand miles away in Municipal Stadium in Philadelphia for the 1948 Army-Navy football game. A little fiddling with dials and there it was, and what a game it was.*

College football was much bigger than the professional game in those days and Army-Navy was as good as it got. President Truman was seated at the fifty-yard line with Fred Vinson, the Chief Justice of the Supreme Court. Most of the cabinet and all of the military's top brass were there, too. Forrestal, Royall, Secretary of the Air Force Symington, and Generals Bradley and Vandenberg were in the stands. Truman sat on the Navy side and the midshipmen behind him

---

* Radio compasses were not actually compasses, they were simply radio receivers that followed signals from ground stations and used an arrow to point to the location. They could be tricky when a plane passed over a ground station because they would swing 180 degrees in an instant as the plane headed away from the station instead of toward its signal.

held up a banner reading: GALLUP PICKS ARMY—the same Gallup Poll that had predicted Governor Dewey would clobber Truman.

The cadets from the U.S. Military Academy at West Point polled even better than Dewey. Undefeated and untied, Army ranked with Notre Dame and the University of Michigan as one of the top three teams in the country. Navy had not won a single game since the middle of the 1947 season. The midshipmen from the Naval Academy at Annapolis had lost thirteen games in a row and were three-touchdown underdogs. Lafferty's crew picked up the game early in the third period and were as surprised as anyone that the score was 14–14. Then Arnold Galiffa, Army's all-American quarterback, marched the cadets down the field to put things right: Army 21, Navy 14. But the midshipmen hung on, their two-hundred-pound fullback Bill Hawkins, injured most of the season, but now playing both offense and defense, carried on almost every play as a fifty-yard Navy drive tied the game with less than five minutes remaining. The crowd was going crazy. The country was going crazy. Lafferty and his crew were going crazy. That's how it ended, a 21–21 tie—on the last play of the game Hawkins knocked down a Galiffa pass deep in Navy territory. The next day's *New York Times* wrote, "Old gaffers home from the sea will be describing this game to their grandchildren a couple of generations from now."

Now, where are we? For ten minutes, Lafferty and his crew looked for Berlin, but it wasn't there and the compass was no help. He switched to an RAF frequency and called Gatow, where a WAF (Women's Air Force) controller told him, "Fly two hundred seventy degrees—straight west."

"How far?"

"Never mind, just fly two-seventy."

In a few minutes, they finally saw a city below, but the airport was on the wrong side of town, and Soviet Yaks were lined up on taxiways. The city was Frankfurt an der Oder, at the Polish border.

They had followed the football game into Poland and were still forty minutes from Berlin over hostile territory. They made it, with no one the wiser. Another crew ended up in Prague, Czechoslovakia, landed, and were treated and toasted as heroes by Czech fliers. Then someone from the U.S. Embassy rushed to the airfield and told them Red Army troops were on the way to arrest them. They were in the air again in minutes, headed for Berlin again. A lost British gasoline tanker—all the gasoline and oil carried into Berlin was on British planes—received a more officious welcome on landing when a uniformed official bicycled up to the plane and asked to see the crew's passports. They had landed, by accident, in Belgium. Papers stamped, they took off again. In another incident, a C-54 broke out of the clouds seventy-five feet above the center of Frankfurt, ten miles from Rhein-Main, because a controller got confused, directing two planes at the same time. It was a dangerous business, every flight.

Pilots were forever fighting the dangers of fatigue and boredom. The most fun some had was flying empty out of Berlin. They would rev the engines up to full power, hold the brakes as hard as they could and then roar on, dropping ten degrees of flap at liftoff, seeing if they could get off the ground in less than a thousand feet. One trick was to put an empty Coca-Cola bottle, or even a cup of hot coffee, on top of the instrument panel in front of the pilot. If the bottle or coffee fell, the pilot paid whatever bill there was at the snack truck that pulled up with each Berlin landing. But that was only part of it: the trick also woke up sleeping pilots—and there was a lot of that, particularly before the replacements began to arrive in larger numbers. On many runs, pilots and copilots alternately slept on cockpit floors, and part of that game was seeing whether the one who was awake could make a landing so soft the other one didn't wake up. A neat trick, but the big danger was the both of them falling asleep. Lieutenant Harold R. Austin and his copilot, Darrel Lamb, both fell asleep on a run, their second of the night, overflew Berlin and woke up at 2 A.M. over the Baltic Sea. Turning around, they flew back and heard on their radio that another plane was six minutes behind schedule. They called in their own number and landed just ahead of the slower plane.

BERLIN AIRLIFT WORKING DESPITE THE WEATHER announced the *New York Times* on November 21. "Therefore," wrote Drew Middleton, "although fogs and mists and low clouds certainly have affected the airlift to a considerable degree, there is as yet no cause for alarm over the shortage of stockpiles in Western sectors of the city."

It did not seem that way to men on the line or in the chain of command. "The weather was lousy all winter," said Bill Lafferty. "You were lucky to see two or three lights if you were coming into Tempelhof." And that was after Tunner had won permission from Washington and from city and church officials in Berlin to install the world's most powerful high-intensity approach lighting system right down the middle of Saint Thomas Cemetery.

Even with the new lights and five hundred tons of sand sprinkled on wet Tempelhof landing strips, on November 30 forty-two flights left the west for Berlin, but only ten made it: seven to Gatow and Tegel, three to Tempelhof. The total cargo delivered that day was eighty-three tons. Food supplies in western Berlin were down to fewer than thirty days. One of the planes that got into Tempelhof was piloted by General Tunner. His radio operator that day, Sergeant Earl Morrison, said: "On final GCA approach to Tempelhof, we spotted the runway threshhold lights at approximately 100 feet of altitude; then the General set the heavily laden C-54 down gently on the pierced steel planking surface. He certainly earned his 'Fog and Smog Club' certificate on that night." Heroics aside, however, the November monthly total was just 113,587 tons, compared with 147,580 in October. The airlift was running 1,490 tons below daily minimum requirements of coal, with 80 percent of that going for industrial use. Most western Berlin families had to make do with twenty-five pounds of coal for the entire winter. The more than 2.1 million people of the west were freezing—and getting only two hours a day of electricity—roaming the city looking for bits of wood to burn. Streetcar service had been reduced by 40 percent and subway service by 50 percent. (The S-Bahn, the city's elevated train service, worked as well as ever because it was the principal mode of public transit in the east and the system was integrated into the western S-Bahn.)

Undersecretary of the Army William Draper, who had been supervising administration of military matters in Germany, was in the country at the time and told his boss, Secretary Royall, that if the fog continued through the end of December, Berlin would be left with no stockpiles. He said, "It looks like curtains . . . We probably would have to run up the white flag."

1

Men of history: Joseph Stalin and Harry S. Truman met only once, at the Potsdam Conference, in July 1945 (above), to establish occupation policy for Germany, dividing the defeated country into four zones and its capital city, Berlin, into four sectors. The military governors of the three allied zones were (below, left to right) General Sir Brian Robertson for the British, General Pierre Koenig for the French, and General Lucius Clay for the Americans.

2

3

From 1945 to 1948, Berlin was governed by a four-power Kommandatura, shown above, with the American commandant, Colonel Frank Howley, and his Soviet counterpart, General Alexander Kotikov, facing each other at the center of the table. The break-up of the Kommandatura over currency issues led almost immediately to the Soviet blockade of the city and to the Allied Airlift, approved by General Curtis LeMay (below, left) and run by General William Tunner (below, right).

4

5

6

"You handle the airlift and I'll take care of the Berliners," Ernst Reuter (left), the elected mayor of Berlin (shown with his assistant, Willy Brandt), told General Clay.

7

"The Cowboy Lift" is what pilots called the early days as they sat waiting for planes at Tempelhof Airport (above). Outside, old C-47s, "Gooney Birds" to the flyers, were unloaded by Germans and Displaced Persons.

9

10

11

Daring young men (clockwise): Captain Kenneth Hawk
Slaker; Rudolph Schnabel, the East German who saved
Slaker; Lieutenant William Lafferty; Lieutenant Gail
Halvorsen, "The Candy Bomber," pushing candy bars
on little parachutes to children below; Lieutenant Noah
Thompson.

12

13

14

15

16

Unloading a C-54, with General Tunner (center, on plane) inspecting (top). Two more daring pilots (above): Lieutenant Guy Dunn and Lieutenant Edwin Gere, who had forty-eight hours to leave law school and his new wife to head for Berlin. A German loader, Kurt Dettmer (below left), and Gerhard Noack, a Luftwaffe mechanic, were recruited to keep Americans flying.

17

18

19

20

A C-54 landing at RAF Gatow over the wreck of a British Avro York transport (above). The first crash, a C-47 that flew into an apartment building near Tempelhof (right).

21

"Black Friday," August 13, 1948, when four planes crashed, this one at the end of a Tempelhof runway (left).

"Rubble women," thousands and thousands of them, some in their best (and only) clothes, some in bathing suits, building a new airport at Tegel in the French sector (above).

Crowds of Berliners, young and old, western and eastern, gathered every day at Tempelhof (below) to watch airlift planes diving for the airport's short runways.

24

CHAPTER 8

"Flying to His Death"

December 6, 1948

"I SEE LIEUTENANT DONOVAN HAS THE DAMN HICCOUGHS AGAIN!"

O N DECEMBER 3, 1948, RUBY PHELPS OF LONG BEACH, California, received a letter from her husband, Captain Billy E. Phelps, an airlift pilot who had won a Distinguished Flying Cross in the war and had escaped death a half-dozen times as a B-17 pilot and prisoner of the Gestapo. But, this time, the letter was different. Phelps, who was waiting for his replacement to arrive at Fassberg, had already flown 167 coal flights to Berlin. He wrote that he was tired and the planes were "flying wrecks" being overused to try to make it to Berlin anytime there was a slight break in the fog.

He had flown twenty-four bombing missions over Germany, including the deepest penetration mission of the war, been shot down once, crash-landed once and been turned over to a Gestapo jail. He waited his turn there as his cellmates—a Frenchman, a German, a Belgian and two young Frenchwomen—were executed. Each, in turn, gave him a "V" for victory sign as one by one they were taken outside to a courtyard and tied to a post in front of a firing squad. He watched from the cell window; the women smiled at him as the shots were fired. Then the Gestapo came for him.

He was taken upstairs, away from the killing ground. He was classified as a prisoner of war and turned over to the Luftwaffe, which sent him to Stalag Luft III. Phelps was there for nine months, until the emaciated American airmen in the camp were marched through knee-deep snow from camp to camp as Russian troops advanced through eastern Germany. He was in a camp outside Nuremberg as American and British bombers came over night after night, killing more than one hundred thousand residents of the city. Phelps escaped twice and was caught twice. On April 19, 1945, at 11:58 A.M.— he remembered the time—his last camp was liberated by the Third Army under General George S. Patton.

Captain Phelps recuperated for more than a year after returning home, had two children with his wife, Ruby Lee—his B-17s were both named "Ruby Lee"—and eventually became operations officer at a U.S. base in Veracruz, Mexico. He volunteered for the airlift, but his letters home told a different story about the men and the flying conditions than the one being told so proudly by the Air Force. In the frenzy to make up for lost time in getting any cargo into the city, the planes weren't being maintained, he wrote. Ruby Lee Phelps, who expected her husband to be home for Christmas, was extremely upset when she read a story in the *Long Beach Independent* of December 6 that a C-54 had crashed near Fassberg the night before. On December 8, the Air Force informed her that Billy was the pilot of that plane. The Skymaster crashed immediately after takeoff at 11:13 P.M. less than a mile from the end of the runway in a light, foggy drizzle. The ceiling was two hundred feet. Phelps, who was twenty-six, was killed along with his copilot, First Lieutenant Willis Hargis of Nacogdoches, Texas, and the flight engineer, Lloyd Wells of San Antonio, Texas.

Lieutenant Edward Dvorak was on the flight rescue team that raced out to the crash site. "As I approached the crash site, it was dark, it smelled from fuel," he said. "And here comes the flight surgeon with remains. I saw the cadet ring on my poker buddy's hand. We'd played poker that night. I'd been in a lot of combat and it never bothered me. But that did."

Edwin Gere had flown two missions with Phelps two nights before, and so he knew the young captain had flown more than 120 hours at night and 36 hours on instruments in the last thirty days. Gere assumed the crash was a result of mechanical failure but he decided not to go to the scene. Wolfgang Samuel, the German boy living near the end of that runway, would write: "One of those C-54s turned over our barracks on a clear December night and then fell like a rock out of the sky. The two pilots were killed . . . Only three years ago they were fighting against my country, and now they were dying for us. The Americans were such strange people . . . I wondered, as only a boy can wonder, what made these people do the things they did?"

Mrs. Phelps did not want to talk much to the reporter, Harry Fulton, who came to the house from the Long Beach newspaper. But she gave him her husband's letters home, one of which arrived after she knew her husband was dead. Fulton wrote:

The grim story of the Berlin Airlift is partially told in Capt. Phelps' letters to his wife . . . They are letters from a man who seemingly sensed he was flying to his death.

They tell of American flyers flying mission after mission with little or no rest between. They tell of flights in all sorts of bad weather—often in overworked planes. Once Capt. Phelps referred to them as "flying wrecks." Twice before Captain Phelps had narrow brushes with death. Both times, he told his wife, an engine caught fire and he was forced to crash land. "I almost got killed," he said in his letter. "I had to lie down and it was almost two hours before I could pull myself together to fill out the flight report."

The official Air Force report of the crash of C-54D, 42-72698, listed "Unknown" for the date and hours since its last inspection, then added, "No record of Depot Overhaul."

"West Berlin has voted," wrote Ruth Andreas-Friedrich in her diary. "Of about one and a half million people entitled to vote, one and a quarter million voted against the politics of the Socialist Unity Party [the communist SED]. An admirable result considering that this decision most likely will have to be paid for with an intensification of the blockade, a winter without coal, nights without light and a permanent diet of dehydrated potatoes, dehydrated vegetables and canned meat. We feel as if we had wings. We feel it's great to be a Berliner. It is wonderful to live in a city that prefers death to slavery, that has decided to suffer more deprivations rather than dictatorship."

The communist-controlled SED boycotted the Berlin City Assembly elections of December 5, preferring to announce that an eastern assembly had chosen a new Lord Mayor for the city, Friedrich Ebert, Jr., whose father had been the first president of the Weimar Republic in 1920. The party did try to campaign, though. A thirty-two-page booklet, *Berlin—Worth a New War?* was distributed throughout the western sectors. Using photographs of Berlin after the Allied bombings of 1944 and 1945, the copy included a slogan: "Yesterday phosphorous, today raisins, tomorrow atom bombs."

Radio Berlin, broadcasting from the Soviet Sector, tried a lighter approach, running a jingle, aimed at housewives:

> *Don't be lured by promises sweet.*
> *Think of the dried potatoes you've had to eat.*
> *Think of all the cut down trees.*
> *And the dark, cold rooms in which you freeze.*
> *Don't vote for the candidates, like a dunce.*
> *Whose parties have already betrayed you once.*

The day before the election, on December 4, *Tägliche Rundschau*, the communist paper, carried a banner headline: THE WESTERN POWERS WILL LEAVE BERLIN IN JANUARY. The story underneath made it clear that when that happened, Berliners who stood with the Allies would pay a price. Posters appeared with this legend: "Stay Away from the Polls. Don't endanger your future . . . Those who vote will be duly noted."

One westerner with power, General Clay, was trying desperately to get into Berlin, not out, for election day. The fog was so bad that the general was required to sign a waiver stating that the Air Force bore no responsibility if there was an accident, and then his plane from Frankfurt was denied landing rights at Tempelhof and Gatow, both at zero-zero in the fog. Finally, he was allowed to land at Tempelhof after an air-to-ground shouting match with Tunner. "When the tower directed us to the taxiway we found the visibility so poor that we dare not move farther down the runway," Clay reported. "We were unable to find the jeep that was sent to guide us and finally reached the unloading ramp guided by an airman under each wing signalling us with flashlights."

More than 86 percent of West Berliners went to the polls on Sunday, December 5, despite its being declared a workday in the eastern sector, to try to prevent voting by the 125,000 westerners whose jobs were on the other side of the sector border. Almost two-thirds chose the Social Democratic Party (SPD), led by Ernst Reuter, giving the party 76 of the 119 seats in the new West Berlin Assembly. The two other democratic parties—the Christian Democrats and the Liberal Democrats—won, respectively, 27 seats and 16 seats. Two days later, the new City Assembly unanimously selected Reuter as "Oberbürgermeister," Lord Mayor—more than two years after the Soviets had vetoed his selection after the 1946 election.

Berlin now had two Lord Mayors. The election institutionalized the new reality of two Berlins, politically divided, though still interconnected by work and family, boulevards and rail lines. The Soviets then announced that all vehicles traveling from East Berlin to the Allied Sectors would be required to receive permits in advance and would be allowed to pass through only one of four new checkpoints. Another indication of separation was that only eighty-five thousand of more than two million western Berliners had registered for the rations being offered in East Berlin. Most of those were people who worked in the east and had usually shopped there before returning home to the west.

In the early morning hours of December 7, RAF Captain Clement Utting was walking through the fog to his York when he was hit by a truck driving across the tarmac. His commander, Donald Bennett, was at his infirmary bedside when Utting regained consciousness.

"Did I crash?" Utting asked. Bennett said, "No, Clem. You did all right."

Utting smiled, closed his eyes and died. The truck that had hit him was running without headlights. Some of the Americans speculated that he had been hit deliberately by a German driver, but there was no evidence to prove that.

An American, Lieutenant Vernon Hamman, was luckier. All four engines of his C-54 iced up at the same time. He set the plane on a glide path toward Tempelhof and hit hard in Saint Thomas Cemetery and almost miraculously bounced up and over the fence around the field, landing on the runway without even blowing a tire.

The fog lifted later that day, December 7. In the next forty-eight hours, American and British planes carried 12,446 tons of food and coal into the three western Berlin airports. Those numbers made the front page of the *New York Times,* but Drew Middleton reporting on December 9 repeated the conventional discouraging wisdom: "Various American and British officials have expressed in the last few days their belief that the Russians, having split Berlin, are now ready to 'wait it out' for the rest of the winter, counting on acknowledged hardships of the coming months to force West Berliners to accept supplies of food and fuel that, according to Soviet propagandists, are waiting in the Soviet sector."

In fact, many American and British officials now believed they were prepared to wait out the winter weather.

Jake Schuffert drew a *Task Force Times* cartoon—"Russia's Winter Hopes"—showing a C-54 flying through a snowman with Stalin's face. AIRLIFT MOVES TO MEET GOAL DURING WINTER was the little paper's headline over two stories that said:

> Several moves are under way to maintain airlift efficiency as winter bears down on Vittles Operations. C-54s and Dakotas are being moved between airports to take advantage of the fact that Gatow has slightly better weather patterns than Tempelhof, gaining 1,000 tons a day . . .

The Army and Air Force are pre-cooking meals for Berlin housewives to save coal in Berlin. There is coal enough for heating one room for two hours a day and about 20 minutes of that is "cooking time" with heat sufficient to boil fluids. Beans, for instance, are pre-cooked for two hours by mess personnel, dehydrated and shipped in bags to families. With but a nominal amount of fuel expended the housewife can heat the food for eating. This is the general procedure for many other foods . . .

FORTY RESERVE WW2 AIR CONTROLLERS CALLED UP was another headline on the page.

Finally, replacement aircrews were coming in larger numbers to Germany and to bases that had been stripped of personnel because of the airlift. "The Second Vittles Generation" they called themselves. Lieutenant Eldridge Williams, the head basketball coach of North Carolina A & T University in Greensboro, a Negro navigator who was one of the original Tuskegee Airmen in the segregated Army Air Corps during the war, was recalled into the military Truman had desegregated in 1947. He was sent first to Laughlin Air Force Base in Columbus, Ohio, and then on to Okinawa. Most others were immediately sent to Great Falls. Lieutenant David Irvin, who had flown thirty B-17 missions over Germany, been shot down and escaped from a POW camp in 1943, was one crew member. His first impression of Great Falls on December 16 was "a long line of C-54s and a long tar-paper shack with coal-burning stoves at either end, a bulletin board with a map pointing to the Mess hall, classrooms and the Officers Club."*

At 7 A.M. the next day he was in a classroom for briefings on the air routes into Berlin. Then weather. Checklists and emergency procedures. Working in cockpit mock-ups. He was in a plane again for the first time on December 27, flying as a copilot on the simulated Berlin

---

* A total of 646 pilots, 487 copilots, 496 flight engineers and 126 mechanics were trained at Great Falls during the airlift.

corridors. By the end of January, he was one of the eighteen pilots in his group of twenty-one to graduate and be put in one of those bucket seats, headed for Westover in Massachusetts. He was there just long enough to see the film *Casablanca* at the base theater and was on his way to Rhein-Main, sitting in the rear of a Lockheed Constellation; the front was reserved for officials of the West German Finance Ministry. He was fascinated by both the rubble and the rebuilding he saw in Frankfurt from the air. He had bombed the city twice in 1944. His first flight was from Rhein-Main as a copilot on a C-54 carrying coal, and these are the notes he took:

"Rhein-Main Tower, this is Big Easy 82, over."

"Big Easy 82, this is Rhein-Main Tower. You are confirmed with a 9 A.M. takeoff. Use runway 33. Copy?"

"Roger, tower. Copy. Will call when taxiing. Out."

"82 cleared for takeoff. Altimeter 29.87. Call when starting turn."

Then over Berlin:

"Tempelhof approach, Big Easy 82, ETA 11:18."

"Roger, Air Controller. Confirm altitude 6,000. Standing by."

"Big Easy, this is Ground Control, Tempelhof, turn left to 270. This is your final approach. Put gear down, flaps as desired. Copy."

"Turn left 267 degrees. No further discussion. We will take over from now on. If you cannot complete the approach, climb to 7,000 feet, on a heading of 270, and contact departure control for further instruction."

"Roger."

"Big Easy 82, this is your final approach controller. Start your descent now, at 500 feet per minute. You are on glide path. Your heading is good. Continue your approach. At 200 feet take over and complete your landing run. Your heading is good, you are 10 feet high on the glide path, lower the nose . . . Good corrections. You are passing through 1,000 feet, one half mile, on glide, on course. Everything looking good. You are now one-quarter mile, passing through 500 feet. If you have runway in sight, continue your approach for landing. Over and out."

He and the pilot, Captain Herman Duty, on the first leg of his last flight, climbed out of the cockpit on a rope ladder so they would not interfere with unloading. Two loaders came in to sweep out the plane. Coffee, doughnuts and pretty girls. Fifteen minutes later Irvin took the left seat and Duty said, "When the plane ahead starts his engines, wait three minutes and start ours." They landed at Rhein-Main at 1:50 P.M. Irvin's next flight was at 3 P.M.: 22,000 pounds of flour and soup.

Pilots such as Duty and Irvin certainly did not think of it this way, but they were revolutionizing aviation. During the same week Irvin arrived, *Task Force Times* ran a short item taken from longer Associated Press stories back home:

> Robert Garrett, an air safety investigator from Washington, representing the Civil Aeronautics Board, is inspecting all operational phases of the airlift and has concluded: "the concept of air traffic control could easily be applied to New York, Chicago and Washington immediately . . . the airlift has advanced the art of traffic control by ten years."

Garrett, the CAB's chief pilot, urged that three airlift techniques be adapted by civilian airlines: a third man, the flight engineer, in the cockpit; standardized instrument panel location and using three altitudes so that even though planes took off every three minutes, they were actually separated by nine minutes from planes immediately ahead of and behind them.

In many ways, the French were peripheral to the airlift. The government in Paris already had political problems with their own communist party—constituting almost 25 percent of the National Assembly—and new "small wars" to retain their colonies in French Indochina, Vietnam, Cambodia and Laos. The French Air Force could supply only two transports, old German trimotored Junkers JU-52s, which flew so slowly they were a danger to everyone else and were pulled off the airlift after flying only a few days.

But, they had their day, December 16, 1948.

Captain Ken Herman, a grandson of onion farmers who had come from Holstein in Germany to Iowa, was taxiing on the new runway at Tegel Airport, preparing to fly west at about 10:30 on that morning. He was stopped by French soldiers in a jeep signaling him frantically to get out of his C-54 and into a drainage ditch near the runway. There was a terrific explosion and he saw his empty plane literally jump sideways. "World War III" was his first thought.

Herman did not know it, but French soldiers had surrounded the airport and nearby streets and were turning away both vehicle and pedestrian traffic. Then they cut the telephone lines to the Radio Berlin station and "detained" Soviet and German employees, including several Red Army soldiers. The French put them under guard in two buses that leisurely toured the city for a couple of hours and then dropped them off in East Berlin. The twenty American officers assigned to the new field had been called to a small reception organized by the French commandant in Berlin, General Jean Ganeval—in fact, they were locked in, too. At 10:45, they were shaken by the same explosion that moved Herman's plane. They rushed to the windows and saw the twin radio towers near the end of the runway crumpling to the ground in a huge dark cloud of smoke. The French had blown up the broadcast towers of Berliner Rundfunk, Soviet-controlled Radio Berlin. Thirty French engineers had enclosed the tower legs in bags of plastique explosive, which had been flown into Tegel the day before by an American, Lieutenant Harold Hendler.

"You will have no more trouble with the towers," said Ganeval, raising a glass of champagne to his American guests.

Captain Herman and his crew climbed back into their plane and flew out over the smoking wreckage. Within three hours, an outraged response arrived in the person of the city's Soviet commandant, Marshal Alexander Kotikov. "How could you do that?" was the French version of Kotikov's opening line.

Ganeval's answer, so they said, was: *"Très simple. Avec le dynamite!"*

Not that simple. Relations between the two commandants were more complicated than that. The Frenchman believed Kotikov had broken his word back in September when the Russian guaranteed safe conduct to the twenty German policemen trapped in the old City Hall in the Soviet Sector and then carted them off to jail or worse. In protesting that action, Ganeval had written to Kotikov: "In a telephone conversation, you and I reached an agreement. I did not doubt your word for a moment and issued my orders accordingly. I still cannot believe that an order guaranteed by you could have been violated in so flagrant a manner. You will find one day that I always keep my word." So he did. In early November he had warned Kotikov that the towers were a danger to air traffic and that if the Soviets did not dismantle them, he would do it by December 16—it was another communication that the Soviets never acknowledged. When Kotikov, who had a heart condition, appeared at Ganeval's office, he was so excited that the French general thought he might die on the spot. Kotikov, his face flushed a deep red, said: "This airfield may cost you dear."

Reporting back to the SDP, Willy Brandt added a note on the explosion: "The following news cannot be published. Before the detonation, adjacent blocks of houses were evacuated. In this context,

French officials arrested 65 Russian citizens. When they were supposed to be released from the temporary detention"—the buses—"all of them insisted on staying. By now, they have been sent to the French zone. I mention this detail because it can be applied to other news about the deserting of Russian soldiers and officials."*

As the cold Christmas of 1948 approached, *Der Club der Insulaner*, an enormously popular RIAS show created weekly by a cabaret performer, Günter Neumann, had a suggestion for the Allies on how to keep Berliners warm on the holiday: "Change the date of Christmas to July 25." Then Neumann added a note about Christmas trees: "Decorations for Christmas will be no problem. The Allies will fly in powdered Christmas trees. All you have to do is add water." A variation on that one had a stork bringing in a flat baby: "Dehydrated. Soak in warm water for twenty minutes . . ." Then, on December 15, Neumann introduced a song with a line to be used on Christmas cards: "The Islander keeps his cool . . ."

> *Der Insulaner verliert die Ruhe nicht,*
> *der Insulaner liebt keen Jetue nicht,*
> *der Insulaner hofft unbeirrt,*
> *daß seine Insel wieder'n schönes Festland wird.*

> *The islander doesn't lose his cool,*
> *the islander doesn't praise the fool,*
> *the islander hopes for the day,*
> *on which his island joins the mainland far away.*

---

* More than one hundred thousand Red Army troops deserted to the West between 1945 and 1948. Most were returned under treaty provisions or roamed the streets of western Berlin, a criminal band preying on civilians—until the deserters learned to present themselves as political refugees and then were allowed legally to stay in the West.

Berliners have always been a sardonic lot, often compared with fast-talking New Yorkers. Here's a couple more from Neumann's *The Islanders Club:*

"It's really cold in Berlin now" . . . "Yeah, well, it's a lot colder in Siberia."

"Don't be afraid, Allies, we are in front of you."

"There's a plane carrying Walter Ulbricht, Wilhelm Pieck and Otto Grotewohl"—the communist leaders of East Germany—"[and] Pieck says, 'What do you think, Otto? Will they be happy and come over to our side if I drop a candy bar with greetings from us?' The pilot turns around and says: 'They would be much happier if I dropped the three of you—and never mind the greetings.' "

" 'Hot frankfurters! Hot frankfurters,' yelled a cart peddler. A lady stopped and asked, 'Are they real pork?' The peddler whispered, 'Maybe there's a little fish mixed in, but you wouldn't notice.' 'Do you mean bow-wow?' the woman said. A passerby looked and said, 'Meow-meow is more like it.' "

"A guy trades a pair of stockings for a can of sardines. The sardines are traded for some coffee, then for cigarettes. The usual, but then along comes a guy who loves sardines. He opens the can and is almost knocked over by the smell. 'Hey, you cheated me, these sardines are rotten.' The first guy says: 'Listen, stupid. They're not for eating, they're for trading.' "*

Berliner Rundfunk, the 100,000-watt radio station that was far and away the most powerful in Germany—in fact in all of Europe—was one of the first things the Soviets took when they got to Berlin in 1945 before the other Allies. And one of the first demands of the Americans was that Radio Berlin be put under four-power control. The Soviets responded by offering the other Allies an hour a week of airtime, supervised by Soviet censors. The Americans turned down

---

* *The Islanders Club*, begun during the airlift, was so popular that it continued for twenty more years, staying on the air until 1968.

that deal and did the best they could, which was not very much at first. In February 1946 they cobbled together an 800-watt station broadcasting seven hours a day over telephone lines. The programming was mainly music. Hardly anyone listened; actually hardly anyone could find the American signal on their old radios. And if they did find the signal they heard mostly classical music, reports of the Nazi war crimes trials in Nuremberg—and static. In June 1947, RIAS was hooked up to an abandoned old tower and a 20,000-watt Wehrmacht transmitter left in Italy when the Germans were driven from that country in 1944. The station's new headquarters was opened on July 6, 1948, two weeks into the blockade of the city—which meant there was not enough electricity for western Berliners to spend much time listening to radios, if they had any. That was when a dozen RIAS jeeps hit the streets with constant newscasts, drawing crowds everywhere in western Berlin. The station also created a telephone service, which allowed Berliners to call and hear the latest headlines. The RIAS reporters became heroes in western Berlin, often being given small gifts by people in the street. One correspondent, Jürgen Graf, loved to tell the story of an old man rushing up to his jeep with two tomatoes, saying, "My tomatoes have come in and I have two, one for you and one for me."

The Russians were among the most loyal listeners of RIAS in the early days, particularly after Clay called a press conference in October of 1947 to say that the Allies would use RIAS to counter attacks on American and British occupation by Radio Berlin and eastern newspapers. *Freedom and Totalitarianism* became a weekly series, repeated several times each day, a translated message from the American military governor.

"Today, two and a half years after the collapse of Nazism," Clay said on November 13, 1947, "we find that fundamental human rights are again disputed—this time by communism. In this series of Thursday evening talks, the United States Military Government will explain the difference between democracy and communism, freedom and totalitarianism. This evening, I shall attempt to outline our basic concepts of freedom and democracy, and contrast them with communist theory and totalitarian practice. In this and the following Thursday evening broadcasts, we will attempt to show the inevitable results of a communist political practice, whose methodology requires the suppression of the individual, and the systematic denial of the basic rights of free men."

Colonel Howley, the advertising man from Philadelphia, knew radio and loved it. He had a plan called "Operation Counterpunch," which often put him on RIAS at the drop of a rumor. When Radio Berlin reported, falsely, during the airlift that babies were dying in the west because of milk shortages, Howley rushed to RIAS to extol the virtues and nutritional value of powdered milk and vitamin-laced baby formula. His greatest triumph, though, involved water. Radio Berlin reported, falsely again, that there were water shortages in western Berlin, which led to long lines at public faucets and to housewives filling bathtubs, sinks, buckets and pots with water, hoarding the stuff as they had done during bombing raids in the war. This time Howley was on the air, not only saying there was plenty of water, but that women should be using more of it, saying: "Forget water shortages. Give your baby a bath. All of you take baths. Use as much water as you want. There's plenty of it!" The panic subsided; the lines disappeared.

It seemed almost comic some of the time, but the war of words would continue through the decades. It was, so to speak, the declaration of Cold War—and OMGUS put three hundred thousand dollars a month into RIAS during the airlift. The Soviets reacted with commentaries like these on Radio Berlin:

RIAS music broadcasts of Tchaikovsky or Mussorgsky have nothing in common with the original compositions except for the notes—everything else, the expression, the pace, the rhythm are falsified. This is, of course, done deliberately. RIAS does not want the listeners to realize the beauty of classical Russian music, but to find it dull. This, too, is nothing but anti-Soviet agitation . . .

Every RIAS broadcast is hostile to peace. Every RIAS broadcast means agitation against the Soviet Union because it is the strongest bulwark of peace in the whole world. All anti-Soviet agitation bears the character of a preparation for war . . .

At the beginning of the airlift, listener surveys indicated that 56 percent of Berliners with radios, east and west, listened to RIAS occasionally. By the end of the year that figure was more than 90 percent. The increase was partly a product of the blockade and airlift when rumors, true and false, swept both sectors of the city hour by hour, and partly a product of the very smart leadership of Colonel William Heimlich, the intelligence officer who had been shocked at the Berlin he saw in 1945. Heimlich, who learned his trade as an announcer and producer at WOSU in Columbus, Ohio, and his assistant, a Russian emigré named Boris Shub, both understood that radio (and propaganda) was about speed, credibility and entertainment. RIAS, which they turned into a real news operation, may have had less wattage than Radio Berlin, but it had quicker and better information—largely because Radio Berlin had to hold information for as long as two days while it was checked by East German and Soviet bureaucracies, including a new Berlin office of TASS, the Soviet news service.

"The Islanders" and other satirical programs provided pointed entertainment. Broadcasting information the Soviets were determined to suppress made RIAS into a respected, even essential, news operation. With the help of a network of informers organized by the SPD, the American station began reporting on Soviet concentration camps in East Germany. Reports called *Schweigen ist Selbstmord—Silence Is Suicide*—began with this introduction:

German countrymen in the Soviet Zone! We want to help you! From now on we will broadcast the truth about conditions under the communist tyranny once a week. Tonight we want to introduce you to two young men who managed to escape from Soviet concentration camps.

The shows ended with:

We appeal to you to join us in order to bring to light the inhumanity of Soviet slavery. Silence is suicide!

Heimlich also began what he called *Spy Reports*. Announcers named East Germans and eastern Berliners believed to be informers for K5, the political police in the Soviet Zone and Sector. The same three drumbeats that introduced BBC German Service reports during the war were followed by a few seconds of silence, and then a whisper: "Attention, Schwerin . . . Attention, Schwerin. Remember the name . . ." It would be the name of a spy in that town.

The show also named corrupt eastern policemen with items such as this one: "Erwin Wolf, Police Sergeant of the 11th Precinct, Magazinstrasse, who lives on Gross Hamburgerstrasse, Berlin N4, is stealing baggage at the Neanderstrasse S-Bahn station."

"RIAS is worse than cyanide," the Soviets broadcast on Radio Berlin. The American station made it their slogan, plastering the "cyanide" quote all over their office walls. Brandt, in his reports back to SPD headquarters, noted the importance of the radio station to German politicians: "The RIAS plays a special role as we reach a large part of the international press through this medium."

It could be dangerous work. Soviet soldiers or agents regularly sought out and beat up RIAS correspondents, kidnapping at least two of them.

• • •

The British handled most of the passenger traffic flying in and out of Berlin. And there was a good deal of it. Many of the more than sixty-eight thousand people evacuated during the airlift were sick. Most were old or quite young; again as many were sick or at least malnourished. To be blunt, they each represented one less mouth to feed. Peter Stanneck, a third-grader who was one of two children in his class chosen in a lottery to be moved to new homes in western Germany, was one of them. His sister, Inge Stanneck Gross, recorded what happened: "Peter was selected as one of 50,000 selected to live in West German castles and mansions . . . Two days after Christmas, he was flown from Gatow. Forty-five kids were there mostly emaciated. No shoes, no winter coats, two seven-year-old twins weighed a total of 75 lbs. He left us after there was an exchange of little presents around a Christmas tree that was flown in. He went to a village called Melsungen near Kassel."

The Soviets branded them concentration camps, saying kids were beaten and starved, working as slaves. But the letters home told another story: "A Swiss Red Cross truck arrived and brought food and clothing," Peter wrote. "Each child received ankle-high walking shoes, clothes and bed sheets. There are even potatoes here, as many as we want to eat. Real potatoes, not dried sticks or powder. And you would never believe the big pile of coal we have, and we also have eternal electric light."

Another boy wrote: "I have milk and eggs which I am allowed to get myself in the henhouse. I already know all the cows and pigs, one of whom is called Lottchen. When I come back you will not know me anymore because I will be so big and strong."

The struggle between Generals Tunner and Cannon climaxed at the end of 1948, actually just before Christmas. Comedian Bob Hope was the cause. Hope, as he had done during the war, organized a troupe of stars and singers and, perhaps more important, beautiful girls, to entertain the men of the airlift, far from home again this Christmas. This was a very big deal, particularly because morale was not always that high among the airlifters, who had thought they would be away from home ninety days at the most. Even Tunner understood that one of the big problems on his bases were "Dear John" letters from women back home who had not seen their men for six months—and did not know when they might see them again.

On December 23, Cannon's office announced the schedule for Hope and his stars, which included the songwriter Irving Berlin, the man who wrote "God Bless America." And on the same flight was the Vice President of the United States, Alben Barkley, and Secretary of the Air Force Stuart Symington. There were to be two performances: one in downtown Wiesbaden on Christmas Eve, near Cannon's staff headquarters but far from the air base, and one in downtown Berlin on Christmas Day for Army occupation troops. The minutes of Tunner's protest to USAFE headquarters read: "General Tunner expressed his extreme displeasure over the Bob Hope show which had been billed as a show for the Airlift."

Actually, he went nuts, demanding that all references to the airlift be removed and threatening to go to Hope himself and to the press. "How do you think this will look in the papers back home?" he shouted. Within hours, shows were scheduled at three airlift bases— Rhein-Main, Fassberg and Celle—and Hope, who had been born in England, scheduled another one himself at Wunstorf to entertain an RAF crowd. Airlift personnel were also given priority for tickets to the Wiesbaden and Berlin performances. "This is Bob—speaking from Fassberg—Hope saying if heating's your goal, call Fassberg for coal," the entertainer began. The biggest laugh from the crowd of 1,500 airmen at Fassberg on December 26 was for this line about Berlin's soupy weather: "Soup I'd settle for—but this stuff has noodles in it."

Berlin—Irving, that is—led a group-sing of the chorus of a song he wrote flying across the Atlantic:

Operation Vittles
We'll soon be on our way
With coal and wheat and hay.
And everything's okay
As in the sky we go
We won't forget to blow
A kiss to Uncle Joe . . .

Stalin, that is.

Tunner did not go to any of the shows. Instead he was having dinner with Symington, who was a captive audience for a carefully prepared list of the airlift commander's complaints about Cannon and Washington. The next day, Tunner gave Symington a tour of airlift facilities, a tour as well scripted as Hope's show. There were a series of "chance" encounters like this one described by Tunner:

" 'Relax,' Symington said for the hundredth time that day. 'I'm Stu Symington. Just wanted to see how you're getting along with that engine.'

" 'Oh, I'm going to get it fixed all right, sir,' the mechanic said. 'But I could do it better if I had better tools.'

" 'What's the matter with your tools?' asked Symington, as the man held up a screwdriver and pliers.

" 'See these?' he asked. 'Well, I bought them myself here in Germany, and they're all I got, and I can't get any more, and they ain't worth a good goddamn.' "

Needless to say, the guy and other mechanics got new tools. Symington also brought along Senator John Chandler Gurney of South Dakota, the Republican Chairman of the Armed Services Committee, to listen to mechanics who had been stationed at Rapid City in his state and flown to Germany on seventy-two-hours' notice, leaving behind their wives and children, who were often unable to pay the rent or buy food. Gurney went back to Rapid City and called a mass meeting of families. The wives got money and soon enough a

C-54 loaded with winter clothing and gifts from the wives was on its way to Burtonwood—along with American steak, eggs, chicken and cans of tuna to supplement the British diet of brussels sprouts and meat pies without meat. With Symington as Tunner's chief advocate in Washington, there were also new barracks and more food. Burtonwood was reorganized from top to bottom, the way Tunner wanted it in the first place.

Some of the guys also got a female boss, as *Task Force Times* reported: "The Airlift ceased to be strictly a man's business recently when Lt. Margaret E. Carver, a United States Navy WAVE from Bonham, Texas, arrived to take over the duties of personnel officer of the VR6 Squadron of the 61st Transport Command Group." A nice touch, but the item failed to mention the British women working as air traffic controllers and the German women actually building runways in high-heeled shoes.

On December 31, American planes flew 5,120 tons into Berlin and British planes brought in another 1,007 tons. The total tonnage for December was 141,438, compared with November's 113,587 tons.

CHAPTER 9

"Stalin Says . . ."

January 30, 1949

O N JANUARY 2, 1949, THE FIRST OF THE AMERICAN PILOTS
assigned to "temporary duty" on the airlift six months earlier was rotated home. Twelve men returned to the United
States. One of them, Lieutenant Robert Bourcey of Watertown, New

York, had flown 189 Vittles missions to Berlin. That same day, forty more men who had served as air controllers during the war were taken from civilian airports and assigned to airlift training centers in Great Falls, Saint Louis, Pittsburgh, Minneapolis, San Antonio and Jacksonville, Florida.

The British had even greater rotation problems. In the first week of January, the British declared that Operation Plainfare would be upgraded to a long-term commitment, which meant planning for a three-year operation. More than 2,500 British draftees who had been scheduled for discharge in September and were still in Germany. Their tours were changed to "indefinite duty." Pilots and crews did not know it, but Tunner's staff had begun working on contingency plans for an airlift that would last ten years.

Fatigue for both Allies had become the greatest problem—the men and their flying machines were wearing out—and there were better maintenance schedules for the planes than for fliers. But even aircraft maintenance was too late sometimes. On January 7, a C-54 headed from Rhein-Main to the big inspection and rebuilding station at Burtonwood in England, a two-hour, forty-five-minute flight, crashed thirty miles from its destination. Six Americans were killed: Lieutenant Richard Wurgel, twenty-six years old, the pilot, from Union City, New Jersey; Lieutenant Lowell Wheaton, Jr., twenty-five, from Corpus Christi, Texas; Sergeant Bernard Watkins, twenty-six, from Lafayette, Indiana; Corporal Norbert Theis, twenty, Cunningham, Kansas; Captain William Rathgeber, forty, Portland, Oregon; Private Ronald Stone, nineteen, Mount Sterling, Kentucky.

It was, however, not only Americans like Lieutenant Bourcey who were going back. By January 1949, twenty thousand "war brides" had gone from Germany to the United States. Another five thousand were flown out to Great Britain. Happy couplings and some broken hearts, too, were part of the occupation and airlift. The nonfraternization films and posters produced by Washington and London were no match for human nature. The rules and regulations, paperwork and permissions for military marriages were dense and complicated, deliberately designed to make those marriages more difficult—and many GIs and Tommies were sent home or on to other assignments when they sought permission to marry locals.

But . . .

Technical Sergeant William Michaels, twenty-seven, of Youngstown, Ohio, a flight engineer on bombing runs over Germany before he was assigned to the airlift, preferred to spend his off-duty time reading and sleeping. Then there came a day in the summer of 1948 when one of his barrack mates persuaded him to come to a café in Celle for a little party. He went and saw a girl across a crowded room. Her name was Anna Kirschbaum. She was twenty-five years old, a concentration camp survivor whose father, a devout anti-Nazi Catholic, had aided parachuted Allied airmen escaping from Germany during the war. She was drafted into the Luftwaffe in 1943, assigned to be a teletype operator and was caught deliberately altering coded messages and sending them to the wrong units. She was charged with sabotage and spent more than a year in jails and a concentration camp near Hamburg. Her weight dropped from 120 pounds to 70 pounds at the end of the war. Now she was healthy again, beautiful. Michaels could not take his eyes off her. He walked up to her and asked to take her out.

"No," was the answer. "You're married."

"I'm not married."

"You look married."

Maybe he did look that way, because he was already in love with Anna.

He finally convinced her and they began taking long walks in the city, talking about a life together. He proposed to her in April 1949. This time she said yes. But then she was in a motorcycle accident that left her with a smashed leg—doctors wanted to amputate—and spent months in a full-body cast. Michaels was reassigned to an air base in Illinois. He wangled a thirty-day pass, went back to Berlin and married his "Annie," as he called her, while she was still in the cast. Michaels returned to the United States while paperwork moved back and forth to allow her to come too. She wrote that she was in intensive physical therapy to walk again and did not want to come to him in a cast—she wanted to walk into her husband's arms. And she did that, at La Guardia Airport in New York on July 4, 1950.

Paul Hawkins, a twenty-year-old Private First Class from Harrisville, West Virginia, a town of 1,200 people, came to Tempelhof with four other mechanics who had been trained to maintain the AN/CPS-5 Medium Range Search Radar, which became so important to air traffic control in Berlin. He had to get used to feeling the presence of General Tunner, who often came by to watch approaches and landings over the shoulders of the young men assigned to work with the new scopes. One of the other maintenance men took him to a small party on New Year's Eve, the end of 1948. He met a German girl there named Eva and before midnight asked if he could see her again. She did not answer, but by the time the party broke up, he realized she did not understand much of what he had said. So he asked again, but added: "Don't think about marriage. I would never marry a German girl."

She knew enough English to answer, "What makes you think I would ever marry you?"

Eleven months and dozens of walks around Berlin later, he did ask, and she did answer, "Yes."

It was not until more than a year and a half later that they got permission from his squadron commander. Hawkins had sixty-five dollars to his name and spent it all on a wedding party in the small apartment they shared on Fuldastrasse. When they returned to West Virginia, his sisters immediately pulled Eva aside and told her, "In America you don't always have to do what your husband tells you to do."

Lieutenant Forrest Ott, twenty-seven, from rural western Minnesota, was in charge of a crew of air traffic controllers at Tempelhof, but he was also a rated pilot and flew 110 airlift missions. He was a little drunk when, in October 1948, he asked the cute blond cashier at the officers' mess, called Columbia House, for a date. Hedda said yes, and after that they spent days off sailing on the small boat he kept on Lake Wannssee. He was rotated out of Berlin in November 1949— and said good-bye to the girl and the military. Back in the States, he wrote her a letter saying it was great fun but he always knew nothing would come of it. But he missed both Hedda and the Air Force. A year after he had come home and many months after his last letter, he wrote to her saying he wanted to come back and get married—if she would have him. He was a civilian by then, so there were fewer bureaucratic problems, and they got married at Columbia House on December 13, 1950. Then he reenlisted in the Air Force.

The day after the crash that killed six Americans, Willy Brandt sent his 145th report to SPD officials back in West Germany. After a number of interviews with Allied officials and some Soviet contacts, he concluded that all concerned wanted to end the Berlin deadlock—all, that is, except for Joseph Stalin. And agreeing that a settlement was desirable, there was no agreement on what that settlement might be:

> In the course of several meetings in the past few days with Allied representatives I have inquired how the relation between Berlin and the West is to be shaped in the future. I have told the British and the Americans that according to my point of view the Russians have probably stopped their original plan to quickly penetrate the whole of Germany . . . Allied circles tend to reckon that an eastern state will soon be formed . . . Among Americans I have heard quite a number of unobjective arguments about remilitarization. People do not want to realize that the debate was, in fact, triggered by the Allies and the Americans . . .

I was among Americans yesterday when the news of Secretary of State Marshall stepping down and his being replaced by Dean Acheson was discussed. This group of people believed that despite Truman's announcement the new foreign minister would probably make new attempts to bring about negotiations and, if possible, a new compromise. I find it especially remarkable what was said about Berlin in this context. A high-ranking officer, mostly concerned with economic questions, emphasized that matters could not continue as before. At some point a compromise had to be reached concerning Berlin. The question was whether a withdrawal could result in advantages in other regions. As possible "return services" in exchange for Berlin's status being changed, he concretely mentioned a.) a peace treaty with West Germany which Russia would de facto recognize, b.) withdrawal from the Russian zone in Austria. It remains to be seen whether he was intentionally aggravating his statements—which is to be assumed—in order to challenge the contrary arguments . . . During the mentioned discussion it was especially emphasized that West Germany was raising its financial and economic contributions for Berlin with great hesitation and under American pressure and that an increase of their helpfulness could not be reckoned with. This attitude, which had made a great impact in American circles, suggested that wide circles in the West would "breathe a sigh of relief" if they could get rid of the burden posed by the Berlin problem . . .

From a different source I learned that several people in Washington, among them Ambassador Bullitt and Chairman of the Joint Chiefs of Staff Omar Bradley, stand up for a normalization of the Berlin problem. People believed negotiations would take place in May or June. Certain American circles have the impression that the Russians are waiting for new negotiations. One of my Scandinavian friends, the Norwegian ambassador, who returned to Berlin from Moscow last month, talked to Bedell Smith, the American ambassador to the Soviet Union, before the latter left Moscow. He indicated that some members of the Politburo believe the time for resumption of negotiations has come. But the important people headed by Stalin do not believe this to be the case.*

Brandt was a talented journalist and political activist, but he did not fully understand the long-range thinking of the men around Truman. Acheson, Kennan and Bradley each had reservations about staying in Berlin, but for different reasons. Berlin was a peripheral interest to the new Secretary of State, whose real desire was for an economically stable and militarily strong West Germany to act as a guardian state between the Soviet Union and its allies and the American allies of Western Europe. Kennan favored a single Germany and the possibility of negotiation that ended with the withdrawal of all occupying forces. Bradley simply did not believe that the Allies had the military power to stay in Berlin once a new Europe was mapped out.

That week, on January 5, General Clay formally asked to be relieved of the European command and retire from the Army. Not for the first time. He regularly asked to be relieved when he disagreed with Washington policy or did not get his way in policy arguments. This time he vented some of his anger in a letter to his friend the Assistant Secretary of the Army, William Draper. Clay had just lost another

---

* The consensus of Soviet historians, according to Viktor Gobarev, the Russian military historian: "Stalin did not think the West would go so far in protecting former enemies. It was his mistake, but no one dared tell him it was failing." Another Soviet scholar, Dr. Alexej Filitov of the Academy of Science in Moscow, concluded that Stalin had considered a blockade as early as October of 1947. Filitov also reported that Stalin was told by Soviet occupation authorities as late as September of 1948 that Berliners' attitudes toward the Soviet Union were improving and that the Allies would soon be forced to make concessions. It was only in December, Filitov said, that Stalin was told the "War of Erosion," a Moscow catchphrase, might not succeed.

battle with Marshall, Lovett and Kennan, who were ordering him to delay plans to equalize the German war debt among the country's population. It seemed the Treasury Department was against it as a tax that would redistribute wealth. "I shall of course carry out the order on equalization," he wrote, then snapped, "which will greatly damage military government's prestige as it makes our word meaningless. When I have done so, I shall request relief."

He was also angry about a "Program for Germany," written by Kennan, which proposed a unified, neutral Germany. Clay had wanted something like that back in 1947, but the Soviet blockade and other developments had turned Clay into an advocate of dividing the country, creating a Western-oriented West German state. One more time Clay was denied retirement. On January 7, Secretary of the Army Royall wrote: "I think it would be harmful for your resignation to be announced at this particular time, as it might lend some color to propaganda that we are relaxing our firm policy toward Russia."

Ironically, the two strongmen of West Berlin, General Clay and Mayor Reuter, now agreed on a vision of the future. Reuter laid out his thoughts in an interview with James P. O'Donnell, the *Newsweek* correspondent who wrote a profile of the German politician for the January 9 issue of the *Saturday Evening Post:*

Airplanes, wonderful. Something you Americans understand so well. But it is unfortunate that it has been called Die Luftbrücke (The Air Bridge) because the days when one dreamed of building a bridge between East and West are over. Here in this Western outpost of Berlin we yearn not for a bridge but a magnet— something in the West strong enough to pull Germany together in that direction. . . . While you debate about the dangers of splitting Germany, the reality is that the Soviets have already done so. . . . We in Berlin will fight to join you. The political currents in Europe will then be reversed from East–West to West–East. The magnetic pull of the West will someday pull Berlin and the East-ern zone back into a united Germany.

Then Clay learned that Acheson was replacing Marshall and Lovett was resigning—and he was persuaded to delay his own exit.

The mayor's office in West Berlin published a pamphlet on January 12 that included a section titled "Airlift Berlin—Daily Life." The day began at 6 A.M. with people dressing and eating by candlelight—a roll and ersatz coffee—then leaving for work early because there was so little public transportation actually running. There was a note say-ing the day's ration card allocated 475 grams of bread per family, one kilogram of pickled vegetables, 62.5 grams of dried vegetables, with an extra ration for diabetics and blood donors. Next was the power schedule listing two 2-hour periods with different times for each neighborhood. Then:

7:45 A.M.—The rapid transit railways with most windows broken, in which there are no lights even when driving through tunnels, are dark and crowded . . .

9 A.M.—In the cold office, people are working in their coats . . . Telephone conversations are interrupted by the engine noise of the airlift planes.

10 A.M.—The Berlin woman trades a bread voucher and a bag full of coal for a couple of cigarettes.

11 A.M.—The dreaded gas man cuts off the gas for four weeks. Someone went beyond the quota.

Noon—The children are coming out of the heated school with lunch. Lessons are taught in three shifts.

12:30 P.M.—Lunch, vegetable soup with potatoes made of dried ingredients.

1 P.M.—The mail brings greetings from the "Golden West" of Germany with descriptions of the life one could live without the blockade.

2 P.M.—Electricity until 4 P.M. The housewife vacuums and irons. Businesses use it to complete necessary work. The hair salons are full. People listen to the radio.

3 P.M.—Aunt Olga from the East sector is visiting. At the sector border, the police took the fresh potatoes and flower pot she wanted to give to relatives. She has electricity, gas, coal and potatoes at home, but would live in the West if she could.

4:30 P.M.—The RIAS truck is delivering news to parts of the city without electricity.

5 P.M.—Closing hour. The last train leaves at 6 P.M. Rush hour at black market intersections.

5:30 P.M.—The bright and heated reading rooms of the occupying powers are filled with Berliners seeking knowledge, light and warmth.

7:30 P.M.—Short visit to the neighbors with a candle in one hand. The Berlin woman has to fight hot wax burns.

8:30 P.M.—Berlin goes to bed because there is no light or coal.

1 A.M.—The alarm clock goes off. There is electricity for two hours. Housework and paperwork is completed. The radio is on.

• • •

On January 13, *Task Force Times* reported that Americans and British planes flew 755 flights into Berlin, carrying 6,677 tons of material, a record except for the Air Force Day marathon during the summer. It was the 205th day of the airlift. Earlier in the week, on the two hundredth day, crowds of Berliners had gathered at Tempelhof to cheer as planes landed one after another. Then, suddenly, they broke through military police lines and onto the field, surrounding pilots and crewmen, clapping them on the back, pressing small gifts, many of them knitted or hand-carved, into the hands of the smiling and embarrassed Americans. There was a sense the Allies were winning, that the airlift would save West Berlin. An Army intelligence survey printed that same day in Washington stated: "Faith in the Airlift and in the willingness of the Western Powers' determination to stay in the city has increased since the beginning of the winter. Unless the situation becomes definitely worse, the population of the West sectors of Berlin may be relied upon to support the policies of the Western Powers through this winter."

It was an unusual winter. The fogs were the worst in at least fifty years, but temperatures were significantly higher than normal, generally in the 30–40 (Fahrenheit) degree range during the day, 30 degrees warmer than during the numbing winter of 1947. In January of 1947 there had been 97 hours of severe frost in Berlin and 281 hours of very severe frost. But this January of 1949, there were none at all. During the nights, however, temperatures sometimes dropped close to zero. Helen Guhse, Ernst Reuter's secretary, said she was opening a bottle of blackberries, canned during the autumn, when it exploded, leaving a black stain frozen on her kitchen wall until the first warm days of spring.

Part of the new Western confidence was related to the obvious success of the counterblockade designed to deprive East German industries of supplies and material that once had been provided by companies in the western sectors of Berlin. The Maxhütte steel complex in East Berlin was advertising for shovels to replace the ones that formerly came from the west. There were also requests for rolled steel sheet, formerly supplied by mills in West Berlin. But business is business—sometimes as usual. An American spokesman, interviewed by the *New York Times*, said: "I'll cite one instance to indicate what's been happening. We have been flying tungsten in by airlift, which is expensive to get and to transport. This rare material has been made into electric bulbs, badly needed by the people of West Berlin—but those bulbs have then been sold and delivered to firms in Soviet-controlled areas. That just doesn't make sense and we propose to halt that flow, effective immediately."

At the same time, a *Times* editorial echoed new confidence: "The latest reports . . . make it plain that if the Russians counted on 'General Winter' to defeat the Berlin Airlift they have made a grave mistake and that the blockade they established to drive the Western powers out of the German capital has boomeranged . . ."

There was a price. The day after the January 13 record delivery of almost 7,000 tons, the *Task Force Times* reported that three more Americans had been killed in another C-54 crash three miles from Rhein-Main. The pilot was Lieutenant Ralph Boyd of Fort Worth, Texas, who had flown twin-engine B-26s during the war and was thirty-two years old, an American Airlines pilot when he was recalled for airlift duty and sent to Great Falls. Lieutenant Craig Ladd, the copilot, thirty, had flown 240 hours of actual combat time during the war, but had only sixteen hours of C-54 time, all at Great Falls. The flight engineer was Sergeant Charles Putnam, forty-four, from Colorado Springs.

The next day, the *Task Force Times* reported that Lieutenant Gail Halvorsen was being rotated back to Alabama after presiding over the dropping of ten tons of candy in six months. He had received four thousand letters from Berliners and innumerable gifts, including china plates, family photographs and stamp collections gathered over decades. He was a national hero by then, a reason the airlift was so popular back home. On the day he returned to the United States, the *San Francisco Chronicle* editorialized: "The forthcoming Congress will be properly concerned with expenses . . . But we agree with General Clay that a pivotal operation like the Berlin Airlift—which will cost less for an entire year than a single day's operation toward the end of WW2—is not the place to start economizing. On the contrary, we consider it would be cheap at ten times the price." *Task Force Times* also reported that health statistics in Berlin in 1948 were better than the year before Operation Vittles began and delivered forty-five tons of medical supplies in six months: "The death rate fell below that of 1939 in the American sector. Weight increases were recorded in all age groups. Polio cases were 1.6 per 10,000 compared with 6.6 in '47." And Alta Jolley finally said yes to her young lieutenant. The Halvorsens were married two months after his TDY in Berlin ended.

That same day, January 14, an old British Handley Page Hastings transport, chartered from Lancashire Aircraft Corporation, collided with a service vehicle on the ground, killing three civilian engineers and a German driver. The British casualties were Patrick Griffin, Edward O'Neil and Theodore Supernat, a British citizen who had been born in Poland and whose father, sister and three brothers had died in German concentration camps. The fourth crash of the month was on January 18. Lieutenant Robert Weaver, thirty, of Fort Wayne, Indiana, who was married and had a one-year-old son, went down ten miles east of Fassberg. Then on January 24, an RAF Dakota crashed in the Soviet Zone, killing Signaler John Grout and seven German passengers being evacuated from Berlin: Gudrun Gisela, Ursula Grasshoff, Irmgard and Emanuel Kelch, Johann Lercher and Gertie and Silvia Zimmerman. The RAF pilots and fifteen other Germans survived.

The crash and the death of the German passengers was treated as a major story by the Soviet-controlled press for several days in both East Berlin and East Germany under headlines like this one:

AIRBRIDGE-DEATHBRIDGE
Senseless evacuation of Berlin children causes tragic victims

A British Dakota carrying 22 passengers, including 17 children and a crew of three, left Gatow airport yesterday and crashed near the Anglo-Russian Zonal border near Schonberg late last night. Search parties led by Russian officers and personnel were sent out immediately ... More and more parents are realizing that they need not have lived in continual anxiety about the journey of their children if they had registered in the east sector for their food and coal rather than remaining in the west sector.

Joseph Stalin, not surprisingly, did not give interviews. He issued *diktats*. That did not stop Western journalists from trying. They telegraphed written questions to the Soviet leader, which piled up on a desk somewhere in the Kremlin—and occasionally, when it suited his purposes, Stalin issued written answers. On January 30, a Sunday, he answered four questions submitted by J. Kingsbury Smith, the European manager of International News Service, the wire service owned by the Hearst newspapers.

The generalissimo was a man of few, usually cryptic, words. The official version was published in *Pravda:*

Q. Would the government of the U.S.S.R. be prepared to consider a joint publication with the government of the United

States of America, to discuss a declaration which confirms that neither the one nor the other government intends to allow a war between them?

A. The Soviet government would be prepared to discuss the question of the publication of such a document.

Q. Would the government of the U.S.S.R. be prepared, jointly with the government of the United States of America, to take steps towards the realization of this peace treaty, for example, gradual disarmament?

A. Of course the government of the U.S.S.R. would cooperate with the government of the United States of America in the carrying through of steps for the realization of the peace treaty and gradual disarmament.

Q. If the governments of the United States of America, the United Kingdom and France agreed to postpone the establishment of a West German state, pending a meeting of the Council of Foreign Ministers to consider the German problem as a whole, would the government of the U.S.S.R. be prepared to remove the restrictions which the Soviet authorities have imposed on communications between Berlin and the Western zones of Germany?

A. Provided the United States of America, Great Britain and France observe the conditions set forth in the third question, the Soviet government sees no obstacles to lifting transport restrictions on the understanding, however, that transport and trade restrictions introduced by the three powers should be lifted simultaneously.

Q. Would Your Excellency be prepared to confer with President Truman at a mutually suitable place to discuss the possibility of concluding such a pact of peace?

A: I have already stated before that there is no objection to a meeting.

The American press seized on the last answer. The lead headline in the *New York Times*, over an Associated Press story on the Smith questions:

STALIN SAYS HE IS NOT AVERSE TO A MEETING WITH TRUMAN; WASHINGTON VIEW CAUTIOUS

The White House, too, initially focused on the idea of a summit meeting, indicating a willingness to discuss a meeting in the United States. Stalin knocked that down, saying his doctors would not allow foreign travel. He wanted Truman to come to Russia, but that was knocked down in turn by the President.

The reaction was quite different at the State Department, where Acheson had just taken over the week before from the retiring George Marshall. Charles Bohlen, director of the "German Group" created by Marshall, telephoned the new Secretary of State at his farm in Maryland and said he thought the most interesting thing about Stalin's words was that the Soviet leader never mentioned currency reform, the original stated reason for the Berlin blockade. Perhaps the omission was deliberate. Perhaps the Russians were ready to back down.

Acheson, after conferring with Truman, waited until his weekly press conference, on Wednesday, February 2, before commenting on Stalin's interview. He dismissed most of what was said as old news, but did respond, very carefully, to the third question: "It is the most interesting exchange of the four . . . There are many ways in which a serious proposal by the Soviet government to restore normal inter-zonal communications and communications with and within Berlin could be made. All channels are open."

The next day, at his news conference, President Truman said his wife would make up the guest room if Stalin wanted to come to Washington. Beyond that, he said, Acheson spoke for the government. In fact, the State Department was desperate to find a back channel to find out what Stalin really meant.

In Berlin, on January 31, General Tunner announced that General Winter be damned, the Americans and British had flown 171,960 tons of cargo into Berlin during January. Another record.

CHAPTER 10

"Zero-Zero"

February 20, 1949

O N THE FIRST DAY OF FEBRUARY 1949, WILLY BRANDT
sent the SPD his longest report to date, number 165, on
the state of affairs on the ground in Berlin:

The Russians have to realize the failure of the blockade of Berlin.
The Western counter blockade has increased the economic diffi-

culties in the Eastern zone. It's with good reason that this problem is explicitly addressed in the Stalin interview. The grocery supplies in the Soviet zone will be catastrophic in the spring and the traffic system is about to collapse. There is frequent news about the shutdown of factories. The conference held by Andre Vyshinsky last week in Karlsbad served to induce representatives of the East to supply the Eastern zone with raw materials, semi-finished products/subassembly, and food. The present success is not overwhelming . . .

Looking at Berlin's development from December 5 onwards, it becomes apparent that the Soviets conducted less infringements/assaults than expected. Although it was intended to transform West Berlin into a ghetto by introducing the new Eastern IDs on February 1, it is announced now that the West Berlin IDs will continue to be recognized in the Eastern sector and in the Eastern zones . . .

Brandt offered the opinion that the Soviets had been ready to make a deal months ago, that they were willing to do as much as possible to prevent or delay a London conference of the Western Allies, which would almost certainly lead to the establishment of a West German state and of an "Atlantic pact," a military alliance led by the Americans. He continued:

It is possible that the Soviets want to gain time, which is understandable with regard to the upcoming creation of the Atlantic pact. The Russians also want to negotiate about the all-German problem. It is widely known that Stalin was already willing to concede during the Moscow talks last summer . . . It would be a success for the Soviets if Germany could be "neutralized" . . . The Russians would like to be involved in the control of the Ruhr and to use the revitalized West German economy for the Eastern zone and reparations.

It is unlikely that an agreement on such a program can be found. An alternative is the maintenance of the border that runs through Germany and the recognition of a Western and Eastern state. This would entail a political equalization of Berlin, which would require different measures than used in the past. Even Moscow must realize this.

The French concept that for security reasons, Germany had to remain weak and that a loose form of state organization as well as a reunion of East and West should be avoided or prevented, gains support by the British . . . The British wish to loosen the ties between the Eastern European states and the Soviet Union. This should be achieved via trade missions that would exploit the fact that the Soviet Union cannot keep up with the import needs of these countries.

Right now, the hope for establishing a balance with Russia plays an important role. It remains to be seen whether the Americans are willing to make concessions to reach this. An American who returned from his vacation a few days ago drew my attention to another threat: in the States, there are only a few people that believe that a peaceful pushing back of Russia from Europe is possible. Some people want a quick military confrontation, while others want to accept the *status quo*.

If the Russians did understand the blockade was a failure, it did not stop the newspapers and magazines in East Germany and East Berlin from printing a steady stream of articles attacking and mocking the Allies.

AIRLIFT PILOTS SUPPLY BLACK MARKET

That was a headline in *Vorwärts* on February 7: "American pilots fly 72,000 cigarettes and 58,000 bars of chocolate to Berlin for the black market each week, besides large quantities of coffee and tinned goods . . . Despite sharp control by English military police, the black market goods inevitably find their way out of the airport to the markets . . ."

AIRBRIDGE SABOTAGE EFFORTS

That was a *Neues Deutschland* headline on February 12: "On 9 February in the Party headquarters of the SPD in Zietenstrasse, Berlin, a secret conference was held by specially selected leaders from the West Zones organizing sabotage acts against the East Zone. In the presence of a group of agents of the Western Occupying Powers stationed in Berlin, undermining orders were given. This is the first time that it has become known that the Airbridge is used as a means of carrying out espionage in the East Zone. A few of the British aircraft carrying mail etc., have thrown out bundles of propaganda literature at certain predetermined spots, where accomplices, previously posted, pick them up and distribute them . . . This courier service has been operating for approximately five weeks . . . The loading of these aircraft is by Press agents in the West Zone who are responsible for choosing the best propaganda material."

AIRLIFT DISASTER

That was a *Vorwärts* headline on February 20: "On Saturday afternoon the fog was thicker over Tempelhof than other parts of the town, and the thickest reported in many years. In spite of radar aids and large fog lamps, the airlift had to be discontinued . . . American pilots are asked to volunteer to make a flight to Berlin when fog conditions are such as to stop normal traffic. There have been no volunteers in spite of the offer of large bonuses."

CLEANLINESS AND HYGIENE A SECONDARY CONSIDERATION

That was a headline in *Berliner Zeitung* on March 1: "For many months we have received complaints, but only in the last few days have definite proofs been obtained regarding the unscrupulous speculations over West Berliner' necessities . . . No sack is washed, cleaned or disinfected. The parcels may be clean on the outside, but who knows what an eight-pound parcel contains? . . . This shows clearly that profit is the primary essential of the airbridge . . ."

THE DECEIT OF THE AIRLIFT

That was a headline in the *Tribune*, another East Berlin newspaper, on March 9, over this analysis: "For Americans, the airlift is good business; the continuation of the profits made during the war. On the other hand, the airlift means increasing debts for the Berliners. Already, at the end of last year, the straight transport costs were about 18.2 million dollars . . . So the airlift leads to financial bankruptcy. The consequences are a transferring of the production of Berlin firms in the West Zones, short working-hours and closing down in Berlin."

Tunner, whose drip-drip-drip graph and chart descriptions did not read particularly well in most newspapers and magazines, agreed to spend a good deal of time with two journalists, Charles J. V. Murphy of *Fortune* magazine and Paul Fisher, the editor of the *Bee-Hive*, the company magazine of United Aircraft Corporation, the manufacturers of the Pratt & Whitney engines that powered both C-54s and C-47s. In the *Fortune* interview, in November 1948, Tunner emphasized that planes were being utilized nine hours a day, compared with three and a half hours a day in normal commercial operations. He also emphasized that at La Guardia Airport in New York or National Airport in Washington, radar-guided instrument landings in bad weather normally took between sixteen and twenty minutes. In Berlin, ground control could bring in plane after plane in less than four minutes each.

Murphy was not sure the airlift would work, but he was certainly impressed with its importance to aviation in the future, writing: "By the Air Force's accounting, it cost the U.S. Government at least $100 a ton to haul coal, flour and other necessities to Berlin. The prospect of making a permanent business of supplying a Rolls-Royce delivery service to the world's biggest poorhouse was one to give pause to even a nation as rich as our own . . . [But] it is no exaggeration to say that the lift . . . has taught American airmen more about the possibilities of mass movement of goods by air than they probably would have learned in a decade of natural development."

Fisher, of United Aircraft, wrote the longest piece published during Operation Vittles. He collected detailed information on everything from spark plug life to propeller pitches, filling an entire issue with airlift coverage, was the reporter who spent the most time with General Tunner, in his office, around airports and in the air. They spoke the same language, loved the same graphs and shared the same confidence that the airlift was succeeding far beyond what even the most optimistic participants had believed when it all began seven months before. Reaching into piles of papers, tapping on charts and boasting, too, Tunner, who was constantly pressuring the Air Force to find him more trained statisticians, said:

> The airlift stands out in aviation like the first page in a wholly new chapter of history. I don't say this idly—but we now know, as we never knew it in the Air Force before, that we can fly anything, anywhere, any time. Climate, mountains, oceans—those can't stop us . . . Given tools of personnel equipment, aircraft, and the steady flow of supplies, cargo can be moved from any point in the

world to any other point in the world, regardless of geography or weather.

Suppose, in a normal world, Frankfurt with its 600,000 people, was thriving. And suppose Frankfurt wanted goods out of St. Louis. As it now stands, the goods must be trucked to a rail terminal, unloaded and reloaded, rail-carried to a port, unloaded and loaded, shipped across the sea, unloaded and loaded, trucked to another railroad, unloaded and loaded again, and carried to Frankfurt where it would be handled twice more. All the handling costs money, and the total transportation times run into weeks, or more likely, into months. Yet by air cargo only two handlings would be necessary, and you could have it within twenty-four hours.

The lessons we've learned from the airlift are tremendously important. Or, if you want it another way, we've proved concretely here some important things we believed all along. We know, for instance, that the future of military air transport—and this inevitably applies to commercial cargo transport—is the big aircraft.

Tunner began talking about a specific airplane, the Douglas C-74 Globemaster, with a capacity of twenty-four tons, ordered by the military in 1942, with the first ones delivered in 1945. But by then the war was winding down and only fourteen were built. Seven of them were used to fly airlift cargo from the United States to Rhein-Main, where it was unloaded and then reloaded into C-54s, because none of the Berlin airstrips could handle the eighty-five-ton weight of a fully loaded C-74. Fisher wrote:

"Look at these figures," he went on, placing a chart on the corner of his desk. "A task force made up of sixty-eight C-74s could haul the 4,500 tons needed in Berlin each day. It takes 178 C-54s to do the same job, or 899 C-47s. With C-74s you would only have to make 5,400 trips a month to maintain your tonnage average, where the C-54s must fly in 13,800 times or the C-47s 39,706.

"The economy runs all the way through. In the C-74 you would need only 16,200 hours of flying time a month, compared to 42,888 in the C-54s or 158,824 in the C-47s. Look at the crews. One hundred and eighty C-74 crews could do the job where we need 465 for the C-54s and 1,765 for the C-47s. The same ratio in maintenance—2,700 C-74 maintenance men could accomplish the job that would require 4,674 on the C-54s, and 10,588 on the C-47s. And finally, you could fly the C-74s on 6,804,000 gallons of fuel, compared to the 8,577,600 needed by the C-54s, or the 14,294,000 the C-47s would need."

That was the way Bill Tunner talked on the record. And he was right. The American and British planes were carrying more cargo each day. Three Americans would claim great credit for the amazing overall efficiency of the airlift: Tunner, the whip; his traffic manager, Major Edward Guilbert; and a brilliant Air Force mathematician, George Dantzig. Guilbert, a Burma veteran, was in charge of ensuring that a load was ready where and when it was needed by each plane, and that distribution trucks were ready in Berlin when that plane landed. Guilbert, using teletype machines, jury-rigged what amounted to an electronic data-sharing system before anyone knew what electronic-data sharing was or what it became in the 1970s: EDI or electronic data interchange. Dantzig, working in the Air Force's comptroller's office, developed "linear programming," which he used to create a giant flight plan based on maximizing supply while minimizing the number of planes and personnel needed to do the job.*

Off the record, out of Tunner's reach, young Americans had their

---

* As a graduate student at the University of California, Berkeley, Dantzig saw two statistical problems on a blackboard and solved both, thinking they were a homework assignment. In fact, they were examples of unproved theorems. That 1939 incident was the basis for the 1997 film *Good Will Hunting*.

own ideas of how to supply western Berlin. A seventeen-year-old corporal, Louis Schuerholz, of Ocean City, Maryland, described one incident this way: "We were assigned to neighborhoods to deliver food and fuel to German homes . . . On one occasion, we drove into East Berlin and approached a Russian fuel dump. We had some Four Roses whiskey, got the guards drunk and took 5,000 gallons of fuel oil which we then delivered to German households in our assigned neighborhoods."

Meanwhile, Willy Brandt was traveling with Mayor Reuter for meetings with officials in London, where he was the first German to be officially received since the war. The Berliner had doubts about British commitment to Berlin, but after a visit with Ernest Bevin, Reuter had no reservations about British determination. The two old socialists had the same emotion about communism: hatred. In his report from London, Brandt portrayed the airlift as an ongoing and growing operation, writing:

I was told from a confidential English source that the Allies were already planning for the airlift for the time period from April 1, 1949, to March 31, 1950. In May/June, a daily capacity of 8,000 tons shall be reached, which means a doubling compared to the best month so far (i.e. January). The English envision, among other things, that the daily food portions are increased from 1,300 to 1,600 tons so that fresh potatoes can be transported to Berlin. Every day, 200 tons of consumer goods, 800 tons of raw materials and more coal for the factories are planned, so that a working week of 38 hours can be ensured. For the next winter, 100 kilograms of coal and 50 kilograms of paraffin oil for each household are planned. The American plan is 700 tons beneath the English. I am mentioning this matter only because it shows that one no longer improvises, but plans long-term ahead.

From there the two Germans went to Paris. As usual, the mood in the two capital cities was quite different. The British seemed steadfast, the French skittish, as Brandt described them:

> Reuter was warmly welcomed in Paris. Prime Minister Robert Schuman, who is fluent in German, stressed that the French government wished for the German unification. François Poncet, the French High Commissioner for Germany, was more reserved, and the officials of the Quai d'Orsay were even more reserved. Contrary to London, people in Paris repeatedly asked: What will happen? What is the solution? What did Stalin's last activity mean?

The Stalin questions were the same in Washington. Acheson, who had been Secretary of State for just a week, conferred with Truman about what to do next in finding out what Stalin meant in his answers to the questions of Kingsbury Smith. They decided to ask Philip Jessup, an American delegate to the United Nations, to try to discuss the matter with the Soviet Permanent Representative, Jacob Malik. "Try to make it sound casual, a matter of personal curiosity," said Secretary of State Acheson, who had told Jessup to come to Washington for a conversation rather than leave a paper trail or take the chance that something might be overheard in a telephone call.

Back at Lake Success, a village on Long Island, where the United Nations was meeting in a renovated factory while its permanent headquarters was under construction on the East Side of Manhattan, Jessup bumped into Malik as they walked into the Security Council chamber for a vote on admitting the Republic of Korea (South Korea) to U.N. membership. They talked about the weather for a couple of minutes, then Jessup asked Malik if he knew whether Stalin had deliberately not mentioned currency reform in the exchange with Kingsbury Smith.

"I don't know," said Malik. "I have no information on that point." Jessup said he would appreciate it if Malik could check and let him know. That was it. Jessup then sent out eight copies of a memo on the conversation, five to his own staff and three to Washington. Bohlen was furious. When Acheson said "secret" he meant secret. In fact, he meant "top secret." The memos were reclassified, called back and destroyed.

But nothing happened. Jessup, named an Ambassador at Large, was transferred to Washington. Meanwhile, the airlift was breaking records again, delivering 152,240 tons in the twenty-eight days of February, an average of 5,437 tons per day.

CHAPTER 11

"A Big Hock Shop"

March 12, 1949

**"NOW THERE'S ANOTHER DIFFERENCE,
YOU GUYS EAT 'EM, WE USE 'EM FOR POKER."**

"THE MOST EXTRAORDINARY THING ABOUT THE AIRLIFT today is that it is no longer extraordinary," wrote *New York Times* columnist Anne O'Hare McCormick on March 4, 1949. "It is taken for granted by the population and occupying forces that it can be continued indefinitely if necessary. Each month proves that it can be stepped up so that next year more coal can be delivered and more power developed for work-making industries. The tension of the early months of the blockade is relaxed, first, because of the growing assurance that the lifeline cannot be broken without war, and, second, because the continuance of the siege without incident makes war appear less probable."

But she added: "That the abnormal is accepted as normal does not make it so, however. Berlin is a fantastic place, in outward aspect and internal strain, the perfect symbol of the deadlock that paralyzes the world. The energy of the Western sector is largely spent holding the line. Berlin stands but obviously it cannot move ahead."

There was a brief confrontation between the Americans and the Soviets in early March, a face-off played up in the American press back home. The Soviets ordered U.S. Army search and registration teams, looking for the remains of soldiers killed during the war, out of the eastern zone, calling them spies. In retaliation, the Americans ordered an eight-man Soviet repatriations mission to leave Frankfurt in the American Zone. The Russians refused to leave, as Clay reported to Washington:

> We did not desire to force entry into the house so we advised [Soviet] Chief of Mission that he could leave house only to return to the Soviet Zone. He refused so we cut off facilities [water, gas and electricity] to house, placed guards and await the departure . . . What is the criticism? . . . We can get them out in five minutes but there could be shooting.
>
> I cannot run this job to please the press. I can carry out orders and if Department of Army does not like my methods, it has only to order its own. If you want us to invite them [the Russians] to dinner, say so. But don't temporize. Either let us force them out

or invite them in. Otherwise, we are laughing stock ... I suppose I don't understand Russians after four years but I do not wonder because I can't understand Americans after 52 years. Please send orders which I will carry out.

No orders came. The eight Soviets left the next day, March 4, without escort or incident.

For all their bravery and determination, the British, impoverished by war damage, simply did not have the resources of the Americans. Mighty Great Britain was broke. In the spring of 1947, the Truman Doctrine was declared after Britain informed Washington it could no longer aid the government of Greece in its battle against communist insurgents. Said Truman on March 12, 1947: "We are the only country to provide that help. . . . It must be the policy of the United States to support free peoples who are resisting attempted subjugation." When the new Labour Prime Minister, Clement Attlee, visited airlift bases on a rainy and windy March 4, the first thing he noticed was that American planes, with nose wheels, landed relatively smoothly, while British planes and C-47s with only tail wheels or tail skids wandered all over the runways as they landed in strong crosswinds. "Why don't we have nose wheels?" he snapped at an RAF officer at Gatow. The reason was that the British planes were just older, but the RAF man, who knew his way around, said, "We'll look into that right away, Prime Minister." That satisfied Attlee, who came home to call the airlift "one of the wonders of the world."

And then there was the indomitable Ernest Bevin, all 250 pounds of him, still recovering from another heart attack, escorted to British and American bases by Tunner. Showing off American equipment, Tunner asked the Foreign Minister if he wanted to see the new American C-97, the military version of the double-decked Boeing Stratocruiser, which, like the C-74, was used to fly heavy equipment from the United States to Rhein-Main. Bevin insisted on climbing the ladder hanging from the cockpit and squeezing through a three-foot hatch. For some reason, the young American opening the hatch and leaning forward to help Bevin had dozens of coins in a shirt pocket and they showered the Foreign Minister as he pulled his way up. The flustered airman reached for the coin shower, letting go of the hatch cover, which fell on Bevin's head. Bevin rubbed his head and laughed at the whole thing. He got even, a bit, when Tunner said he wanted to show him some "organizational charts."

"Organizational?" said the Foreign Minister. "What kind of word is that, 'organizational'? There is no such word in the English language. You Americans made it up."

The average cargo delivered to the three Berlin airports by the Americans and the British reached 6,328 tons per day at the beginning of March—more than had been coming into the city by railroad and canal before the airlift began. New lighting systems, including bright devices called "strobe lights," which flashed and streaked along from tower to tower almost pulling planes to the landing strip, were operating at Tempelhof, Gatow and Tegel. New paper bags, costing less than a penny per trip, were developed to carry coal.*

But planes were still wearing out. On March 4, on a flight over Soviet-occupied territory in eastern Germany, from Wiesbaden to Berlin, the right wing of a C-54 piloted by Lieutenant Royce Stephens of San Antonio, Texas, burst into flames. Four men, including two traffic controllers hitching a ride, bailed out, but Stephens didn't make it and died in the crash near the town of Langensalza. The four

---

* The surplus duffel bags lasted between fifteen and twenty flights before they needed repair. The repair work, it turned out, was being secretly done by an East German company until the Soviets discovered the work and closed that factory. In March 1949, the bags, which cost $3.80 each, were replaced by sturdy paper sacks costing only thirty cents apiece.

survivors were taken to a Russian hospital and then turned over to Americans in Berlin. On March 11, a German policeman named Kurt Zulsdorf was killed in the fog and dark when he walked into the propeller of an RAF York transport at Gatow. There were two more crashes during the month—nine British airmen were killed in just seven days between March 15 and March 22. Even so, the airlift had defeated General Winter—and more and more industries in East Berlin and East Germany were shutting down because of a lack of supplies and materials kept out by the Allied counterblockade. With negotiations in Washington, London and Paris concluding agreements which would establish a separate West Germany, a new country of 45 million people, and a North Atlantic Treaty Organization, originally called the "Atlantic Pact," a military and economic alliance including all the countries of Western Europe, Moscow was becoming almost as isolated as West Berlin. The rumors that Stalin was looking for some way to end the blockade were now coming from Moscow rather than Berlin.

It was on March 14 that Philip Jessup, now in Washington, received the telephone call from Jacob Malik asking him to stop by at the Soviet Mission to the United Nations the next time he was in New York. Jessup was on the first plane the next day, March 15, going straight from La Guardia Airport to the Soviet Mission, a mansion at the corner of Sixty-eighth Street and Park Avenue. Malik was waiting for him with an interpreter. They exchanged small talk about health. The Russian complained of lumbago. The America had burned his hand putting out a stove-top fire. Then Malik read slowly from a typed sheet: Stalin's decision not to mention currency reform, said the interpreter, was "not accidental."

There was nothing casual about the meeting. Jessup reported back to the State Department: "The Soviet interpreter had the translation of this formal message already typed out in English and read it off." In the prepared statement, Malik also said that currency reform could be discussed at the Foreign Minister level, at the four-power conference already being planned in Paris. Jessup than asked whether that meant the blockade of Berlin would be lifted after the conference. Malik said he had no instructions about that.

"Why don't you ask?" said Jessup, who then returned to Washington to report to Charles Bohlen, heading the small "working group" on the blockade negotiations—if they were actually negotiations. On the same day in Berlin, Soviet soldiers were building concrete and steel barricades across streets at the border between the eastern and western sectors of the city. The CIA, which had many sources among East German policemen, had already warned Washington that would happen:

> The complete sealing of Soviet sector streets leading into the western sectors is to be carried out soon. With the exception of a few main thoroughfares, the streets will be closed with wooden barriers. Traffic through the streets still open will be closely checked by foot patrols. Vehicles attempting to pass from the Soviet sector to the western sectors without a proper police permit are to be summarily confiscated . . . On the U-Bahn and S-Bahn, police are under instructions to confiscate all packages larger than briefcases. There is no legal basis for such confiscation . . . The police met with scattered resistance from outraged passengers. Railroad personnel showed passive resistance and in many cases, gave passengers warning or concealed parcels.

All that turned out to be just another futile attempt to stop goods being smuggled into West Berlin from the east. The official American estimate of the black market trade was that it was adding two hundred calories a day to the food rations in West Berlin. And in East Berlin, officials tried again. Policemen received these orders the same week: "Absolutely all vehicles are to be checked in addition to trucks and their trailers and horse-drawn vehicles, also cars and handcarts. The inspection should not be conducted in a superficial fashion. It must include the trunks of cars. With trucks, special attention must be paid to the possibility of a false bottom in the loading area and to any other hollow spaces that could be used as hiding places."

Even with smuggled food sometimes available, there were few feasts in Berlin. *Der Telegraph*, in the western zone, featured airlift recipes: jam made from rotten apples, black bread fried in candle grease, pancakes cooked in machine oil.

The black market in Berlin was making a lot of people rich, and many of those people were Americans. The Associated Press sent one of its front-line feature writers, Hal Boyle, to write about that. His story, which moved on the wire on March 12, was headlined:

P.S.—BERLIN'S A BIG HOCK SHOP
Americans—and Their Wives—Making a Fast Buck

Boyle's story was written as a letter from an ex-GI who had stayed in Berlin to a buddy who had gone back to the States and was having a hard time:

Didn't I say you was a jerk ever to leave Germany? I'm working for military government here in Berlin, and bunked up with two guys in an eight-room house a Nazi used to own. It costs us $30-a-month each and that takes care of the furniture, a housekeeper and a fireman . . .

All the guys who got out of uniform didn't get out of the black market, Joe. It ain't as crowded as it was, but there are still plenty of sharp elbows between me and a fast dollar. Some of the elbows belong to American wives here. They bought up all the fine furniture, antiques and Meissen china in Berlin with cigarettes . . . Those biddies really plundered Berlin.

A lot of the boys are buying diamonds now—the last things left to the Kraut fraus. Boy, do they hate to turn loose from their sparklers, but they need the grub more. Here's one that will bring a laugh. One officer's wife tried to send to the States seven concert grand pianos . . .

There was another trick Americans played in the early months of the occupation. Identical "Occupation Marks"—"scrip" rather than currency—were issued to the soldiers of all four of the occupying powers in 1946, which allowed capitalist American soldiers to sell cigarettes or watches to communist Soviet troopers at exorbitant prices, say five Occupation Marks for a nickel pack of Lucky Strikes—and then cash the five Occupation Marks they received to U.S. Army paymasters for five dollars to be sent home to their families. Before higher-ups caught on, more than $200 million had been shipped stateside. As Gerhard Rietdorff learned the hard way, there were Americans who cheated, stuffing paper into empty cigarette cartons, exchanging them for marks and then racing away in their jeeps, laughing.

And there were Americans who were incorruptible. Corporal Joe Trent, who supervised loaders at Celle, was a regular at a hotel bar in Hannover. There came a day when a German in a new suit and tie sat next to him and said he would give Trent a Volkswagen for a thousand pounds of sugar. He figured the guy was making bootleg schnapps and told him to get lost. First Lieutenant Albert Lowe of Bergoo, West Virginia, had piloted fifty B-24 bombing missions over Berlin when he was called back up, and in December 1948 flew the first of his 267 Vittles missions. One day he climbed into his C-54 and saw a well-dressed couple inside the plane. The man took out a stack of American currency and offered Lowe ten thousand dollars if he would let them ride along to western Germany. His answer: "Get the hell off my airplane." Another pilot took the couple—and ended up being court-martialed for smuggling.

• • •

In March, Clay repeated one more time that he wanted to retire from the Army as soon as possible, but that he knew he could not leave while Berlin was under siege. What he did not know was that Moscow and Washington were talking through Jessup and Malik. Only a dozen or so Americans, all in the State Department or White House, knew what was happening—and they were still not convinced the Soviets were serious. One who knew was Clay's political advisor, Robert Murphy, and he was ordered by his State Department superiors not to tell the military governor. Secretary of the Army Kenneth Royall did not know, either. In fact, that same week Royall sent a secret memo to Acheson, recommending that the Allies withdraw from the city when a West German government was established and a western city, Bonn, would be named as the new capital of a federal republic. Saying that the airlift could not continue indefinitely, Royall concluded by bringing up Clay's old proposal of sending an armed convoy down the 110 miles of Autobahn from West Germany into Berlin: "If we are to remain in Berlin, consideration should be given to establishing a land route there even at the risk of an untoward incident."

Clay, too, was a man who had secrets or secret agendas. On September 28, 1948, six months before, he had cabled, again "Top Secret," the Department of the Army: "Request authority to proceed with British and French agreement at early date to make Western currency sole legal currency in Western sectors. This is essential to protect our position in case Soviets split city politically."

He was authorized then to try to reach an agreement with the British and French. That took almost six months. The British were skeptical and the French adamant, both preferring a separate Berlin currency controlled by the four occupying powers to end the confusion and economic chaos caused by Westmarks and Eastmarks of, officially, equal value—although on the street and in shops a Westmark was worth five Eastmarks. Then Reuter's visit to London and discussions with Bevin in February changed the situation, as Clay reported to Washington: "London's views have changed. British now express their readiness to make West currency legal tender in Berlin. This is a real step forward."

Indeed it was. Reuter had persuaded Bevin that currency change-over "means the definitive recognition that [West] Berlin belongs to the West." It took another month to persuade the French—just as it had taken months to get the French to join the United States and Britain in the June 20, 1948, currency reform that was a factor in triggering the Soviet blockade. In that one, Clay and Robertson had bluntly told the French commander, General Koenig: "Too bad. You stop the banks in your zone from taking the new currency. We're going ahead. Period."

Koenig reported back to Paris. A midnight session of the French National Assembly was called, and they voted to accept that currency reform for the three zones of West Germany.

Now, six months and one airlift later, the French finally agreed to the exclusive use of Westmarks in the three Allied sectors of Berlin. On March 17, without seeking new authorization from his superiors at the Pentagon or anyone else in Washington, Clay sent a top-secret cable to the Department of the Army, which began:

> Joint press release on currency change-over now fixed at 1800 hours Berlin time 20 March 1949 ... The United States, the United Kingdom and French military governors after consulting with the responsible German authorities in Frankfurt and Berlin, and in response to the unanimous resolution of the City Assembly on 4 November 1948, have today decided that from March 20th the Eastmark shall cease to be the sole legal currency in Western sectors of Berlin ... A copy of the release will be sent to Soviet headquarters just before it is made public.

"The Third Ordinance for Monetary Reform," as it was called, was another complicated piece of business, but its major provision was that Eastmarks would not be accepted for rent or food. With each Westmark worth roughly five Eastmarks, the ordinance ruled that persons working and receiving rations in the western sector would be paid in Westmarks. Men and women who lived in the west but worked in the east could exchange 60 percent of their Eastmark wages for Westmarks, and those working and drawing rations in the east could exchange 30 percent of their Eastmark wages. Berliners who lived in the east and worked in the west would receive 10 percent of their pay in Westmarks. With the 5-to-1 exchange rate, westerners were given a tremendous financial advantage over their eastern brethren—as West Berlin became, economically, part of West Germany.

Berlin was now two cities, first politically and now economically. And Germany itself was effectively split into two countries as well.

On March 21, the day after the Westmark was established as the official currency of West Berlin, Malik called Jessup again. He told the American that if a definite date was set for the foreign ministers meeting, the blockade could be ended before the conference. But he also added that the Soviets wanted to be sure that the creation of a West German state would not be announced before the Paris conference. It was Jessup's turn to say he had no instructions on the matter, though he knew that weeks of preparation would be necessary before the establishment of what would officially be the Federal Republic of Germany—and be called West Germany.

Acheson ignored Royall's memo and the idea of sending a convoy down the Autobahn. Even Clay now had doubts, teletyping the Pentagon that he thought a convoy had a 3-to-1 chance to succeed with combat, but that even had his old plan worked, the railroads and canals would still be blocked. Jessup's memorandum of his frustrating talks with Malik made its way to President Truman's desk in late March, and the President authorized Jessup to reveal what had been said during the talks to the British and French ambassadors to the United Nations. The British Foreign Office was not pleased at all when the message reached it that night, telling Bevin in a cover note, "This is a decidedly amateur way of doing business with the Russians." But Bevin, an amateur himself, thought it was worth a try. He was due to arrive in Washington in a few days for conferences with Acheson and Schuman and told the professionals to wait for his return. "Watch this," Bevin scrawled on the memo from New York. "Stalin may now raise the blockade." At the same time, President Truman signed off on continuing the clumsy dialogue with the Soviets—and to keeping them secret from the professionals in the U.S. military, beginning with Clay.

Clay sensed that something was happening, not in Washington but in Moscow. On March 29, he learned that Marshal Sokolovsky, his Russian counterpart and onetime friend, was being recalled to the Soviet capital to become Deputy Defense Minister, presumably a promotion. But Clay thought it might also mean Soviet policy was shifting. He became even more convinced when Sokolovsky's departure was followed by a formal letter from his successor, General of the Army Vasily Chuykov, the commander of Red Army forces during the Battle of Berlin: "Dear General Clay: I have the honor to inform you that V. D. Sokolovsky has been assigned to a new post . . . I have assumed the duties of Commander and Chief of the group of Soviet forces in Germany and Chief of the Soviet Military Administration in Germany. Sincerely, V. I. Chuykov."

That kind of diplomatic nicety from the Russians was so surprising that Clay immediately sent a "Confidential" cable to Washington saying: "Soviet courtesy of this type is so unusual that I attach significance to it as a possible preliminary move to a settlement which would be intended to prevent West German government."

There was, of course, more going on than Clay knew. On April 1, the British and French foreign ministers, Bevin and Schuman, arrived in Washington to sign the agreements for the signing of the new North Atlantic Treaty, creating NATO, the North Atlantic Treaty Organization. Then Bevin and Schuman were briefed extensively by Secretary of State Acheson on the Jessup-Malik talks and agreed that the American ambassador-at-large could tell the Soviet ambassador that he had authority to negotiate in the name of all three Allied governments. On April 4, the two foreign ministers and Acheson, along with representatives of nine other countries— Belgium, Canada, Denmark, Iceland, Italy, Luxembourg, the Netherlands, Norway and Portugal—signed the documents creating NATO, beginning with this introduction:

> The Parties to this Treaty reaffirm [that they] are determined to safeguard the freedom, common heritage and civilisation of their peoples, founded on the principles of democracy, individual liberty and the rule of law. They seek to promote stability and well-being in the North Atlantic area . . . They are resolved to unite their efforts for collective defence and for the preservation of peace and security.

The thirteen articles of the treaty pledged economic cooperation, joint military action and provisions for the addition of countries other than the original signatories:

> The Parties will contribute toward the further development of peaceful and friendly international relations by strengthening their free institutions, by bringing about a better understanding of the principles upon which these institutions are founded, and by promoting conditions of stability and well-being. They will seek to eliminate conflict in their international economic policies and will encourage economic collaboration between any or all of them.
>
> In order to more effectively achieve the objectives of this Treaty, the Parties, separately and jointly, by means of continuous

and effective self-help and mutual aid, will maintain and develop their individual and collective capacity to resist armed attack . . .

And then the most important provision:

The Parties agree that an armed attack against one or more of them in Europe or North America shall be considered an attack against them all and consequently they agree that, if such an armed attack occurs, each of them, in exercise of the right of individual or collective self-defence recognised by Article 51 of the Charter of the United Nations, will assist the Party or Parties so attacked by taking forthwith, individually and in concert with the other Parties, such action as it deems necessary, including the use of armed force . . .*

    The Parties may, by unanimous agreement, invite any other European State in a position to further the principles of this Treaty and to contribute to the security of the North Atlantic area to accede to this Treaty . . .

So, four years after they were Allies in a world war, the Western powers had drawn the lines of what would be called the "Cold War."

---

* The definition of "armed attack" was specified "on the territory of any of the Parties in Europe or North America, on the Algerian Departments of France, on the territory of or on the Islands under the jurisdiction of any of the Parties in the North Atlantic area north of the Tropic of Cancer; on the forces, vessels, or aircraft of any of the Parties, when in or over these territories or any other area in Europe in which occupation forces of any of the Parties were stationed on the date when the Treaty entered into force or the Mediterranean Sea or the North Atlantic area north of the Tropic of Cancer."

CHAPTER 12

"Here Comes a Yankee"

April 16, 1949

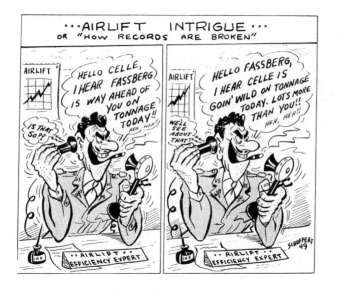

D IE *NEUE ZEITUNG,* ONE OF THE AMERICAN-FINANCED
newspapers in western Berlin, reported on its front page
on April 1 that it had been authorized to break the secrecy
around the construction of an underground railroad tunnel from

western Germany more than 120 miles into western Berlin: "The biggest project of the post-war era, probably the most gigantic project of all time, has been finished under the most difficult conditions in the strictest secrecy . . . The blockade of West Berlin has been broken. The subterranean bridge is working. On Friday morning at 0.600 hours, the first train left . . . Prominent members of the Western military governments, the chief, and a special reporter of *Die Neue Zeitung* participated in the first ride . . ."

The reporter asked the chief engineer, identified as S. H. Monzens of Detroit, Michigan, what would happen if the Soviets bored into the tunnel. That would be a serious hostile action that could lead to war, Monzens answered. He added: "It has not been forbidden by the Potsdam Agreements to build a tunnel through another zone. If the Russians wanted to build a tunnel from Moscow to Calais, we definitely wouldn't interefere with them."

"A great day, April the First!" the story concluded. April Fool!

Meeting in Washington during the first days of April, Acheson, Bevin and Schuman drafted a joint proposal for ending the Allied counter-blockade and for ending the Soviet blockade. On April 5, Jessup went to New York again to read that position paper to Malik:

1. Reciprocal and simultaneous lifting of the restrictions imposed by the Soviet Union since March 1, 1948 [the first day Soviet troops had stopped and boarded an Allied train headed for Berlin], on communications, transportation and trade between Berlin and the Western Zones of Germany and the restrictions imposed by the three powers on communications, transportation and trade to and from the Eastern Zone of Germany.

2. The fixing of a date to be determined for a meeting of the Council of Foreign Ministers.

• • •

Two days later, April 7, was a momentous one for both West Germany and western Berlin. In Washington, Secretary of State Acheson and foreign ministers Bevin and Schuman issued a joint communiqué making it official and public that the Allies intended to end military government of their occupied zones in West Germany and join with the German Parliamentary Council in Bonn to create an autonomous—not independent, but autonomous—"German Federal Republic," with Bonn as its capital. The West German parliamentarians, of many parties, were delegated to write a "Basic Law," a constitution of their own.

Under the title "Principles governing exercise of powers and responsibilities of US-UK-French Governments following the establishment of German Federal Republic," the three signers declared in part: "Generally speaking, the German Federal Republic shall be at liberty to take administrative and legislative action, and such action will have validity if not vetoed by the Allied authority. This means that military government will disappear and that the function of the Allies shall be mainly supervisory."

Berlin was not mentioned in the communiqué, to the great disappointment of politicians in West Berlin, beginning with Mayor Reuter, who had hopes that the Allies and the West German Parliamentary Council would announce that the city would be the twelfth *land* (state) of the Federal Republic. Still, on that same day, Reuter reported on his visits, by invitation, to the capitals of the three Allies, Paris, London and Washington. Particularly in England and the United States, he was treated as a hero in a three-week tour of major cities. And he was convinced for the first time that the Americans would not back down on Berlin and, in fact, would go it alone if necessary. He gave an enthusiastic report to the West Berlin Assembly that day, reporting among other things that the House Appropriations Committee had voted the day before in Washington to provide $43 million in new funding for the airlift, added to the more than $300 million provided up to then, most of it from the budget of the Air Force. With other funding the United States had spent at least $300 million to keep the planes flying since June. Reuter's report was summarized in the annual report of the Magistrat: "The visit to the United States publicly demonstrated that Berlin in the meantime had become a symbol of the will to freedom for the whole world. The warm and enthusiastic reception which was given the city's officials in Washington, New York and many other cities constituted a recognition of the behavior of the German population. This recognition could not have been shown more impressively."

Willy Brandt was even more direct in reporting on his conversations with Reuter and Allied officials after the trip in a flurry of reports marked "Highly Confidential" to SPD officials in West Germany on April 9:

> We did not need to worry that the Americans would abandon us in case the Russians changed their policy. When this topic was discussed in Washington, Reuter was interrupted by the comment that it was out of the question that there would be a return to the past . . . It seems the Russians have become insecure and are looking for a way to lift the blockade . . .
>
> It is possible that the Soviets want to gain time which is understandable with regard to the upcoming creation of the Atlantic Treaty. The Russians also want to negotiate about the entire German problem.

Brandt offered the opinion that an agreement between the four World War II Allies was now impossible and then repeated a bit of his February 1 report: "Sovereignty has to be assumed by the German populace . . . The Germans have to declare their interests . . . An alternative is the maintenance of the border that runs through Germany and the recognition of an Eastern and Western state. This would entail an equal political division of Berlin. . . . Even Moscow must realize this."

There was no doubt Moscow realized that the blockade was not only failing but had been a major factor in Allied determination to transform West Germany from an occupied territory into a separate state. Germany would now officially, as well as effectively, be divided into two countries, with Berlin a jointly occupied disputed territory in the middle of one side. Ironically, the Allies worried that the Soviets would react to the Washington communiqué by immediately lifting the blockade and appealing for a single, united Germany in an attempt to confuse and stall the ongoing debates about the Basic Law in Bonn and in the three Western capitals. "Such a move is expected by a number of top [American] officials," reported Drew Middleton in the *New York Times* on April 9. "These officials realize that the blockade, which long ago ceased to be a menace, is one of the factors that has impelled German opinion toward a West German state and that its removal might bring about a re-examination of the entire question of unity versus partition by the Germans."

One indicator of the political impact of the blockade and airlift was the positive reaction to the Washington communiqué by Dr. Konrad Adenauer, the anti-Nazi mayor of Cologne before the war, who was president of the Parliamentary Council and leader of the Christian Democratic Union, the dominant conservative party in West Germany. The *New York Times* reported that the Christian Democratic leader was now pledging to push forward passage of the Basic Law as quickly as possible. Two weeks before the blockade began, on June 10, 1948, Adenauer had reacted to the so-called London Recommendations—the original Allied draft proposal for joint governance of a West German state—by saying: "Germans have no choice but to oppose these Allied Recommendations to preserve our honor before posterity."

The events of the past ten months had transformed both the

victors and the vanquished. The determination of the Americans and the British and the bravery of West Berliners produced statements like these, the first from a Christian Democratic parliamentarian, the second from Social Democratic Party national headquarters in Hannover:

> Yesterday and today there have been many justified, but harsh, words said in criticism of military government . . . I believe it is necessary that a friendly word as well be said to the Allied powers, and that it may be formulated as follows: "We recognize, and we are happy, that the attempt of Russia to conquer Berlin has been thwarted by your resistance—we hope forever."

> We must show the Berliners that we comprehend the importance of their struggle. But we must also make it clear that the Western powers, by their actions in Berlin are defending the interests of all Germans. For we should not forget that Berlin's fate is also ours.

Willy Brandt's reports on April 9 also included a "Strictly Confidential" assessment of the mood of General Clay:

> General Clay has asked a few diplomats to his office to explain to them that he continued to believe that a division of Berlin was the best solution. Last summer, the French were in favor of abandoning Berlin, while the British were uncertain. Even in Washington, the question was controversial. It seems to me that Clay wants to outline his role during the Berlin crisis, as it will appear in diplomatic records. Clay allegedly said he supported a preemptive war against the Soviet Union. Such a war would be decided by the Air Force and would entail extensive destruction of Europe.

If Clay said that, it may have been an angry reaction to the news, told to him by his British counterpart, General Robertson, of the Jessup-Malik conversations—kept secret from him by both the State Department and the White House. On April 12, Secretary of State Acheson had suggested to President Truman that he inform the Chairman of the Joint Chiefs, Omar Bradley, and Clay of what was happening. But Truman, worried about leaks, waited a week before he told his generals. In the third week of April, even as Washington and Moscow were preparing statements on the end of the blockade and rumors, Clay was not officially informed. Newspapers, at least officially, knew more than the European commander. Rumors and reports of a settlement were beginning to appear in American and British newspapers, including the *New York Times*, which reported the diplomatic gossip on its front page of April 17, under the headline:

EAST AGAIN SEEKS
FREEDOM OF TRADE
IN GERMAN ZONES

Soviet Believed by Many to
Be Looking for Excuse to
Lift Berlin Blockade

No one in the military of either the United States or the Soviet Union officially knew of the negotiations going on at the United Nations and in Washington and Moscow. The Allies just kept flying, bringing into Berlin's three airports an average of more than 6,300 tons a day—a total of 197,160 tons for the month. Ground controllers at Tempelhof were landing a plane every three or four minutes, and the turnaround time for C-54s—landing, unloading and getting back into the air—was as low as fifteen minutes. Another new tonnage record was set on April 11, when British and American planes brought in 8,246 tons. The Navy, which used only its own mechanics and maintenance crews, announced that its planes were operating at 155 percent efficiency, spending 12.2 hours of each twenty-four hours in the air, compared to nine hours for Air Force transports.

By April, the number of incidents between Russian planes and Allied transports had passed seven hundred, even though pilots often did not bother filing the harassment reports because that would just mean more debriefing and paperwork. One of the incidents that was never reported involved Peter Izard, the young RAF corporal whose job was supervising loaders but who grabbed every chance he could to fly. On a mission from Wunstorf to Gatow in a Handley Page Halton, a four-engine bomber converted to transport work, Izard was sitting in the jump seat behind the copilot when a Yak buzzed them again and again, coming so close that the British pilot was forced to bring his starboard wing almost to the vertical. "What the hell," the pilot said, and kept going into a slow 360-degree barrel roll—an amazing aerobatic feat for a plane weighing more than forty tons. When the Halton was upside down, Izard's seat broke loose and he was flying in space with cigarette packs and everything else not bolted down.

One report that was filed was by a Navy pilot, Ensign Bernard Smith, who counted twenty-two Yaks on his tail one clear night. RAF Squadron Leader David Bevan-John was in the copilot's seat instructing a pilot making his first run into Gatow when there was an explosion beside the plane and the sky turned green. "Jesus, that's flak," he said, grabbing the controls from the new guy, who had wandered out of the corridor and over a Soviet air base, drawing bursts of anti-aircraft fire.

On the American side, Lieutenant Charles Allen became the only pilot whose plane was hit by Russian fire, at least as recorded officially. Though it was probably an accident, a Soviet ground-to-air missile scraped across his nose two feet from the front landing gear door, causing relatively little damage to anything except the nerves of Allen and his crew.

Noah Thompson, the Vermont farmer, may also have been hit. Flying 2571, a C-54 with a history of problems from Gatow back to Fassberg one bright midnight, there was a tremendous explosion behind him. "We're going down," he thought, but he couldn't see anything unusual in the air or on the ground and all the instruments seemed to show normal readings. He sent his flight engineer, Paul Bradshaw, back to look.

"The whole floor is blown apart back there," Bradshaw reported. "I think it's over the hydraulic accumulator"—the reservoir for the fluid that controlled a range of functions. "It looks like it might have blown up." Checking again, Thompson saw that the hydraulic pressure was zero—that meant no flaps, no brakes, no steering. The landing gear, however, normally powered hydraulically, had a backup: the wheels could be lowered by a hand crank, which was what Bradshaw was doing as Tex Newcombe, the copilot, called to the Fassberg tower: "Hydraulic fluid all over the place, we don't know what else. Have the fire truck, crash wagon and ambulance stand by."

Thompson came in nose-high, hoping the dragging tail would slow the plane on the short (six thousand feet) runway and that he could steer by revving and slowing the engines on both sides.

"Tex," Thompson yelled, "pull the emergency air brake lever." But Newcombe and Hawkins together could not move the thing; the plane was going to roll until it hit something. Thompson let go of the useless steering column and grabbed the emergency brake on his side. He pulled with all his might and it worked, throwing the three of them against the windshield as the wheels locked. C-54 2571 stopped two feet from the airfield's fence.

By then, American pilots, called up from civilian jobs, included the chief pilots of both United Airlines and American Airlines. The former chief pilot of Trans World Airways, D. M. Tomlinson, who had been recalled to service as an Air Force captain, a deputy to Tunner, told the *Task Force Times:*

I go out to Wiesbaden or Rhein-Main bases just for the pleasure
of seeing these youngsters perform . . . I doubt if ever in history
there has been such sustained precision flying as these crews are
doing here. When we came in and set up the task force, I would
have sworn, for instance, that you could not make ground-
controlled landings at intervals better than twenty minutes apart.
I had to be shown. They showed me. Day after day they bring
them in at three-minute intervals, and it's a magnificent job of flying and a magnificent job of communications work that makes it
possible . . . The aviation earnings from this job will be enormous
even years from now. We have about 600 flying crews, and every
one of those crews could form a cadre around which you could set
up an instrument flight training program. They've certainly
opened up my eyes.

Extraordinary piloting was ordinary on the airlift. If anything
could go wrong it usually did. Lieutenant Joseph Lauter, flying from
Fassberg, could hardly keep his C-54 level on a night flight to Tempelhof. For more than an hour he muscled the plane along, using ai-
lerons to stay level and land in Berlin. The problem, a common one,
was too much gasoline, meaning too much weight—and in this case
all the extra gas, two hundred gallons of it, were in the left wing tanks,
so the plane kept trying to drop off in that direction.

But for Bill Tunner, it was all going too well. By the beginning of
April, he had 225 American C-54s and 154 assorted British planes.
There were 75 more in maintenance sheds or at Great Falls. "Willy-
the-Whip" thought his men were settling in, becoming too compla-
cent with no real enemy now that the weather was improving. His
answer, as usual, was competition. One of the first things he had done
as commander of the task force was to break up the planes he had into
squadrons—and then pit squadron against squadron, airfield against

airfield, particularly Celle versus Fassberg, the two RAF bases, only twenty-five miles apart.

So, Tunner's staff came up with "The Easter Parade," an Easter present for the people of Berlin. The idea was to whip up the troops and use every plane and every trick in the book to deliver record tonnage from noon on Saturday, April 15, to noon on Easter Sunday, April 16. The plan was a secret, but it got to General Joseph Cannon's office; the general himself was in the United States, not coincidentally, which gave Tunner the freedom to plan the day.

Tunner was everywhere that day, cheering and goading. Life imitated art, or at least imitated Jake Schuffert's cartoons. The sergeant caricatured the general's style in adjoining panels under the headline: AIRLIFT INTRIGUE or "How Records Are Broken." The first panel showed an officer shouting into a telephone: "Hello, Celle, I hear Fassberg is way ahead of you on tonnage today!! Heh Heh!!" The second showed the same officer shouting: "Hello, Fassberg, I hear Celle is goin' wild on tonnage today. Lots more than you!! Heh, Heh!!" On the morning of the 16th, Tunner visited Fassberg and walked the place with the base commander, Colonel Coulter, who was bragging about being 10 percent over his delivery quota, and said, "That's fine, Colonel, but of course it's not up to what they're doing over at Celle. They're really on the ball over there." Coulter's first reaction was to have a "Beat Celle" banner hung at the end of Fassberg's busiest runway. Then the general drove over to Celle and told his men there about the banner. In the middle of all that, Cannon's deputy, General Robert Douglas, called Tunner to say, "I don't want to discourage you, Bill, but even if you have a lot of tonnage but it drops off the next day, Joe's going to raise hell."

Tunner, who used the big-day strategy when he commanded the Hump runs from India to China in World War II, answered that he knew from experience that overall tonnage would be higher than before the parade. The exercise was in morale, not weight lifting.

At noon on Saturday, sergeants assigned to operations offices at each air base raced out to the big "Howgozit!" scoreboards and revised the daily quotas. The new numbers added up to ten thousand tons. That was the first time most crews figured out what had been happening the past few days as more and more coal was brought into the western fields by train and truck and all leaves were canceled. Looking at the board, Lieutenant Eugene Wiedle saw that his squadron's usual goal had been almost doubled to a thousand tons.

Desk officers suddenly appeared to do some flying. Major Albert Schneider, a squadron commander at Rhein-Main, looked out his office window and saw a C-54 pulling out of the takeoff line and heading for a parking dock. He sent out a man to find out why and the pilot said her engines were leaking too much oil. Schneider then ran out, told the pilot to get down and climbed in himself to fly the thing to Berlin.

Soon enough, a plane was landing or taking off in Berlin every 30.9 seconds. The sky was alive above the three airports and Germans gathered along the tracks of the Tempelhof U-Bahn station to watch. In the air, pilots were loving it. C-54 number 5555, which liked to call in as "Four Nickels," announced itself, "Here comes small change on the range." Number 77 called in, "Here comes seventy-seven, a bundle from heaven, with a cargo of coal for the daily goal." Another poet of the sky contributed: "Here comes a Yankee with a blackened soul, bound for Gatow with a load of coal."

Down on the field at Tempelhof, Ensign Bernard Smith watched in amazement as a landing C-54 cartwheeled off the runway and broke in half. As the crew ran for safety, a ten-ton truck filled with German workers pulled up to unload the coal aboard. General Clay called Tunner and said, "I don't know what you're doing, but keep it up." The Soviet representative in the Air Safety Center at Tempelhof—the Russians had exercised their right to be there throughout the airlift—rejected a protest over harassment by a Yak fighter by saying the planes were coming in so fast he could not understand the scopes and charts all around him.

The controllers did. The parade ended when someone ran out to the last plane with a bucket of red paint and sloppily wrote the score under the side window of the cockpit:

TONS: 12,941
FLIGHTS: 1,398

The total of coal delivered was the equivalent of the payload of six hundred fifty-car trains. And the daily airlift total after that never dropped below nine thousand tons. The loads were changing, too, as life in western Berlin became a bit more comfortable. On April 20, a C-54 brought in two hundred thousand seedlings to begin the remaking of the Tiergarten and other city parks. Two days later a C-74 brought in the components to build a new power plant. By then, in a five-day period, including the Easter Parade, the airlift delivered more tonnage than trains had before the blockade.

A week after the Easter Parade—and three days after Bradley and Clay were officially told of the Jessup-Malik negotiations—the *New York Times* and other American papers reported on April 21 that the United States had received "feelers" about lifting the blockade from Soviet diplomats at the United Nations. The next day, at his weekly news conference, President Truman denied that. There had been no "peace feelers," said the President, and he did not expect any. When reporters pressed him, citing reports that the United States was willing to resume four-power talks at a Conference of Foreign Ministers on the future of Germany, Truman declined to answer, saying there were too many "ifs" in the questions.

It was TASS that officially broke the story of the negotiation. On April 26, the Soviet news agency reported, according to the Associated Press:

> LONDON, TUESDAY, APRIL 26—Russia said today she would lift the blockade of Berlin if the Western powers would set a date for the Big Four Foreign Minister's meeting on Germany.
>
> In a statement datelined Moscow and distributed in London, Tass reported that Jacob A. Malik, the Soviet delegate to the United Nations Security Council had given Russia's view to Philip C. Jessup at Lake Success March 21.

The dispatch, which was transmitted around the world but not at home in the Soviet Union—Voice of America and Radio Free Europe broadcasts to the Soviet Union were jammed—listed only two conditions, basically a rewording of the secret Allied message of April 5. The Soviet communiqué, as translated by the Associated Press, read:

> 1. A Big Four Foreign Ministers council should meet to discuss a separate currency for Berlin, "together with other questions bearing on Germany."

> 2. If a date can be agreed for such a meeting "reciprocal restrictions on communications and trade could be lifted before the meeting."

TASS then released a fairly accurate account of the Malik-Jessup meetings, which had begun on February 15.

The *New York Times* headline, across three columns of the front page the next morning, April 27, read:

U.S. NOW SEES THE WAY CLEAR
TO END THE BERLIN BLOCKADE
AND RESUME PEACE PARLEYS

A smaller headline characterized the Soviet statement as "a surprise." The second paragraph of the *Times* story read: "The statement was made in a State Department communiqué, issued 24 hours after agreement had been reached on the formation of a West German federal republic, which the Soviet blockade was designed to prevent."

Another paragraph was ludicrous: "President Truman, who indicated that he knew nothing about any Soviet negotiations on ending the Berlin Blockade, finally got a report on those negotiations today from Dr. Jessup."

The next day Jessup traveled the familiar route from Washington to Park Avenue for another meeting with Malik. The talk inside was again over one detail after another. But there was a difference: when Jessup arrived, he found himself encircled by a crowd of dozens of reporters and photographers from around the world. The American was back on April 29 and so was the press. But all Jessup and Malik were doing was reading statements to each other from their superiors in Washington and Moscow. In fact, one of Malik's bosses, Deputy Foreign Minister Andrei Gromyko, was actually there. The ambassadors finally came out, but all they would say was that they had had a "satisfactory" talk. The next day Jessup was back again, this time accompanied by the British and French ambassadors to the United Nations, Lord Alexander Cadogan and Jean Chauvel.

Meanwhile, in Berlin, General Clay announced that he expected that the Western Germany Parliamentary Council would approve a constitution—the Basic Law—by April 15 and that the Federal Republic of Germany would come into being before the middle of July.

• • •

The Clay announcement came on the same day that the most important journalist in Washington, James Reston, the *New York Times* Washington bureau chief, wrote a long analysis of the events of the past months that obviously reflected the thinking and concerns of the State Department or at least of Secretary of State Acheson and his closest aides. It was a classic Washington tactic and story: a semiofficial message to our allies and adversaries under the headline:

U.S STAYS SKEPTICAL IN NEGOTIATING
WITH RUSSIA
Feeling Prevails That Offer to End Blockade Is a Maneuver Only

"Outwardly our officials will continue to assume the best Soviet motives as the President, Secretary of State Acheson and Dr. Jessup have done all week," wrote Reston. "But privately they are skeptical and assume the worst."

What the Russians are doing, some observers here believe, is merely seeking by a new tactic the same objectives they always had. All along they have sought to build up the eastern zone of Germany, which they control, and tear down the Western zones . . . For a long time, by employing bold and even ruthless diplomacy, the Russians succeeded in this policy fairly well. They gained control over eastern Germany. They gained, at Potsdam, a voice in Western Germany. They gained reparations for all Germany. They managed for a time to block the economic revival of Western Germany.

When this policy led to the coordination of United States and British zones and when we countered with the political organization of Western Germany, the European Recovery Plan [the Marshall Plan] and the North Atlantic Treaty, the Russians resorted to force in Berlin and merely succeeded in hastening the economic, political and military organization of the West.

> Now they appear to have a new tactic . . . seeking to negotiate
> us out of there by an interesting appeal to the German people . . .

Reston, or his sources, speculated that at the promised Council of Foreign Ministers meeting, the Soviets would propose to establish a single German government and the withdrawal of all foreign occupation forces from the country. Such a withdrawal would leave the Red Army on the eastern border of Germany while U.S. forces would be thousands of miles away. That, of course, was one reason the United States was pushing ahead so fast with the establishment of a new country, the Federal Republic of Germany, created by the Basic Law being negotiated in Bonn. As another American diplomat, quoted in a *Times* story by Drew Middleton, said, "If Germany is united as a result of the Council of Foreign Ministers, it will be a communist state within five years . . ."

CHAPTER 13

"We Are Alive!"

May 12, 1949

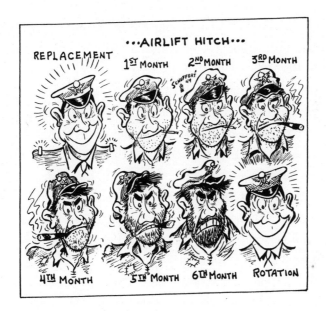

BERLIN BLOCKADE WILL END MAY 12

THE HEADLINE WAS IN LIGHTS, MOVING AROUND THE TOP OF the *New York Times* Building in Times Square on May 5, 1949.

In East Berlin the next day, the headline in *Neues Deutschland* read:

THE POLICY OF PEACE IS SUCCESSFUL . . .
GENERAL CLAY STRUCK DUMB

The official document both sides were commenting on was a single paragraph submitted to Trygve Lie, the Norwegian who was Secretary-General of the United Nations: "We, the representatives of France, the United Kingdom and the United States of America on the Security Council have the honor to request that you bring to the attention of the members of the Security Council the fact that our Governments have concluded an agreement with the Union of Soviet Socialist Republics providing for the lifting of the restrictions which have been imposed on communications, transportation and trade with Berlin."

On the Kurfürstendamm, the main shopping street of West Berlin, the news was coming from Rudolf-Günter Wagner, speaking through the loudspeaker on the fender of his RIAS jeep: "Agreement has been reached between the three Western powers and the Soviets regarding the raising of the Berlin Blockade and the holding of a meeting of the Council of Foreign Ministers. All communications, transportation and trade restrictions imposed by both sides . . . and between Berlin and the Eastern zones will be removed on May 12 . . ."

Not that anyone really heard him. The jeep could not move because the street was a lot more crowded than Times Square on New Year's Eve, and Berliners were cheering so loudly that all they could hear was themselves. Occasionally a group chanted: *"Hurra! Hurra! Wir leben Noch!"* "Hooray! Hooray! We are alive!"

A *Times* reporter, Sydney Gruson, telephoned the Operations Room at Tempelhof to get reaction from the Americans there. Lou Wagner, the private from New Jersey who used to test for ice on the runways by racing jeeps up and down the pierced metal planks, answered. "We're jumping up and down for joy. That's what we're doing," said Wagner, who had come in early. He had woken up at

4 A.M.—because there was not enough noise. Few planes were flying that early morning. "We've shown them what we can do," said another enlisted man. "They'll think twice about trying us out on this one again." The military policeman on guard outside the airport said, "This means better times. Better chow. And the chance to get the hell out of here."

Corporal Wagner, who kept a diary, wrote: "Ten hundred Zulu Time. Not one aircraft engine heard all day. This is it. Rotation at last. Goodbye, Berlin. *Es war Wunderbar!*"

Going out onto the streets, Gruson asked the first German he met, a policeman, what he thought and the man answered: "What can we be expected to think of after living for ten months under blockade? We want life to be a little easier. We want more light, we want more gas, and perhaps more than anything, an end to dehydrated potatoes."

The wording of the agreement was simplicity itself, only 171 words, including:

1. All the restrictions imposed since March 1, 1948, by the government of the Union of Soviet Socialist Republics on communication, transportation and trade between Berlin and the Western zones of Germany and between the Eastern Zone and the Western zones will be removed on May 12, 1949 . . .

2. All the restrictions imposed since March 1, 1948, by the governments of France, the United Kingdom and the United States, or any one of them . . . will also be removed . . .

3. . . . On May 23, 1949, a meeting of the Council of Foreign Ministers will be convened in Paris, to consider questions relating to Germany and problems arising out of the situation in Berlin . . .

• • •

Four days before the trains and trucks rolled, Johanna and Willi Last were married on May 8 in their local church. There was no heat, of course, and the bride wore a coat made from a horse blanket. The registrar performing the wedding wore a parka and his words came out like puffs of smoke through the hood. The wedding dinner was soup with a few carrots and potatoes. The worst thing during the blockade was eating in the dark. But, said the bride, that had advantages, too: "The next day you'd see there were worms in the potatoes. But, you know, it was meat for us."

Most of the men and women who battled the blockade of Berlin heard that it was over from each other. Sergeant Hugh Tosone, a chief mechanic at Rhein-Main, heard the news on the radio and rushed over to the plane his crew was working on and told them to knock off. "It's over," he said. "It's over."

But it wasn't, really, at least for many of the pilots, the aircrews and thousands of others who made up the airlift. Neither the Americans nor the British made announcements at the bases and airports in West Germany and West Berlin, because a decision had been made by Allied leaders to continue the airlift until October 31, 1949, so that supplies of food and fuel and industrial materials could be stockpiled in case the Soviets tried it again. The work went on; there was just less of it.

Lieutenant Edwin Gere heard the news after landing at Fassberg and he did what a lot of pilots did that day: grab a ride to Flynn's Inn, halfway between Fassberg and Celle, where they toasted each other, the airlift, the German workers and anybody or anything else that came to mind. It was *the* place, a grand old mansion, rumored to have been the hunting lodge of the chief of the Luftwaffe, Hermann

Göring, or just a very fancy whorehouse with its thirty bedrooms and acres of manicured gardens. The mansion had been appropriated by Captain N. C. Flynn, the housing officer at Fassberg, as an R&R—rest and recreation—center for officers. He set up a famous bar and a good dining room and rented out rooms at fifty cents a night. Men came to use the tennis courts, the bowling alleys and swimming pool. Some of them came to visit their wives, who had moved in upstairs, abandoning Air Force housing at an old resort, Bad Mergentheim, a beautiful place on a river, but almost two hundred miles from their husbands at Fassberg.

Bill Palahunich, the Ukrainian-speaking sergeant, was back in the United States, having dinner with his father, when they heard the news on the radio. "Great," he said. "But it will start someplace else."

"I'm glad you're home and safe," said his father, who had left the Ukraine at the age of sixteen. "But you're right. You can never trust a Russian. . . ."

Both Guy Dunn and Gail Halvorsen were in the air when the end was announced. Dunn was flying engines from Mobile to Rhein-Main and was told as he landed at Lajes Field in the Azores. Halvorsen, the "Candy Bomber," was flying from Brazil to Mobile. He heard the news when he landed and felt a surge of happiness. Then he went to the officers' club to celebrate, having two glasses of orange juice rather than his usual one.

"I'm gonna miss it," said Corky Colgrove. "I was having a hell of a good time."

A lot of the Germans supervised by men, or boys, like Colgrove, had some of the same feelings. "We were skeptical and we were worried about what we would do next," said Walter Riggers, the inspector at Fassberg. "I enjoyed working with the Americans. In fact, they asked me to work in the Philippines and said I could get American citizenship in five years. I would have done it, but there was this local girl . . ."

Gerhard Noack, the loader, said: "We were glad to have helped the Berliners, but our second thought was what would become of us." But then he was offered a job by the British at Celle. The same kind of thing happened to Kurt Dettmer. He had a friend who repaired typewriters at Rhein-Main and they were both offered jobs with an American contractor, IBM.

"We mechanics did not celebrate," said Günter Metzger. "We liked working there . . . But it was over."

On May 12, Soviet newspapers carried for the first time a TASS dispatch saying that the blockade had ended. The exact wording of the lead: "The Western Allies have issued orders to lift the Berlin Blockade."

At one minute after midnight on May 12, the lights went on again all over Berlin. The Soviets, exactly according to the negotiated settlement, had thrown the switches that reconnected western Berlin to the giant Klingenberg power station in the eastern sector. At the same moment, floodlights went on 105 miles to the east in Helmstedt, the border between the British and Soviet sectors. The long wooden barriers blocking the Autobahn to Berlin were lifted in the white glare of spotlights, as American radio correspondents—Charles Collingwood of CBS, Merrill Mueller of NBC and Martin Agronsky of ABC—broadcast live back to the United States. Soviet-controlled Radio Berlin made a single announcement: "At this moment, all traffic and trade restrictions between the Soviet Zone of Germany and the western zone and within Berlin imposed since January 1, 1948, are being lifted on the orders of the four occupation powers."

In Berlin, American First Lieutenant William Frost, holding a bouquet of lilacs handed to him by a young woman named Johanna

Kraapz, and his driver, Private Horace Scites, took off for Helmstedt as the lights went on. The first British car to leave Berlin, carrying Captain Allan Hutchinson of the Royal Horse Guards, was waved on by a smiling Russian guard at the British-Soviet checkpoint. Coming the other way, British trucks, loaded with fresh vegetables and fruit, the first one carrying a thousand pounds of cucumbers, roared to life and sped down the road to the old capital city. A gray Ford convertible, driven by a United Press correspondent, Walter Rundle, easily passed them and led the procession into Berlin, arriving at 1:46 A.M. As he stopped, the waiting crowd of Berliners, who had been literally dancing in the streets, surrounded the convertible and placed a wreath of roses around his neck. He noticed that lights in cafés and apartments were rapidly switching on and off; Berliners were happily playing with light switches, a commonplace luxury denied them for the past 324 days.

Then came the trucks into Berlin, decorated with the green of spring branches. The first train, carrying correspondents from newspapers and radio stations from around the world, left Helmstedt at 1:23 A.M., with nineteen others carrying coal, food and mail lined up behind it and draped in American, British and French flags. British soldiers aboard serenaded other passengers with "It's a Long Way to Tipperary!" It reached Berlin at 5:08 A.M.

"We heard on the radio the starting of the first train," Christa Ruffer wrote in her diary. "We danced and were so glad. There was food. I ate fish."

The City Assembly, the parliament of western Berlin, held a special session in Schöneberg City Hall. After a reading of the names of the seventy-nine men who had been killed in the airlift, Mayor Reuter said: "In our great demonstrations in the summer of the past year, we called on the world for help. The world heard our cry. We are happy to have here in our midst, as a guest, the man who together with his two colleagues took the initiative in organizing the airlift in the summer of last year. The memory of General Clay will never fade in Berlin. We know for what we have to thank this man . . . We will never forget what he has done for us."

A crowd of three hundred thousand Berliners were gathered as Reuter and Clay came out of the building on May 12 and declared a holiday in the city. The mayor said: "The blockade is ended. The attempt to force us to our knees has failed, frustrated by our steadfastness and firmness. It failed because the world heard our appeal and came to our assistance. It was frustrated because even though everything seemed against us and even though it took faith to move mountains for us to survive, we have finally won. Berlin will always remain Berlin."

He repeated what he had said inside: "The memory of this man will never fade in Berlin."

Clay responded: "The end of the blockade does not merely mean that trains and trucks are moving again. It has a deeper significance. The people of Berlin have earned their right to freedom and to be accepted by those who love freedom everywhere. The people of Berlin ranked with the American and British pilots who fed the city as the real heroes of the blockade."

Robert Lochner, Clay's translator, was stunned when he looked over at the man who had been compared to a Roman emperor. Lucius Clay was crying.

Standing behind his commander, Howley, the American city commandant, who had been promoted to brigadier general in January, turned to one of his staff and said, "This is their Valley Forge." At the same time, it was announced that Dr. Konrad Adenauer, the president of West Germany's Parliamentary Council, who had just been informed that the Allied military governors had approved the Basic Law, was promising that West Germany would always retain its ties to Berlin. Roars of "Bravo!" rose from the crowd. West Berliners knew that for much of the blockade, many in West Germany, afraid of war and alienated by Berlin's arrogance over the centuries, would have been just as happy if all of that city had been engulfed by the Soviets. That, after all, would have left West Germany as a country attached to Western Europe without the complications and dangers of supporting and listening to the fast-talking Islanders of the old Prussian capital city.

In fact, one of the political triumphs of the airlift had been to bond ordinary citizens of western Germany to their kin in Berlin. By the end of the blockade, a two-pfennig surcharge had been added to postage in the western zones to buy supplies for the western sectors of the besieged city. Some voluntarily paid ten and twenty pfennig for "Help Berlin" stamps on their mail. In Westphalia and Saxony, citizens had organized one-day fasts and had brought their food to Allied air bases for transport into Berlin. The city of Bremen sent twenty million cigarettes to western Berlin, and Schleswig-Holstein donated two million pine seedlings to replace the trees of the city's parks and woods. "Give aid to our beleaguered countrymen!" shouted the town crier in the old walled town of Melsungen, in Hesse. The townspeople gathered in the square and donated the equivalent of four railroad freight cars of grain, dried fish and vegetables to be transported to Berlin. The airlift united the country-to-be that would be called West Germany.

Alice Sawadda, a twenty-nine-year-old secretary, went to a café on the Kurfürstendamm with her boyfriend and they did what they had talked about and fantasized about for months: they ordered two hot chocolates and cake. But they could not finish their treat. They were not able to handle food that rich.

The last military governor of West Germany—Clay was replaced by a civilian, John McCloy—left his headquarters on Kronprinzallee on

May 15. The general was exhausted. Most Berliners thought he was leaving because the blockade was ending, but in fact, his retirement date, the subject of dozens of teleconferences and memos over the past year, had actually been set before he knew of the secret blockade negotiations going on in New York. It was a Sunday, the day of the weekly American parade on what had been Hitler's Grafenwöhr parade ground, which Clay usually attended—and did again this day. The entire American military contingent, thousands of men, marched by their commander, then a flight of P-47 Thunderbolts flew over the field in a formation spelling out the word "C-L-A-Y." They were followed by a flight of F-80 Shooting Stars, the United States' first jet fighter, and a seventeen-gun salute. Then the general and Mrs. Clay left for Tempelhof. The time of Clay's departure was not announced, but word got around and more than a half-million Germans stood silently in tribute along the route as the general's car drove the four and a half miles to the airport. The pilot of the C-54 that took the Clays to Rhein-Main was Lieutenant Bill Lafferty. It was his last mission. A week later, the City Assembly, led by Mayor Reuter, renamed Kronprinzallee. It was now Clayallee.

As his tour finally ended on September 1 and he headed back to the States and his job as deputy director of MATS, General Tunner prepared the Air Force's required "Lessons Learned" report on the airlift, beginning with the job descriptions of the 32,900 U.S. service personnel and 23,000 civilians, including Germans. Classified "Restricted Secret," the report emphasized central command and the utilization of local, foreign labor—stating that Tunner's use of 5,000 German mechanics had been an almost unqualified success:

> The Task Force Commander should have full control of all personnel and equipment needed to accomplish his mission . . .
> Because of the extreme shortage of trained military personnel

during the first four months of the Airlift operation, it was found that an augmentation to the maintenance family group was necessary. Aircraft were arriving in the Theater faster than logistical support could be placed into effect. This situation was relieved by authorizing each squadron to employ 85 German mechanics. Without this assistance it would have been impossible for the Airlift to perform as it did during November, December and January . . . Manpower requirements for German personnel used in aircraft maintenance have been established at approximately 7.0 Germans per allocated aircraft. This supplements an average crew of 12 airmen in organizational maintenance per allocated aircraft . . . It was found necessary to employ approximately 5,000 foreign personnel on aircraft maintenance . . . There were 27 cases of suspected sabotage at Airlift bases, only four were definitely proved. The saboteurs were unknown . . . [And fewer than one hundred German and foreign loaders and mechanics were fired during the airlift.]

Tunner went on:

To maintain the economic stability of Berlin industry, it was necessary to provide an outlet for finished manufactured products. These items varied from delicate instruments and chemical supplies to heavy machinery and industrial equipment. The remainder of the backhaul from Berlin consisted of empy coal and flour sacks, vehicles, mail, personnel and personal belongings . . .

On a short-haul operation of this type an overall aircraft utilization of 10 hours per day on C-54's can be maintained . . . All traffic, regardless of weather conditions, is considered as being conducted as under Instrument Flight Rules, and no variations are allowed in any of the approach patterns . . . The comparative number of accidents per 100,000 hours of flying: Air Force overall, 59; Airlift Task Force overall, 26.

And finally:

MASS CARGO BY AIR FEASIBLE. Given the tools of personnel, equipment, aircraft, and the steady flow of supplies, cargo can
be moved from any point in the world to any other point in the
world, regardless of geography or weather.

The official U.S. Air Force count on categories and numbers of reported harassment incidents by Soviet forces was 773, including:
buzzing, 77; close flying, 96; flak, 54; air-to-air fire, 14; flares, 59;
radio interference, 82; searchlights, 103; rockets, 4; balloons, 11.
There were certainly hundreds more that went unreported, because
for pilots any complaint just led to filling out more forms; they were
met by paperwork jeeps as they landed. When military archives were
opened in Moscow after the fall of the Berlin Wall and the collapse of
the communist government, historians found very little on the airlift.
The Soviets often did not index records of unsuccessful operations or
else just destroyed them. For whatever reason, no records were found
that indicated the Soviets had any war plans regarding the airlift. One
historian, Viktor Gobarev, former deputy director of the Soviet Institute of Military History, regarded the airlift as a template for the un-
written rules of the Cold War: "Self-discipline. Russians don't try to
shoot down your planes and Americans don't try to push armed con-
voys through our territory."

The airlift actually continued through the end of September 1949,
stockpiling food, fuel and medical supplies for use if the Soviets once
again tried to blockade the city. The final shutdown was a month earlier than the announced date of October 31 because Allied and city
officials concluded that more than enough material was warehoused
in the city to allow time to restart the airlift if there were ever another

blockade. There were two more fatal crashes during the extended airlift, both of them in July. On the 12th, a C-54 crashed on a flight from Celle to Gatow when its number 3 and 4 engines both quit, killing three Americans: the pilot, Lieutenant Robert von Luehrte of Covington, Kentucky, a thirty-six-year-old World War II veteran with fifty B-17 missions, who had been working as a restaurant equipment salesman when he was called up and sent to Great Falls; copilot Lieutenant Donald Leemon of Green Bay, Wisconsin; and Sergeant Herbert Heinig of Indianapolis. Four days later, five RAF men were killed when a Handley Page Halston piloted by I. R. Donaldson crashed during takeoff at Tegel.

Thirty-nine British citizens, RAF regulars and civilians, and thirty-two Americans were killed during the airlift, along with nine or more German airlift employees. The official U.S. tally of the cost of the operation was calculated at about $350 million.

The British and Americans began closing down their air bases in West Germany, beginning with Celle on July 31. The last American airlift flight from Rhein-Main—the airfield remained open as the "Gateway to Europe"—was on September 30. The pilot, Captain Perry Immel, flying his 403rd mission, was accompanied by a squadron of C-54s behind him. Painted on the side of his plane was: "Last Vittles Flight—1,783,573 Tons."

The British flew 542,236 tons. The pilot of their last flight landed at Gatow on September 23. The Dakota had this message painted on its side: "Positively the Last Flight . . . Psalm 21, Verse 11." That psalm reads: "If they plan evil against you, if they devise mischief, they will not succeed."

EPILOGUE

AMERICAN AND BRITISH PLANES CONTINUED TO DELIVER more than 240,000 tons of cargo to Berlin through the end of July 1949, when night flights were suspended. In August, the total dropped to 77,759 tons and then, in September, to just 16,151 tons. It was over. The focus shifted to diplomacy.

The Council of Foreign Ministers finally met in Paris on June 23, 1949, a day short of a year from the beginning of the Berlin Blockade. The Soviets, represented by Vyacheslav Molotov and then a new foreign minister, Andrei Vishinsky, argued in both public and closed sessions for a return to the rules and conditions of occupied Berlin before the airlift. The Soviet proposal called for a reinstatement of the Kommandatura, the four-power governing system, with each occupier having veto power. The Western Allies rejected that idea, and the conference ended on July 20 without agreements of any kind. In rejecting a return to the status quo ante, the Allies confirmed the status quo post-airlift: two Germanies and a divided Berlin.

That status was still unofficial, but in the weeks and months after May 12, the two new countries emerged. The Soviet Union had lost its gamble that the Allied powers could be forced out of Berlin without a war—and concentrated on legally consolidating its hold on East Germany with East Berlin as its capital. The Federal Republic of Germany, West Germany, officially came into being on September 15, 1949, after parliamentary elections and the election, by the new parliament, of Konrad Adenauer of the Christian Democratic Union, the principal conservative party, as the first chancellor. The formation of the German Democratic Republic was announced by the Soviet Union on October 7, 1949. Provisions making West Berlin part of West Germany were "suspended for the time being," but the city could send representatives to the new western parliament, located in Bonn. On the same day the western republic was instituted, the State Department replaced the Army as the American occupying authority. The title of Military Governor, Clay's title, was replaced by the Office of High Commissioner for Germany.

On October 21, 1949, the United States, Great Britain and France approved the incorporation of West Berlin into the Federal Republic. On November 9, the three Western Allies and the Soviet Union signed a declaration allowing the Federal Republic and the Democratic Republic, two separate German nations, to apply for membership in the United Nations.

There are several sets of statistics concerning the airlift. The official U.S. Air Force numbers include: total cargo delivered to Berlin—2,325,809 tons, 1,783,573 of those by the Air Force and 542,236 tons by the Royal Air Forces of Britain, Australia and New Zealand, along with private aircraft chartered by the British government. The total number of flights into Berlin was recorded as 277,569—189,963 by the Americans, and 87,606 by the British and their Commonwealth partners. A total of 81,843 tons of material stamped "Manufactured in Blockaded Berlin" were flown out of the city by American and British planes.

• • •

In January 1952, *Der Abend* in West Berlin sponsored a contest in which Berliners were asked to write short essays answering the question "What do you remember about the airlift?" Many of the hundreds of submissions were similar, using phrases like these: "The world respected us." . . . "The world was watching us." . . . "The world cared about us."

The man who appealed to the world in 1948, Ernst Reuter, died of a heart attack at the age of sixty-four, on September 29, 1953. More than 750,000 Berliners—one of every three people in West Berlin—came out for a memorial service at City Hall or lined the route to the cemetery. The United States was represented by the High Commissioner for Germany, James B. Conant, and the new commander of the U.S. Air Force in Europe, Lieutenant General William Tunner.

On the night of August 13, 1961, alarmed and weakened by the number of East Germans—as many as two thousand a day—seeking political asylum in the West by crossing from East to West Berlin, the East German government, with the backing of the Soviet Union, erected barbed-wire barriers just inside their own territory along the border that had divided the city since 1945. The barbed wire was then replaced by a brick and concrete wall. President John F. Kennedy's first reaction was to send retired General Lucius Clay to Berlin as his personal representative with the rank of Ambassador-at-Large. The wall was torn down on November 9, 1989, by both East and West Berliners as citizen unrest toppled the government of the Soviet Union and its Eastern European allies. Germany was reunified into a single country, with Berlin as its capital, on October 3, 1990, when East Germany was absorbed into West Germany under provisions of the Basic Law approved in 1949.

In May 1999, the Airlift Gratitude Foundation, originally founded by the West German government to give financial aid to American and British veterans of the airlift and their families, sponsored a fiftieth-anniversary celebration of the day Operations Vittles and Plainfare ended. The local newspaper in Vacaville, California, the *Reporter*, published an article by Sally Miller Wyatt on a local resident, retired Air Force Colonel Earl von Kaenel, an airlift pilot who went to Berlin for the anniversary ceremonies. As Lieutenant von Kaenel, fifty years before, he was the pilot with the pregnant wife who arrived in Hawaii just after he left for Berlin. Young Lieutenant von Kaenal's thirty-day TDY stretched into nine months and when he was finally reunited with his wife, Mitzi, he met his infant daughter, Susan, for the first time.

A few days later, the *Reporter* printed a letter from another local resident, Heike Krautschick, who wrote: "How often I have silently thanked the people involved in the Berlin Airlift for literally creating a life for me and my family. How ironic that one of the very people responsible lives here in Vacaville where I too have made my home. I cannot thank Earl von Kaenel enough for his flights during the Airlift. How does one measure the gift of a new life, of countless opportunities, of living in peace and being able to see your own children thrive full of hope for the future . . . Thank you again, Earl von Kaenel, from the bottom of my heart."

The Germans who worked on the airlift were also invited to the ceremonies at Tempelhof. Gerhard Noack, the loader from Fassberg, was near the Tempelhof U-Bahn station when he heard a man with an American voice talking to a souvenir seller about what had happened there so long ago.

"Five marks? You want five marks for that?"

"Bill Morrisey!" said Noack. The American turned around and the two old men hugged each other.

Ten years later, at another ceremony, Kurt Dettmer, the Fassberg mechanic, saw an American he thought he recognized. The Germans at the field would normally begin conversations by saying *"Was ist los?"*—literally "What is loose?"—but used as "What's happening?" One American there would always answer *"Der Hund ist los"*—"The hound is loose."

Dettmer said, *"Was ist los?"* The American turned to him with a grin and said, *"Der Hund ist los."*

• • • •

This is a later word on others written about here:

Ruth Andreas-Friedrich left Berlin at the end of 1948 and worked as a journalist in Munich. She died in 1977. *Underground Berlin*, published in 1989, was taken from Andreas-Friedrich's diaries covering the years 1938 to 1945, when she was a member of "Onkel Emil," a resistance group of artists and writers and teachers who helped Jews escape from Nazi Germany. *Battleground Berlin*, published in 1990, covered the years 1945 to 1948.

Jack O. Bennett, the chief pilot of American Overseas Airlines, made 650 trips into Berlin during the airlift. Some credited him with flying the first airlift flight in his stripped DC-3, before it was called an airlift. He became a pilot for Pan American Airways and lived in Berlin until he died in 2001.

Ernest Bevin resigned as Foreign Secretary of Great Britain in March 1951 and died a month later.

Willy Brandt, the young Social Democratic Party correspondent in Berlin, became Chancellor of the Federal Republic of Germany after serving as Mayor of West Berlin. He won the Nobel Peace Prize in 1971 for his efforts to try to reduce tensions between West and East Germany.

Lucius Clay was the Chairman and Chief Executive Officer of Continental Can Company from 1949 to 1962. Later, he became a partner at Lehman Brothers. He died in 1978 at the age of eighty-one. His autobiography, *Decision in Germany*, was published in 1950.

Lawrence "Corky" Colgrove left the Air Force as a sergeant on the day before the Korean War began. He worked as a mechanic for United Airlines for thirty-five years and owned a liquor store in Denver, which he sold after twenty years.

RAF Flight Lieutenant John Curtis stayed in the service and became Air Marshal Sir John Curtis.

Kurt Dettmer worked as a shop foreman and then test director for the company that made Germany's Leopard tanks. He then worked at the Institute for Materials Science at the Technical University of Braunschweig.

Walter Dougan remained in the RAF. His service included six more years in Germany, training Luftwaffe pilots. After leaving the service, he taught engineering at Dawlish College in Exeter.

Guy Dunn retired from the Air Force as a Lieutenant Colonel after thirty years and became a home builder in Arizona.

James Forrestal's mental condition continued to deteriorate until he was hospitalized at Bethesda Naval Hospital just outside Washington. He leaped to his death out of a seventh-story window on May 21, 1949, nine days after the end of the Berlin Blockade. Legend has it that his last words were "The Russians are coming!"

Edwin Gere left the Air Force as a captain in 1953. He earned a Ph.D. in political science at Pennsylvania State University and taught at the University of Connecticut and the University of Massachusetts for thirty-five years. In 1990, his family gathered at Keuka Lake in

New York State and persuaded him to write a book about the airlift, titled *The Unheralded*.

Edward Guilbert used the lessons he learned tracking cargo into Berlin to create what is now called electronic data interchange (EDI), a computerized system for shipping and receiving information and tracking now used by tens of thousands of companies around the world. He became the leading civilian advocate of EDI, using the Berlin experience to create inventory and distribution systems for large commercial operations, among them Kmart and Wal-Mart.

Gail Halvorsen retired as a colonel in the Air Force in 1974. His last posting was as commander of Tempelhof. An elder of the Church of Jesus Christ of Latter-Day Saints, he was Assistant Dean of Student Life at Brigham Young University for ten years. He also wrote a book in 1990 about his Berlin experiences, *The Berlin Candy Bomber*.

Paul Hawkins became a Baptist minister after leaving the Air Force.

Frank Howley returned to the advertising business in Philadelphia and lectured widely on his Berlin experience. He wrote a book titled *Berlin Command*, published in 1950. He became Vice Chancellor of New York University in 1952, retiring in 1967.

Fred Hulke worked as a technician for International Business Machines (IBM) in Germany for thirty-five years.

Peter Izard stayed in the Royal Air Force for thirty-six years, retiring as a squadron leader.

Helmut Kohl, the boy who remembered receiving a CARE package, was the Christian Democratic Chancellor of the Federal Republic when East Germany collapsed and became the first Chancellor of a reunited Germany in 1990.

Alexander Kotikov returned to the Soviet Union after the airlift and all references to him or his service were removed from the *Great Soviet Encyclopedia.* In other words, he became a "nonperson."

Curtis LeMay, as Commander of the Strategic Air Command, became a four-star general in 1951, the youngest four-star since Ulysses S. Grant. He retired from the Air Force in 1965. He ran for Vice President of the United States in 1968 on a third-party ticket headed by Alabama Governor George Wallace. He died in 1990. His autobiography, *Mission with LeMay*, written with MacKinlay Kantor, was published in 1965.

Günter Metzger became an administrator with the Gerling Insurance Group. When the airlift was over, each mechanic was presented with a certificate of service. Metzger showed me his in Fassberg sixty years later: "In appreciation of the services so ably performed by Günter Metzger, which greatly contributed to the success of the Berlin Airlift . . . Theron Coulter, Colonel, United States Air Force."

Earl Moore became a dentist in Dallas, Texas, and was the president of the Berlin Airlift Veterans Association during the time I wrote this book.

William Morrisey left the Air Force and spent twenty-four years as an air traffic controller, working for the Federal Aviation Administration.

Gerhard Noack worked as a printer and was the managing director of Heide-Druck printing company for twenty-four years.

Forrest Ott retired from the Air Force as a lieutenant colonel.

William Palahunich, the Ukrainian-speaking sergeant, left the Air Force in 1951, entering Eastern Kentucky University and working as a football coach and physical education instructor after graduation before going back to his first love, farming.

Elisabeth Poensgen was one of tens of thousands of Germans who answered newspaper advertisements by a schoolteacher and writer named Walter Kempowski asking for letters and diaries. He collected them into what is now the Kempowski Archive in Berlin.

Gerhard Reitdorff became a licensed tour guide in East Berlin, escorting tour groups from Western countries. "The authorities knew I was anticommunist but they needed me as a VIP guide because I could speak other languages. The tourists were crazy from propaganda. They would feel my shirt because they thought it would be made of paper." Still, when the Berlin Wall came down in 1989, he did not consider it "liberation." He considered it "occupation," and he did not enter West Berlin until three weeks later. "I was literally shaking all over," he told me. "I was so afraid of capitalism."

Henry Ries, the photographer who took many of the iconic airlift photos, became an American citizen after the war and a staff photographer for the *New York Times*. In 2003, he was awarded Germany's Officer Cross of the Order of Merit, the highest award the country gives to foreigners. He died in 2007.

Walter Riggers worked for the RAF at Fassberg until 1956, before joining the German Army and retiring in 1975.

Wolfgang Samuel retired as a colonel in the U.S. Air Force and has written six books.

Ernst Schmidt became the director of the sewage works in his hometown of Hermannsberg.

Jake Schuffert continued working for the Air Force as a civilian graphic designer until his retirement in 1988. He also drew cartoons for various aviation publications.

Kenneth Slaker remained in the Air Force, achieving the rank of lieutenant colonel. He remained in contact with **Rudolph Schnabel**, who worked for the German Post Office for many years.

Vasily D. Sokolovsky became Chief of Staff of all Soviet military forces and a member of the Soviet Central Committee. He died in 1968.

Ulrich Stampa made his way to Argentina after the airlift to work in Juan Perón's Instituto Aerotécnico with Dr. Tank. He lived well with a wife and three children and proudly showed me photographs of his home in Córdoba. He returned to Germany when Perón was overthrown in 1955 and the Tank team scattered over the world. He became an expert in wind power, designing propeller setups to generate electrical power all over Europe—and supported right-wing parties in Germany. At one point in a long interview at his home in Bremen, he said almost explosively: "There were no Jews killed in the camps. My father worked at Auschwitz. Those stories around the world are all Jewish lies. I'm not saying the camps were paradise, they were not, but no one was killed there."

Noah Thompson went home to Vermont and bought a dairy farm, which he ran for thirteen years. He then became director of the Extension Service of the University of Vermont.

William Tunner won a third Distinguished Service Cross for leading the Combat Cargo Command during the Korean War. He became Commander of the U.S. Air Force in Europe and then Commander of the Military Air Command. He retired in 1960 because of heart problems. He died in 1983.

Louis Wagner served in the Korean War, then went into radio and television, producing the 11 P.M. news for WKYW-TV in Philadelphia. He worked as a correspondent called "Captain Lou," a local Charles Kuralt reporting on leisure. He also wrote a syndicated column for years and retired to South Carolina, flying his own small plane a couple of times a week.

Eldridge Williams, the former Tuskegee navigator, decided to stay in the Air Force after the airlift, retiring as a lieutenant colonel in 1971. He became executive director of personnel of the Dade County (Miami) Public School District, retiring in 1985.

NOTES

CHAPTER 1: "CITY OF ZOMBIES"

2   *"Robert Murphy"*: Mark-Arnold-Foster, *The Siege of Berlin* (London: Collins, 1979), p. 35. All future references are to "Foster."

4   *There were hundreds of thousands:* Deployment numbers from Roger G. Miller, "To Save a City," Air Force History and Museum Program, p. 30. Miller estimated that the Red Army had 500,000 to 1 million combat-ready troops in Germany. All future references are to "Miller."

4   *"The English political officers"*: Social Democratic Party Archives, Bonn, Germany. All future references are to "SDP Archives."

5   *Allied statisticians:* Miller, p. 31.

5   *six months of medical supplies:* Richard Collier, *Bridge Across the Sky* (New York: McGrawHill 1978). All future references are to "Collier."

5   *Dr. Eugene Schwarz:* James Romero, *Skyblue 79*, self-published, 2005, p. 84. All future references are to "Romero."

6   *Colonel Frank Howley:* Frank Howley, *Berlin Command* (New York: Putnam, 1950). All future references are to "Howley."

6   *RIAS, "Radio in the American Sector"*: *Time*, February 14, 1949; Petra Galle, *RIAS Berlin und Berliner Rundfunk 1945–1949* (Munster: Lit Verlag, 2003).

7   *"looking like a Roman emperor"*: *New York Times Magazine*, July 4, 1948, p. 6; *New York Times*, April 17, 1978, p. 1.

7   *destroy every Soviet airfield:* Archive of Robert E. Frye, producer/director of *The Berlin Airlift*, a co-production with WETA-TV, Washington, D.C., originally broadcast on PBS in July 1998. All future references are to "Frye Archive."

8   *"a logical outgrowth"*: Curtis E. LeMay and MacKinlay Kantor, *Mission with LeMay* (Garden City, N.Y.: Doubleday, 1965), p. 411. All future references to "LeMay."

8   *military governor, General Robertson:* Miller, p. 23.

9   *his superior, General Bradley:* Jean Edward Smith, *Lucius D. Clay: An American Life* (New York: Henry Holt, 1990), p. 476. All future references are to "Smith."

9   *Clay's answer, via teleconference: The Papers of General Lucius D. Clay, Germany 1945–49*, vol. 2, edited by Jean Edward Smith (Bloomington: Indiana University Press, 1974), p. 622. All future references are to "*Papers.*"

10 *William Heimlich:* National Security Archive, George Washington University, gwu.edu/-nsarchive/coldwar/interviews/episode-4.

11 *Henry Ries, a Jewish Berliner:* Letter to family, September 9, 1945.

11 *"a city of the dead . . . city of zombies":* Miller, p. 3.

11 *"Chronic hunger has taken":* Collie Small, "Berlin's Winter of Fear," *Collier's*, February 21, 1948, p. 17.

12 *Lutz Rackow:* Interview.

12 *Red Army deserters:* Frank Donovan, *Bridge in the Sky* (New York: David McKay, 1968), p. 23. All future references are to "Donovan."

12 *Gerhard Rietdorff:* Interview.

13 *Geoff Smith, an RAF mechanic:* Von Uwe Forster, Stephanie von Hochberg, Ulrich Kubisch, and Dietrich Kuhlgatz, *Aufrag Luftbrücke: Der Himmel über Berlin* (Berlin: Deutsches Technik Museum, 1998), p. 110. All future references are to "Forster."

13 *marked "Bird Dog":* Harold Hendler: Interview.

15 *WESTERN POWERS:* Paul Steege, *Black Market Cold War* (New York: Cambridge University Press, 2007), p. 190. All future references are to "Steege."

15 *At the end of the war:* Collier, p. 33.

16 *Clay's staff had estimated:* Anthony Mann, *Comeback: Germany 1945–1952* (London: Macmillan, 1980), p. 104. All future references are to "Mann."

17 *Elisabeth Poensgen:* Letters in Kempowski Archive, Berlin.

17 *Ruth Andreas-Friedrich: Battleground Berlin by Ruth Andreas-Friedrich*, translated by Anna Boerresen (New York: Paragon House, 1990), p. 108. All future references are to "Andreas-Friedrich."

18 *Inge Godenschweger:* Frye Archive.

20 *"Analysis of the materials":* Miller, p. 17.

20 *Central Intelligence Agency:* Ibid.

21 *"For many months": Papers*, p. 568.

22 *Stalin responded:* Vladislav Zubok and Constantine Plekhanov, *Inside the Kremlin's Cold War* (Cambridge, Mass.: Harvard University Press, 1996), p. 52.

22 *Very few Soviet documents:* Viktor Gorbarev: Taped interviews, Frye Archive.

23 *commanders cabled Molotoy:* Miller, p. 25.

26 *Christian Seaford:* Edwin Gere, *The Unheralded: Men and Women of the Berlin Blockade and Airlift* (Shutesbury, Mass.: Andrus, 2005), p. 180. All future references are to "Gere."

26 *"It seems important": Papers*, p. 702; "Airpower as a Tool of Foreign Policy: Two Case Studies," Pentagon Report A805524.

27 *"The evacuation of family":* Lucius D. Clay, *Decision in Germany* (New York: Doubleday, 1950), p. 366. All future references are to "Clay."

27 *"Remember this":* Lucius Clay Oral History, July 17, 1974, Harry S. Truman Library, Independence, Mo. All future references are to "Truman Library."

28 *"This is the disintegration":* Robert Jackson and Patrick Stevens, *The Berlin Airlift* (Wellingsborough, U.K.: 1988), p. 37.

28 *"It was under these conditions"*: Truman Library.
28 *"Karlshorst on June 28"*: Memo to the President from CIA Director Rear Admiral R. H. Hillenkoetter, June 30, 1948, Declassified October 4, 1977, Truman Library.
28 *"[counter] blockades"*: Avi Shlaim, *The United States and The Berlin Blockade: A Study in Crisis Decision-Making* (Berkeley: University of California Press, Berkeley, 1983), p. 378. All future references are to "Shlaim."
30 *"We stay in Berlin"*: *Foreign Relations of the United States 1948*, Vol. 2, p. 930.

CHAPTER 2: "ABSOLUTELY IMPOSSIBLE!"

31 *Lieutenant William Lafferty:* Interviews and correspondence.
32 *Tempelhof Airport in Berlin:* BBC News, August 7, 2008; *Things* magazine, summer 1999; lunch at Tempelhof, summer 1999; Kim Murphy "A Drive to Save Tempelhof, Base of the Berlin Airlift," *Los Angeles Times*, April 26, 2008, p. 1; "The Mother of All Airports," *Der Spiegel*, April 25, 2008.
33 *The airlift was a British:* Interviews with Bernd von Kosta, Alliierten Museum and Archive, Berlin; Her Majesty's Office of Stationery, London; Waite letter to Lady Tedder, June 9, 1948, Liddell Hart Centre for Military Archives.
35 *Ernest Bevin:* Frank Roberts Interview, National Security Archive, George Washington University, Washington, D.C.
36 *"Well, me lad"*: Ibid.
39 *Lieutenant J. B. McLaughlin:* Interviews and correspondence.
39 *Captain William A. Cobb:* Interviews and correspondence.
39 *Corporal James Spatafora:* Frye Archive.
39 *"In London"*: Collier, p. 103.
40 *Jack O. Bennett:* Stewart Powell, "The Berlin Airlift," *Air Force* magazine, Vol. 81, No. 6, June, 1998.
40 *Lieutenant Fred V. McAfee:* Interview and correspondence, *The Bee-Hive* magazine (published by United Aircraft Corporation, East Hartford, Conn.), Fall 1948, Vol. 23, No. 4, p. 14. All future references are to *"Bee-Hive."*
40 *was based in Guam:* Lieutenant Glenn Truitt, Frye Archive.
41 *"We fly in two hours"*: Klaus Scherff, *Luftbrücke Berlin.* (Stuttgart: Motorbud, 1976), p. 61. All future references are to "Scherff."
41 *First Lieutenant William J. Horney: Task Force Times*, October 20, 1948.
41 *Lieutenant Charles Widmar:* Interview and correspondence with Mrs. Mary Widmar.
41 *"Seldom, even in time of war"*: *United States Armed Forces Medical Journal*, Vol. 3, No. 11, 1948, p. 1253.
42 *Arthur Lidard:* Correspondence; Samuel, p. 165.
42 *Lieutenant Guy Dunn:* Interviews and correspondence.
42 *Lieutenant Gail Halvorsen:* Interviews and correspondence.
44 *Private First Class L. W. "Corky" Colgrove:* Interviews and correspondence.
44 *With all the wild energy:* Collier, p. 98.
44 *weathermen and ground control operators: Task Force Times*, July 23, 1948.

44 *Noah Thompson:* Interviews and correspondence; Noah Thompson, *A Pilot's Story: Flying in the 1940s* (Rutland, Vt.: Academy, 1995), p. 117.

46 *"Thirteen GIs worked": Time,* July 12, 1948.

46 *glide slope path . . . was 40 to 1: OMGUS: Four Year Report,* 1945–49.

47 *The Sunderlands:* Collier, p. 78.

48 *Flight Lieutenant John Curtis:* Frye Archive.

49 *Lieutenant John Townsend:* Correspondence.

49 *"We are receiving":* Teleconference TT-9300, Top Secret—Eyes Only, Bradley to Clay, April 2, 1948.

50 *Edwin A. Gere, Jr.:* Interviews and correspondence.

51 *pour gasoline over the garbage:* Captain Karl Mautner, U.S. liaison officer to Berlin, government interview, Library of Congress.

52 *Corporal Spatafora:* Frye Archive.

52 *Staff Sergeant Robert Evans:* Correspondence. Evans wrote this in one letter: "I have had a long and satisfying life, a marriage of 50 years, two great kids. But as I look back I think perhaps my participation in the airlift was the most important thing I've done and I'm intensely proud of that."

52 *Roger W. Moser, Jr.:* Interviews and correspondence; Roger Moser Jr., "Recollections of the Berlin Airlift," *ATC Journal,* January 1999.

53 UNIVERSAL INTERNATIONAL NEWSREEL: Frye Archive.

54 *Newsreels in Great Britain:* Frye Archive.

54 *Ernst Reuter:* Miller, p. 3; David E. Barclay, unpublished biography of Ernst Reuter; James O'Donnell, "The Mayor Russia Hates," *Saturday Evening Post,* February 5, 1949, p. 109.

56 *"The man has the mentality":* Barclay, p. 50.

57 *"Everyone was afraid of him":* Ann Slater interview, Frye Archive.

59 *"they no doubt mean it":* Andreas-Friedrich, pp. 230–31.

CHAPTER 3: "COWBOY OPERATION"

62 *Major Edward Willerford: Bee-Hive,* p. 9.

62 *Lieutenant Leonard Sweet:* Colonel Wolfgang W. E. Samuel, *I Always Wanted to Fly* (Jackson: University Press of Mississippi, 2001), p. 26. All future references are to "Samuel."

63 *the tonnage they were able to deliver:* General T. Ross Milton, "The Berlin Airlift," *Air Force* magazine, July 1968.

63 *First Lieutenant Leland Williams:* Gere, p. 203. Interview with Peter Hagen, Sag Harbor, N.Y.

63 *Group Captain Noel Hyde:* Ann and John Tusa, *The Berlin Airlift* (Staplehurst, Ky: Spellmount, 1998), p. 165.

64 *Walter Lippmann: New York Herald Tribune,* July 17, 1948.

64 *"The Western countries": Economist,* July 24, 1948.

64 *Cornelius Whitney:* Miller, p. 80.

64 *Arthur Vandenberg: Presidential Studies Quarterly,* Wiley & Blackwell, Hoboken, N.J., Summer 1980.

65 *"Jim wants me to hedge":* Harry S. Truman, *Memoirs* (New York: Doubleday, 1955).

65 *Major General William Tunner:* William H. Tunner, "Over the Hump," USAF Warrior Studies, Office of Air Force History, 1964. All future references are to "Tunner."

67 *Major General Laurence Kuter:* Roger Launius and Coy F. Cross II, "MAC and the Legacy of the Berlin Airlift," Military Airlift Command, Scott Air Force Base, April 1989, p. 29. All future references are to "Launius and Cross."

67 *Private Tom Henshaw:* Frye Archive.

70 *Lieutenant Robert Miller:* Donovan, p. 47.

70 *in Morse code:* Collier, p. 20.

70 *Robert Murphy:* Miller, p. 41.

71 *"Present tension in Berlin":* Ibid.

71 *Two days later:* Tunner, p. 162.

72 *3,200 companies:* Gaertner Report, Hoover Institution.

73 *"They cannot drive us out":* Clay, p. 367.

73 *Now, on July 21:* Collier, p. 92 ff.

74 *"[The airlift] would involve":* NSC Memorandum for the President, July 16, 1948, Box 220, President's secretary file, Truman Library.

74 *Lovett offered this opinion:* HST Museum, Meeting Discussions, 1948, Box 220, MAC Legacy, p. 17.

75 *Marshall's concern:* Foreign Relations of the United States [FRUS] August 26, 1948. Vol 2, p. 1085.

76 *Silverplate:* Miller, p. 25; Samuel, p. 71.

78 *"We have ordered":* Scherff, p. 159.

78 *Sergeant William Palahunich:* Interviews and correspondence.

80 *The Soviets also set up:* William Stivers, "The Incomplete Blockade: Soviet Zone Supply of West Berlin, 1948–49," *Diplomatic History* 21, no. 4, 1994, pp. 569–602.

81 *By the end of the year:* Brandt, p. 196; Steege, p. 217.

82 *"I expect you to produce":* Tunner, p. 158 ff.

83 *"Joe Smith was a good man":* Tunner, Frye Archive.

84 *"Two American flyers":* Los Angeles Times, June 28, 1998, p. 1.

85 *JCS 1067:* Order issued May 15, 1945.

85 *"That is the hand":* Frye Archive.

85 *American posters everywhere:* "Es begann mit einem Kuss ... It Started with a Kiss: German-Allied Relations After 1945" (edited by Florian Weiß), Jaron Verlag, published by Allied Museum, Berlin, 2005, pp. 5–13.

85 *"Veronikas":* Howard K. Smith, *Events Leading Up to My Death* (New York: St. Martin's Press, 1996), p. 180.

86 *"Gee, Mac":* New York Times, August 28, 1949.

86 *"We were lectured":* Frye Archive.

87 *"This could be poison":* Lou Wagner, interviews and correspondence.

87 *"There were not enough coins":* Reitdorf interview.

88 *Juergen Graf:* Interview, Frye Archive.

88 *Norbert Podewin:* Interview.

88 *"Westerners suddenly":* Interview.

88   *Gail Halvorsen, the pilot:* Interview and correspondence; Gail S. Halvorsen, *The Berlin Candy Bomber* (Bountiful, Utah: Horizon, 1997).
89   *Herschel Elkins:* Ibid.
90   *Ten-year-old:* Gere, p. 174.

CHAPTER 4: "BLACK FRIDAY"

94   *In western Berlin during:* Rodrigo, p. 118.
94   *five categories:* Ibid.
95   *In England at the same time:* David Kynaston, *Austerity Britain, 1945–1951* (London: Bloomsbury, 2007).
95   *David Lawrence:* Frye Archive.
95   *Soviet Premier Stalin invited:* Clay, p. 516.
96   *"If, as suggested by":* Notes, cabinet meeting, September 10, 1948, Truman Library.
96   *The KI, the Committee of Information:* David E. Murphy, Sergei Kondrashev and George Bailey, *Battleground Berlin: CIA vs. KGB in the Cold War* (New Haven, Conn.: Yale University Press, 1997), p. 62.
97   *"The actual operation":* Tunner, p. 162.
98   *The French had no planes worth:* Wolfgang Huschke, *The Candy Bombers* (Berlin: Metropol, 1999), p. 134. All future references are to "Huschke."
99   *PLUTO:* www.historic-uk.com/England/History/UK/England-History/Mulberry andPLUTO.
100   *"Black Friday":* Tunner, p. 152 ff.; Lafferty, interview and correspondence.
102   *David Bevan-John:* Collier, p. 136.
104   *Sergeant Bill Palahunich:* Interviews and correspondence.
104   *Molotov, on August 15 in Moscow:* Michael Narinskii, "Soviet Union and the Berlin Crisis," Fondazione, Italy, 1997, p. 67.
105   *Tunner said nothing:* Bettinger interview, Frye Archive.
105   *the mimeograph publication: Task Force Times,* August 23, 1948.
106   *" 'What's the yelling about?' ":* Tunner, p. 181.
107   *Two played that game:* Rodrigo, pp. 89–92.
107   *"The Americans will leave":* Collier, pp. 51–56.
107   *network television documentaries:* Frye Archive.
108   *SLAVES SERVING:* Rodrigo, p. 89.
108   *"Stop! Stop!":* Mann, p. 132.
109   *Gerhard Noack:* Interviews and correspondence.
111   *Young Allied soldiers:* Fred Hall interview.
111   *John Collyer:* Frye Archive.
112   *Shoes were a prize:* Miller, p. 84.
112   *Elisabeth Poensgen:* Letters, Kempowski Archive.
112   *CARE, the Cooperative:* Interviews and correspondence, Anthony Williams, CARE; CARE Archive.
113   *"Trapped in the pressure":* New York Times Magazine, August 15, 1948.
114   *"Frau Bergerebuss": New York Times,* August 15, 1948.

CHAPTER 5: "WE ARE CLOSE TO WAR"

116 *Lieutenant Richard A. Campbell:* Correspondence.

117 *"People begged for food":* Unpublished memoir, Charles L. "Pat" Patterson.

121 *A* Time *correspondent: Time,* September 6, 1948. www.time.com/time/article/ 0,9171,77948.00.html.

121 *"They manhandled three":* Smith, p. 832.

122 *More than 250,000 people: New York Times,* September 10, 1948.

124 *a week later: New York Times,* August 13, 1948.

124 *Captain Kenneth Slaker:* Interviews and correspondence; Kenneth Hawk Slaker, *A Military Pilot's Exciting Life and Visit from the Hereafter* (Raleigh, N.C.: Ivy House, 2008), p. 97.

126 *"You have to eat now": The Berlin Airlift,* PBS broadcast, *The American Experience.*

128 *"WESTERN OFFICIALS WORRIED": New York Times,* September 27, 1948, p. 1.

128 *"I have a terrible feeling":* Harry S. Truman, *Years of Trial and Hope,* (New York: Doubleday 1955), p. 148.

129 *Phillip Graham:* Shlaim, p. 339.

129 *"The American people would crucify you":* Ibid.

CHAPTER 6: "RUBBLE WOMEN"

132 *softball . . . 16 to 2:* John Chadra, interview in *Sarasota Herald-Tribune,* Sarasota, FL, June 25, 2009, p. A1.

132 *The Veronikas: City of Burden, Sin.* Forster, p. 163.

133 *"About the most bleak": New York Times,* February 3, 1949.

133 *Great Falls:* Miller, p. 79; History of Malmstrom Air Force Base, www.malmstrom .af.mil.historymalmstromhistory.asp.

134 *Jake Schuffert:* Information from Berlin Airlift Veterans' Association.

135 *On October 8: Tägliche Rundschau,* October 8, 1948, p. 1.

135 *Whether those numbers:* Steege, p. 226.

136 *None of this was secret:* Collier, p. 30.

136 *"If the officers":* Steege, p. 227.

136 *"See that guy":* Halvorsen, interviews and correspondence.

137 *"These guys are good":* Bee-Hive, p. 20.

137 *Günter Metzger:* Interview.

138 *Walter Riggers:* Interview.

138 *Fred Hulke:* Interview.

138 *RAF Sergeant John Overington:* Frye Archive.

139 *"They were the roughest games":* David Williams interview, Frye Archive.

139 *Ulrich Stampa:* Interview and correspondence.

140 *Kurt Dettmer:* Interview.

140 *Private First Class Johnny Orms:* Gere, p. 209.

140 *That cold night: Task Force Times,* October 2, 1948.

140 *Lieutenant Howard S. Myers:* Powell, "The Berlin Airlift," *Air Force* magazine, Vol. 81, No. 6, June 1998, p. 57. Archived at www.afa.org/magazinejune1998/0698 berlin.asp. All future references are to "Powell."

141   *Robertson's residence:* Gere, p. 149.

141   *John Hopkins:* Lafferty interview.

141   *cut down trees:* Howley, p. 232.

142   *On October 13, General Clay:* Teleconference TT-1406, Papers, p. 896.

142   *Then, Dulles himself landed:* Andrei Cherny, *The Candy Bombers* (New York: G. P. Putnam, 2008), p. 430. All future references are to "Cherny."

143   *"I suppose you realize":* Teleconference TT-1406, Papers, p. 900.

143   *LeMay's last day:* Miller, p. 51; Tunner, p. 189.

144   *Leonard Sweet:* Samuel, p. 23.

144   *"You Yanks":* Gere, p. 93.

144   *Anthony Cecchini:* Rodrigo, p. 122.

145   *"It's just a little":* Rodrigo, p. 93.

145   *"Just give me the woid":* *Time*, October 18, 1948. www.time.com/time/article/ 0,8816,799308,00.html.

145   *"Master Pilot Dougan":* Gere, p. 147.

146   *Clay returned to the United States:* *New York Times*, October 21, 1948, p. 1.

146   *"It is the considered opinion":* Shlaim, p. 364.

146   *The Central Intelligence Agency:* Cherny, p. 436.

147   *"The Soviet planners":* *New York Times*, October 22, 1948, p. 1.

148   *"It broke my heart":* Earl Moore interview, Frye Archive.

148   *Lieutenant Bill L. Cooley:* Powell, p. 59.

149   *problem for aircrews was still fatigue:* Rodrigo, p. 32.

150   *"Peter came into the world":* David Binder, *The Other German* (Washington, D.C.: New Republic Books, 1975), p. 130.

152   *an American flag dropped:* History of the 503rd Engineering Corps, USAF.

CHAPTER 7: "IT LOOKS LIKE CURTAINS"

157   *full-time airlift service began at Tegel:* *New York Times*, November 5, 1948.

157   *Navy RD5s arrived:* Tunner, p. 214; Miller, pp. 93–95.

157   *was ceremoniously handed a putty knife:* Letter from Captain Meyer Minchen, U.S. Navy.

157   *"I was thief, a good one":* Dr. Laurin interview, Frye Archive.

158   *"Vittles Bowl":* *Task Force Times*, November 5, 1948.

158   *"One C-54 would firewall":* Colgrove interview.

159   *"This is Big Easy":* Lafferty, interview and correspondence.

159   *bungee cords:* Lt. Col. Joseph Lauter, quoted in Samuel, p. 42.

160   *bring back several falcons:* Romero, p. 93.

160   *Lieutenant Earl Hammack:* Frye Archive.

160   *A famous RAF:* Huschke, p. 227; Gere, p. 154.

161   *Lieutenant George H. Nelson:* Samuel, p. 19.

161   *"bulb removed":* Samuel, p. 19.

161   *"Risks were taken":* Hendler, Samuel, p. 37.

161   *"Our Father which art":* Robert Jackson and Patrick Stephens, *The Berlin Airlift* (Northampshire, U.K.: 1998), p. 125.

161 *Hewitt LeBlanc:* Miller, p. 89; correspondence, February 6, 2007.

162 *hired veteran German weathermen:* Rodrigo, p. 186.

162 *"The ceiling is unlimited":* Task Force Times, December 21, 1948.

163 *Louis Wagner:* Interview and correspondence.

163 *"I don't need advice":* Tunner, Frye Archive.

164 *"How does one get":* "The Fassberg Diary" was given to me by William Lafferty.

165 *Two days later, on November 15: Washington Post,* May 11, 1998, p. A18; *Himmel über Berlin,* p. 267.

165 *In Berlin, both western:* Ann Stringer, "Berlin Today: One Family's Story," *New York Times Magazine,* January 2, 1948.

166 *Wolfgang Samuel:* Wolfgang Samuel, *German Boy* (Jackson: University of Mississippi Press), p. 358.

167 *flew several gravestones:* Lafferty interview.

167 *"The March of Dimes":* The American family activities were reported on regularly in *Task Force Times,* notably on January 8, 1949.

167 *"Westchester-on-Wannsee": New York Times Magazine,* November 30, 1948.

168 *Ann Slater:* Frye Archive.

168 *James Sutterlin:* Frye Archive.

168 *ninety-three checkpoints: New York Times,* December 19, 1948.

168 *"Lorries from the Balkans":* Interviews and correspondence.

169 *"There are holes all over": New York Times,* March 17, 1949.

169 *"Those young Russians":* Interviews and correspondence.

169 *Sergeant George Gibbons: Task Force Times,* November 22, 1948.

170 *Lieutenant Gere wrote back:* Interview, Alfred University News Bureau.

170 *On November 27, Bill Lafferty:* Interviews and correspondence.

170 *Army-Navy football game: New York Times,* November 28, 1948.

172 *Coca-Cola bottle:* Samuel, p. 29.

172 *both of them falling asleep:* Letter, Russell Koolhof, June 22, 2006. Also, Samuel, p. 33.

174 *"It looks like curtains":* Draper, Oral History, Library of Congress, p. 69; interview by Jerry Hess, 1972.

CHAPTER 8: "FLYING TO HIS DEATH"

175 *Captain Billy E. Phelps:* Hoover Institution Archives, Security and Intelligence, Interrogation of Billy E. Phelps, POW #4817, Germany, June 14, 1945; Harry Fulton, "Pilot's Death Bares Three Dramatic Stories," *Long Beach Press-Independent,* December 9, 1948.

177 *Lieutenant Edward Dvorak:* Powell, www.afa.org/magazine/june1998/0698berlin.asp.

177 *Edwin Gere had flown:* Interviews and correspondence.

177 *Wolfgang Samuel:* Samuel, *German Boy,* p. 368.

179 *"Don't be lured":* Donovan, p. 185.

180 *Clement Utting:* Gere, p. 194.

181 *Vernon Hamman:* Frye Archive.

182 *Lieutenant David Irvin:* Colonel David Irvin, Jr. *Highway to Freedom* (Paducah, Ky.: Turner, 2002), p. 13.

184 *"Robert Garrett": Task Force Times,* December 20, 1948.

185 *Captain Ken Herman:* Frye Archive.

185 *General Jean Ganeval:* Thomas Parrish, *Berlin in the Balance* (Reading, Mass.: Perseus, 1998), p. 277: *New York Times,* December 17, 1948.

187 *Der Club der Insulaner: Time,* February 14, 1949.

188 *"There's a plane carrying": New York Times Magazine,* November 30, 1948.

188 *"Hot frankfurters!":* Donovan, p. 156.

189 *"My tomatoes have come in":* Jurgen Graf interview, Frye Archive.

190 *"RIAS music broadcasts":* Galle, p. 291.

192 *"We appeal to you":* Galle, p. 302.

192 *"Erwin Wolf":* Donovan, p. 171.

193 *"Peter was selected":* Inge Stanneck Gross, *Memories of War and Its Aftermath* (Eastsound, Washington: Island in the Sky, 2005), p. 174.

193 *The Soviets branded them:* Donovan, p. 185.

193 *Comedian Bob Hope:* Tunner, p. 194 ff.

194 *Irving Berlin: Task Force Times,* December 23, 1948.

195 *dinner with Symington:* Miller, p. 52; Tunner, p. 196; *Task Force Times,* December 24, 25, 26, 1948.

195 *"What's the matter":* Donovan, p. 159.

195 *John Chandler Gurney:* Samuel, p. 66.

CHAPTER 9: "STALIN SAYS . . ."

197 *On January 2, 1949: Task Force Times,* January 4, 1949.

198 *Pilots and crews did not know:* Tunner, p. 223.

199 *William Michaels:* Gere, p. 111; Joseph Werner, *Berlin Airlift: Brides and Grooms Created* (Stony Brook, N.Y.: Water Edge, 1997), p. 83.

200 *Paul Hawkins:* Werner, p. 57.

200 *Forrest Ott:* Werner, p. 137.

203 *That week, on January 5: Papers,* p. 973.

204 *"I think it would be harmful": Papers,* p. 977.

205 *The day began at 6 A.M.: Luftbrücke Berlin,* Ein dokumentarisches Bildbuch (Berlin-Grunewald: Fritz Moser, 1949), p. 59.

207 *"Faith in the Airlift": New York Times,* January 19, 1949.

208 *advertising for shovels: New York Times,* December 16, 1948.

208 *"I'll cite one instance": New York Times,* January 19, 1949.

210 *"AIRBRIDGE-DEATHBRIDGE":* Rodrigo, p. 143.

210 *Joseph Stalin, not surprisingly:* Michael D. Haydock, *City Under Siege* (Dulles, Va.: Brassey's, 1999), p. 265; Parrish, p. 311.

CHAPTER 10: "ZERO-ZERO"

219 *Charles J. V. Murphy: Fortune*, November 1948, p. 89.

219 *Paul Fisher: Bee-Hive*, p. 30.

222 *EDI:* "Sam Walton's Secret Weapon," *Audacity* (published by *American Heritage*, New York), Spring 1996. All future references are to "Sam Walton's Secret Weapon."

223 *Louis Schuerholz: Task Force Times*, February 21, 1949.

224 *Philip Jessup:* Philip Jessup, "Park Avenue Diplomacy—Ending the Berlin Airlift, *Political Science Quarterly* 87, no. 3 (1972), p. 360 ff.; *New York Times*, April 30, 1949; Dean Acheson, *Present at the Creation* (New York: Norton, 1969), p. 267 ff.

CHAPTER 11: "A BIG HOCK SHOP"

227 *"The most extraordinary thing": New York Times*, March 5, 1949.

228 *There was a brief confrontation: Papers*, p. 1038.

229 *"Why don't we have": New York Times*, March 6, 1949.

230 *"Organizational?": Tunner*, p. 202.

230 *New paper bags:* Miller, p. 86; *New York Times*, April 25, 1949.

231 *It was on March 14:* Jessup, p. 360 ff.

232 *"The complete sealing":* Berlin-East Germany OSS-CIA files at www.Paperless Archives.com.

232 *"Absolutely all vehicles":* Steege, p. 255.

234 *said he would give Trent a Volkswagen:* Joe Trent interview; www.konnections.com/airlift/trent.

234 *Lieutenant Albert Lowe:* Gere, p. 56.

235 *"If we are to remain":* Miller, p. 175.

235 *"Request authority to proceed": Papers*, p. 881.

236 *"Joint press release": Papers*, p. 1045.

237 *On March 21, the day after:* Jessup, p. 360 ff.

238 *"Dear General Clay":* Miller, p. 181.

CHAPTER 12: "HERE COMES A YANKEE"

242 *"The biggest project":* Rodrigo, p. 192.

242 *"1. Reciprocal and simultaneous":* Jessup, p. 360 ff.; *New York Times*, April 28, 1949, p. 1.

245 *"Germans have no choice":* W. Phillips Davison, *The Berlin Blockade: A Study in Cold War Politics* (Princeton: Princeton University Press, 1978), p. 283.

246 *"Yesterday and today":* Ibid., p. 284.

248 *By April, the number of incidents:* "Summary of Corridor Incidents," Memo, ALTF/IN/cc, USAF Office of Information.

248 *"Jesus, that's flak":* Collier, p. 147.

248 *Lieutenant Charles Allen:* Charles S. Allen, "A Personal Account," www.konnections.com/airlift/callen.

249   *"We're going down":* Thompson, p. 125.

250   *"I go out to Wiesbaden":* D. M. Tomlinson, *Task Force Times*, April 9, 1949.

250   *Lieutenant Joseph Lauter:* Frye Archive.

251   *"Beat Celle":* Task Force Times, February 24, 1949.

253   *"the Easter Parade":* Tunner, p. 221; Miller, p. 99; *New York Times*, April 17, 1949, p. 1; Lafferty interview; Wagner interview.

253   *had received "feelers":* New York Times, April 21, 1949, p. 1.

253   *"peace feelers":* New York Times, April 22, 1949, p. 1.

255   *The next day Jessup traveled:* New York Times, April 28, 1949, p. 1.

256   *"U.S. STAYS SKEPTICAL":* New York Times, May 1, 1949, p. 1.

CHAPTER 13: "WE ARE ALIVE!"

260   *A* Times *reporter, Sydney Gruson:* New York Times, May 5, 1949; Wagner interviews and correspondence.

262   *Johanna and Willi Last:* Frye Archive.

262   *Sergeant Hugh Tosone:* Interview.

262   *Lieutenant Edwin Gere:* Interviews and correspondence.

263   *Bill Palahunich:* Interviews and correspondence.

263   *Guy Dunn:* Interviews and correspondence.

263   *Corky Colgrove:* Interviews and correspondence.

264   *Gerhard Noack:* Interviews and correspondence.

264   *Kurt Dettmer:* Interviews and correspondence.

264   *Günter Metzger:* Interviews and correspondence.

264   *William Frost:* New York Times, May 12, 1949.

266   *Robert Lochner:* Frye Archive.

266   *his commander, Howley:* New York Times, May 16, 1949.

267   *Alice Sawadda:* Parrish, p. 325.

268   *As his tour finally ended:* "A Preliminary Report to Commanding General, United States Air Force in Europe and Air Officer Commanding-in-Chief British Air Forces of Occupation by Commanding General, Combined Airlift Task Force, CALTF June 20, 1949."

271   *On the 12th, a C-54 crashed:* Huschke, p. 265.

EPILOGUE

273   *finally met in Paris:* New York Times, June 7, 1949.

274   *There are several sets of statistics:* Miller, p. 108 ff.

275   Der Abend: Municipal Archives, Berlin. Donovan, p. 182.

275   *On the night of August 13, 1961:* Richard Reeves, *President Kennedy: Profile of Power,* (New York: Simon and Schuster, 1993), p. 209 ff.

275   *In May 1999:* Vacaville *Reporter,* May 2, 1999, p. 1; May 6, 1999, p. 8.

276   *Gerhard Noack:* Morrisey, Noack interviews.

276   *Ten years later:* Dettmer interview.

277   *Jack O. Bennett:* *Toronto Globe and Mail,* September 10, 2001.

279   *Edward Guilbert:* "Sam Walton's Secret Weapon."

282   *Jake Schuffert:* National Museum of the USAF.

282   *Kenneth Slaker:* Interview.

282   *Ulrich Stampa:* Interview.

282   *Noah Thompson:* Interview.

283   *Louis Wagner:* Interview.

BIBLIOGRAPHY

Acheson, Dean. *Present at the Creation*. New York: Norton, 1969.

Airlift Gratitude Foundation. "Blockade and Airlift: Legend or Lesson." Berlin, 1988.

Alliierten Museum, Berlin. *Es begann mit einem Kuss*. Berlin: Jaron Verlag, 2006.

——. *Pioneers of the Airlift*. Berlin: Nishan, 1998.

Auftage Luftbrücke: Der Himmel über Berlin, 1949. Berlin: Nicolai, 1998.

Andreas-Friedrich, Ruth. *Battleground Berlin: Diaries 1945–1949*. New York: Paragon House, 1990.

Arnold-Forster, Mark. *The Siege of Berlin*. London: Collins, 1979.

Aviation Operations Magazine. *A Special Study of "Operation Vittles."* New York: Conover-Mast, 1949.

Bennett, Lowell. *Berlin Bastion*. Frankfurt: Fred Rudel, 1951.

Binder, David. *The Other German: Willy Brandt's Life and Times*. Washington, D.C.: New Republic Books, 1975.

Bohlen, Charles. *Witness to History*. New York: Norton, 1973.

Bradley, Omar. *A Soldier's Story*. New York: Henry Holt, 1951.

Bradley, Omar, and Clay Blair. *A General's Life*. New York: Simon and Schuster, 1983.

Cherny, Andrei. *The Candy Bombers*. New York: Putnam, 2008.

Clay, Lucius. *Decision in Germany*. Garden City, N.Y.: Doubleday, 1950.

Collier, Richard. *Bridge Across the Sky*. New York: McGraw-Hill, 1978.

Davison, W. Phillips. *The Berlin Blockade: A Study in Cold War Politics*. Princeton, N.J.: Princeton University Press, 1978.

Donovan, Frank. *Bridge in the Sky*. New York: David McKay, 1968.

Forster, Uwe von, Hochberg, Stephanie von, Kubisch, Ulrich, and Kuhlgatz, Dietrich. *Auftrage Luftbrücke: Der Himmel über Berlin*. Nicolai, Berlin, 1998.

Gaddis, John Lewis. *The Cold War*. New York: Penguin, 2005.

Gere, Edwin. *The Unheralded*. Shutesbury, Mass.: Andrus, 2004.

Giangreco, D.M., and Robert E. Griffin. *Airbridge to Berlin*. Provato, Calif.: Presidio, 1988.

Gross, Inge Stanneck. *Memories of World War II and Its Aftermath*. Eastsound, Wash.: Island in the Sky, 2005.

Hagen, Yvonne. *From Art to Life and Back*. New York: Xlibris, 2005.

Halvorsen, Gail. *The Berlin Candy Bomber*. Springville, Utah: Horizon, 1997.

Hammond, Thomas T., ed. *Witnesses to the Origins of the Cold War*. Seattle: University of Washington Press, 1982.

Haydock, Michael. *City Under Siege*. Washington, D.C.: Brassey's, 1999.

Howley, Frank. *Berlin Command*. New York: Putnam, 1950.

Huschke, Wolfgang. *The Candy Bombers*. Berlin: Metropol, 1999.

Irvin, David W. *Highway to Freedom: The Berlin Airlift*. Paducah, Ky.: Turner, 2002.

Judt, Tony. *Postwar*. New York: Penguin, 2005.

Launius, Roger, and Coy Cross. *MAC and the Legacy of the Berlin Airlift*. Scott Air Force Base, Illinois, 1989.

LeMay, Curtis, with MacKinlay Kantor. *My Story*. Garden City, N.Y.: Doubleday, 1965.

Man, John. *Berlin Blockade*. New York: Ballantine, 1973.

Mann, Arthur. *Comeback*. London: Macmillan, 1980.

Mastny, Vojtech. *The Cold War and Soviet Insecurities*. New York: Oxford University Press, 1995.

McCullough, David. *Truman*. New York: Simon and Schuster, 1992.

Middleton, Drew. *The Struggle for Germany*. Indianapolis: Bobbs-Merrill, 1949.

Morris, Eric. *Blockade*. New York: Stein & Day, 1973.

Murphy, David E., Sergei A. Kondrashev, and George Bailey. *Battleground Berlin: CIA vs. KGB in the Cold War*. Yale University Press: New Haven, 1997.

Naimark, Norman. *The Russians in Germany*. Cambridge, Mass.: Belknap, 1995.

Parrish, Thomas. *Berlin in the Balance*. Reading, Pa.: Addison-Wesley, 1998.

Pearcy, Arthur. *Berlin Airlift*. Shrewsbury, England, Airlife, 1997.

Provan, John, and R. E. G. Davis. *Berlin Airlift: The Effort and the Airplanes*. McLean, Va.: Paladwr, 1998.

Roberts, Frank. *Dealing with Dictators*. London: Weidenfeld & Nicolson, 1991.

Rodrigo, Robert. *Berlin Airlift*. London: Cassell, 1960.

Romero, James. *Skyblue 79—Over and Out*. Self-published, 2005.

Samuel, Wolfgang. *Coming to Colorado*. Jackson: University Press of Mississippi, 2006.

———*German Boy*. Jackson: University Press of Mississippi, 2000.

———*I Always Wanted to Fly*. Jackson: University Press of Mississippi, 2001.

———*The War of Our Childhood*. Jackson: University Press of Mississippi, 2002.

Scherff, Klaus. *Luftbrücke Berlin*. Stuttgart: Motorbuch Verlag, 1976.

Schrader, Helena. *The Blockade Breakers*. Gloucestershire, U.K.: Sutton, 2008.

Schuffert, John. *Airlift Laffs*. Berlin Airlift Veterans Association, San Antonio, Texas, 1999.

Shlaim, Avi. *The United States and the Berlin Blockade*. Berkeley: University of California Press, 1983.

Slaker, Kenneth Hawk. *A Military Pilot's Exciting Life and Visit from the Hereafter*. Raleigh, N.C.: Ivy House, 2008.

Smith, Jean Edward. *Lucius D. Clay*. New York: Henry Holt, 1990.

————, ed. *The Papers of Lucius D. Clay*. Bloomington: University of Indiana Press, 1974.

Steege, Paul. *Black Market, Cold War*. Cambridge, U.K.: Cambridge University Press, 2007.

Sutherland, Jon, and Diane Canwell. *The Berlin Airlift: The Salvation of a City*. Gretna, La.: Pelican, 2007.

Thompson, Noah C. *A Pilot's Story: Flying in the 1940s*. Rutland, Vt.: Academy, 1995.

Truman, Harry S. *Memoirs*. Garden City, N.Y.: Doubleday, 1955.

Tusa, Ann, and John Tusa. *The Berlin Airlift*. New York: Sarpedon, 1988.

Werner, Joseph. *Berlin Airlift: Brides and Grooms Created*. Stony Brook, N.Y.: Wateredge, 1997.

Williams, Francis. *Ernest Bevin*. London: Hutchinson, 1952.

Zubok, Vladislay, and Constantine Pleshakov. *Inside the Kremlin's Cold War*. Cambridge, Mass.: Harvard University Press, 1996.

ACKNOWLEDGMENTS

Without taking anything away from all the people who helped me do this book, the research and writing were a pleasure because of two wonderful women, one generous man and two wonderful organizations. The women are my assistant, Susan Gifford, and my interpreter, translator and guide in Germany, Regine Wosnitza. The man is Robert Frye, a television producer who led me through hundreds of hours of interviews and films he collected and archived in making three films on Berlin and the Berlin Airlift for the Public Broadcasting System. The first organization is the Berlin Airlift Veterans Association; the second is the American Academy in Berlin.

Among the many things Sue did for me as I wrote was to survey every member of BAVA, those daring young men of 1948 and 1949, many of them featured in this book. Two BAVA officers—W. C. (Dub) Southers and Lewis Dale Whipple—helped me contact airlift veterans. Regine, with the help of the German writer and student of the airlift Wolfgang Hutschke, tracked down Germans who worked for the Allies, and scheduled visits and interviews all over the country. My home in Berlin was the American Academy, where I was a Holtzbrinck Distinguished Visitor for several weeks in 2007. The academy, which was founded by Ambassador Richard Holbrooke while he was the United States envoy to the country, is designed to foster German-American studies, and it does that and much more under the leadership of Gary Smith and his talented staff. The view—overlooking Lake Wannssee—is good and so is the food, but the best thing there is the companionship and stimulation of living with other writers, teachers and artists, each engrossed in his or her own projects. I loved every minute and was productive every day. You can't ask for more than that. I thank my friend John Rielly for leading me to the academy.

I am also grateful for the help of Byoung Hwa-Wang, who did German translations for me at the University of Southern California. I owe a lot, as usual, to librarians and archivists in four countries—the United States, Germany, England, France and Russia—and most particularly to Bernd von Kostka and Dr. Helmut Trotnow at the Alliierten Museum in Berlin; Carol Ledenham of the Hoover Institution Archives in Palo Alto, California; Stella Lopez at the Annenberg School for Communication at the University of Southern California; and Dr. Jeffrey Underwood of the National Museum of the U.S. Air Force. My agent and friend, Amanda Urban, helped keep the Reeves family in business. And to Alice Mayhew, my editor of more than twenty-five years, and her assistant, Roger Labrie, thank you one more time.

Finally, I want to thank the daring men, not so young anymore, who invited me into their homes and lives to talk about their service and bravery in the amazing adventure called the Berlin Airlift.

RICHARD REEVES
NEW YORK

INDEX

myth, 107; newsreels about, 53–54; purpose of, 3–4, 5, 14–15, 208, 212, 236, 255; Soviet views about, 80. *See also specific person*
Boettgen Orphanage, 169–70
Bohlen, Charles, 74, 129, 212, 225, 232
Bonn, Germany, as capital, 235, 243, 274
Bourcey, Robert, 197–98
Boyd, Ralph, 208
Boyle, Hal, 233–34
Bradley, Omar: and American withdrawal from Berlin, 9; Clay's relationship with, 7, 9; and Clay's trip to Washington, 74, 75; and debate about airlift, 74, 75, 146, 202, 203; and evacuation of American "dependents" from Berlin, 49, 50; evacuation of family of, 50; and Soviet arrest of Berlin police, 122
Bradshaw, Paul, 249
Brandt, Peter, 150
Brandt, Willy: airlift views of, 223; and British commitment to Berlin, 223; and Clay-German relations, 120; and Clay-Reuter meeting, 58; and future of Germany, 244–45; honors and awards for, 277; as journalist, 4–5, 55; London trip of, 223; optimism of, 78–79; Paris trip of, 224; and possibility of war, 81; professional career of, 277; RIAS views of, 192; and Soviet-Allied relations, 150–51, 201–3, 215–17, 244; Soviet blockade views of, 81, 215–16; and Soviet offering of food and fuel for Berliners, 80–81; and SPD, 4–5, 55, 78–79, 186, 201; and Tegel explosion, 186–87; views about Clay of, 120, 246; warnings of, 81
British: airlift as idea of, 33–37; airplanes of, 76–77, 83; call up and reassignment of crew and planes by, 44, 47; and Clay's currency plan, 235–36; commitment to Berlin of, 223; and creation of German Federal Republic, 243; and future of Germany, 8, 217; Germans' interaction with, 52, 85, 138–39; and lifting of Soviet blockade, 265; newsreels of, 54; pessimism about airlift by, 128–29; rationing by, 94, 95; resources of, 229; and strength of troops in Germany, 4, 28; U.S. joint operations with, 98–99; views about Americans by, 48. *See also* Allies; *specific person or topic*
Burtonwood (air base), 69, 100, 119, 156, 196, 198

C-47 airplanes, 38–40, 51, 62, 65, 69, 82, 83, 84, 105, 140–41, 152, 219, 229
C-54 airplanes: American fleet of, 83; Clay's request for additional, 74, 77; crashes of, 140, 141, 177, 198, 208, 271; and "The

Easter Parade," 252; German mechanics for, 136–37, 138; and "Lessons Learned" report, 269; and loading competition, 116; maintenance of, 69, 70, 156, 160, 161–62, 249, 250; Navy as source of, 148; pilot training in, 133, 134, 182; Pratt & Whitney engines in, 219; at Tegel, 185; tonnage deliveries of, 98; transfer to Germany of, 40, 41, 42, 43, 63; Tunner's desire for more, 105; turnaround time of, 247; and weather conditions, 158, 165, 181
C-74 Globemaster airplane, 221–22, 229
C-97 airplanes, 229–30
Camp Trauen, 109–10
Campbell, Richard A., 116–17
"Candy Bomber," 89–91, 108, 208–9
Cannon, John K., 144, 145–46, 163–64, 165, 193–95, 251
CARE (Cooperative for American Remittances to Europe), 112–13, 279
Carter, N. Dean, 51
Carver, Margaret E., 196
Cassady, George, 42
Cecchini, Anthony, 144–45
Celle (air base), 84, 98, 109, 111, 119, 131–132, 140, 141, 194, 251, 271
Central Intelligence Agency (CIA), 20, 28–29, 63, 72, 146, 232
charity/donations, 113, 157, 167, 170, 195–196, 267
Chataigneau, Yves, 95
Chauvel, Jean, 255
Chevasse, Nick, 164–65
children, evacuation of, 193
Christian, William, 89
Christian Democratic Union, 72, 180, 245, 246, 274
Churchill, Winston, 35
Chuykov, Vasily, 238
Ciro's, 39
Civil Aeronautics Board, 184
Civil Aviation Authority (CAA), 52
Clark, Joan, 167
Clay, Lucius DuBignon: and air corridor plan, 23; airlift views of, 26–27, 34, 73, 75, 147, 209; and Allied Control Council, 22; and Allied withdrawal from Berlin, 9, 22; and American troops as "high school kids," 85; armed convoy idea of, 6, 7–8, 34, 235, 237; authority and power of, 7; and B-29 Superfortress airplanes, 76; and beginning of airlift, 26, 36–37; and Berlin Wall, 275; Bradley's relationship with, 9; Brandt's views about, 120, 246; and creation of German Federal Republic, 255; and currency issue, 13, 16, 27, 95–96, 235–236; description of Berlin by, 11; and deterioration of American military, 27;

INDEX

INDEX

INDEX

INDEX

ABOUT THE AUTHOR

Richard Reeves is the bestselling author of three presidential biographies: *President Kennedy*, *President Nixon*, and *President Reagan*. A syndicated columnist and winner of the American Political Science Association's Carey McWilliams Award, he lives in New York and Los Angeles. He is Senior Lecturer at the Annenberg School for Communication at the University of Southern California.